BUILDING KNOWLEDGE IN EARLY CHILDHOOD EDUCATION

A focal point of early childhood education is how young children build knowledge and the ways that practitioners, parents and carers can help them to do so. Many adults find it challenging to identify what knowledge young children are building and how they do so, making it difficult to support young children's learning and development in the most effective ways. This essential guide will help you to identify and develop young children's knowledge and understanding in early years settings, not only in terms of statutory requirements but far beyond them.

Building Knowledge in Early Childhood Education draws on empirical research findings from the *Young Children As Researchers* (YCAR) project to examine everyday activities and reveal the means that young children use to build knowledge and understanding, as well as exploring the similarities between learning behaviours in early childhood and adult life.

Interweaving everyday activities in practice with research and theory, this book covers:

- how young children construct knowledge;
- learning, problem-solving and exploring;
- concepts and conceptualising in early childhood;
- evidence-based decision-making;
- how young children behave as researchers.

Offering practical advice and suggestions to create opportunities that identify and facilitate young children's own constructions of knowledge and understanding, this book is essential reading for practitioners, students and all those interested in the theories surrounding young children as researchers.

Jane Murray is Senior Lecturer in Early Years Education at the University of Northampton, UK. She is also a qualified headteacher and a former early childhood teacher.

Research informed professional development for the early years
TACTYC (Association for Professional Development in Early Years)

The books in this series each focus on a different aspect of research in early childhood which has direct implications for practice and policy. They consider the main research findings which should influence practitioner thinking and reflection and help them to question their own practice alongside activities to deepen knowledge and extend understanding of the issues. Readers will benefit from clear analysis, critique and interpretation of the key factors surrounding the research as well as exemplifications and case studies to illustrate the research-practice or research-policy links. Supporting the development of critical reflection and up to date knowledge, the books will be a core resource for all those educating and training early years practitioners.

Exploring the Contexts for Early Learning
Challenging the school readiness agenda
Rory McDowall Clark

Building Knowledge in Early Childhood Education
Young children are researchers
Jane Murray

Forthcoming titles:

Places for 2 Year Olds in the Early Years
Supporting learning and development
Jan Georgeson and Verity Campbell-Barr

Supporting Abused and Neglected Children in the Early Years
Practice, policy and provision
Sue Soan

BUILDING KNOWLEDGE IN EARLY CHILDHOOD EDUCATION

Young Children Are Researchers

Jane Murray

LONDON AND NEW YORK

First published 2017
by Routledge
2 Park Square, Milton Park, Abingdon, Oxon OX14 4RN

and by Routledge
711 Third Avenue, New York, NY 10017

Routledge is an imprint of the Taylor & Francis Group, an informa business

British Library Cataloguing in Publication Data
A catalogue record for this book is available from the British Library

Library of Congress Cataloging in Publication Data
A catalog record for this book has been requested

ISBN: 978-1-138-93793-2 (hbk)
ISBN: 978-1-138-93794-9 (pbk)
ISBN: 978-1-315-67601-2 (ebk)

Typeset in Bembo
by Saxon Graphics Ltd, Derby

CONTENTS

SERIES EDITORS' PREFACE

Professor Emerita Janet Moyles and
Professor Jane Payler

Welcome to the second volume in the new, inspiring TACTYC book series. As part of the Association for Professional Development in the Early Years, TACTYC members believe that effective early years policies and practices should be informed by an understanding of the findings and implications of high quality, robust research. TACTYC focuses on developing the knowledge base of all those concerned with early years education and care by creating, reviewing and disseminating research findings and by encouraging critical and constructive discussion to foster reflective attitudes in practitioners. Such a need has been evident in the resounding success of events such as our conferences where speakers make clear connections between research and practice for delegates. Early years practitioners and those who support their professional development engage enthusiastically with early childhood research and understand how it is likely to impact upon, and enhance, practice. They acknowledge that research has a distinct role to play in effective work in early years education and care, and that they should be part of a 'research-rich education system'.

TACTYC is an organisation with a specific focus on the professional development of all those involved in early childhood with the express purpose of improving practices to enhance the well-being of young children. Its reputation for quality research and writing includes its international *Early Years* journal. This book series is likely to be popular with those who value the journal as it will add to its range and scope. Our aim for the series is to help those who educate and train early years practitioners at all levels to understand the implications and practical interpretation of recent research and to offer a rationale for improving the quality and reach of practice in early years education and care.

It is not always easy for busy trainers and practitioners to access contemporary research and translate it into informed and reflective practice. These books are intended to promote the benefits of applying research in an informed way to develop quality pedagogical practices. Each individual book in this series will explore a range of different topics within a theme. This second book considers the issues involved in *children building knowledge as researchers*. It teases out the implications of research and theory about how practitioners understand, interpret and articulate the complex processes and outcomes that are inherent in the ways young children interact with the world to construct knowledge. This exciting book identifies how young children's everyday activities, thinking and actions exemplify research behaviours in similar ways to academics. The ideas are presented in a clear, unambiguous way, while acknowledging the often complex relationships between what we know and what is possible in practice.

Interest in this phase of education and care has been growing exponentially in the last few years and there is now a rich source of early years research on which writers may draw. The claim is frequently made that policies are 'evidence-based' but this is not the same as rigorous, impartial research. Many policy and practice documents purport to be based on 'evidence', but this depends to a large extent on the political framework and ideology in place at different periods in time – few governments have the scope in their relatively short elected periods to give strategic consideration to the complex implications of different research outcomes for policies and practice. What is politically and economically expedient at the time is too often the driving force behind decisions about young children and their families.

All the writers in this series have been asked to present their particular focus, and to outline the issues and challenges within that framework, which are relevant for early years practitioners. Exploring aspects of early years practice, based on research and sound theoretical underpinning, the writers will offer guidance on how findings can be analysed and interpreted to inform the continuing process of developing high quality early years practice. They will examine the research background to each topic and offer considered views on why the situation is as it is, and how it might move forward within the frameworks of imposed curricula and assessments. They will offer thoughtful advice to practitioners for dealing with the challenges faced within that particular focus and will suggest relevant follow-up reading and web-based materials to support further reflection, practice and curriculum implementation. Each book will also identify where further research is needed and will help tutors, trainers and practitioners to understand how they can contribute to research in this field.

Early years education and care is universally contentious, especially in relation to how far those outside the field, for example, politicians and policy-makers, should intervene in deciding what constitutes successful early years pedagogy, curriculum and assessment. The main focus of the series will be on practice, policy and provision in the UK, but writers will also draw on international research perspectives, as there is a great deal to learn from colleagues in other national contexts.

The series particularly targets readers qualified at Level 6, or students on such courses, preparing for roles in which they will be expected to educate and train other practitioners in effective early years practices. There will be many others who will find the books invaluable: leaders of early years settings, who often have an education, training and professional development role in relation to their staff (and may well be qualified at Level 6 or beyond), will similarly find the series useful in their work. Academics and new researchers who support the training and development of graduate leaders in early years will also appreciate the books in this series. Readers will benefit from clear analysis, critique and interpretation of the key factors surrounding the research as well as exemplifications and case studies to illustrate the links between research and policy as well as research and practice. The books will support the development of critical reflection and up-to-date knowledge and will be a core resource for all those educating and training early years practitioners.

In summary, research-based early years practice is a relatively new field as much of practitioners' work with young children over recent years has been based on the implementation of policy documents which are often not grounded in rigorous, clear, unambiguous research evidence. The main aim of the TACTYC series is to help tutors and trainers to enable practitioners to become more informed advocates for provision of high quality services for children and their families. This will be achieved by promoting the benefits of applying research in an informed way to develop the quality of practice.

ACKNOWLEDGEMENTS

I am most grateful to the children, practitioners, parents and professional researchers who contributed in many valuable ways to the *Young Children As Researchers* project: thank you. I also extend my sincere gratitude to the Support Editors, Anita Soni and Nancy Stewart, who have given their time to review and provide constructive feedback on the book chapters. For their unstinting encouragement and inspiration, I thank Stephen, Jemima, Will and Fergus.

I am grateful to publishers who have consented to the use or adaptation of figures and tables in this book which previously appeared in my other *Young Children As Researchers* publications:

Figure 2.1	Plural paradigm model[4]
Figure 2.2	Jigsaw methodology[2, 3, 4, 6]
Figure 2.3	YCAR epistemological barriers[6]
Figure 2.4	YCAR epistemological categories[6]
Figure 3.1	Building blocks for exploration[5]
Figure 4.1	Building blocks for finding solutions[5]
Figure 4.5	Pedro's sugar construction[1]
Figure 5.1	Building blocks for conceptualisation[5]
Figure 5.19	The climbing frame[1]
Figure 6.1	Building blocks for basing decisions on evidence[5, 6]
Table 2.1	Research behaviour framework (RBF)[3, 4, 6]
Table 2.4	YCAR epistemological factors in young children's everyday behaviours[3, 4]

Notes

1 Murray, J. (2012) Young Children's Explorations: Young children's research? *Early Child Development and Care.* **182** (9): 1209–1225. DOI: 10.1080/03004430.2011.604728

2 Murray, J.M. (2013) Young Children's Research Behaviour? Children aged four to eight years finding solutions at home and at school. *Early Child Development and Care.* **183** (7/8): 1147–1165.

3 Murray, J. (2014) Researching Young Children's Worlds. In T. Waller and G. Davis (Eds) (2014) *An Introduction to Early Childhood.* 3e. London: Sage, pp. 325–345.

4 Murray, J. (2015a) Can Young Children be Researchers? In H. McLaughlin (Ed.) (2015) *Children and Young People's Participation in Policy, Practice and Research*. London: National Children's Bureau, pp. 48–63.
5 Murray, J. (2015b) Young Children as Researchers in Play. In J. Moyles (Ed.) (2015) *The Excellence of Play*. 4e. Maidenhead: McGraw-Hill Education, pp. 106–124.
6 Murray, J. (2016) Young Children are Researchers: Children aged 4–8 years engage in important research behaviour when they base decisions on evidence. *European Early Childhood Education Research Journal*. **24** (5): 705–720. DOI: 10.1080/1350293X.2016.1213565

1

INTRODUCTION

Located at the heart of early childhood education are the ways that young children build knowledge and the ways that practitioners, parents and other adults help them to do so. Based on empirical research evidence, this book provides practical guidance for early childhood leaders, tutors, practitioners, parents and students to identify, understand, interpret and articulate the complex processes and outcomes that are inherent in the ways young children interact with the world to construct knowledge. The book is also about how adults might support children in that endeavour.

Outstanding leaders and excellent practitioners in early childhood education understand the importance of interweaving knowledge about their practice and their children with evidence-based research and theories in our field. This book is a framework that brings together these aspects to understand young children's actions. Drawing on research findings from the *Young Children As Researchers* (YCAR) project, the book shows how young children construct knowledge when they are engaging in their everyday activities at home and in their early childhood settings, in ways that are congruent with research behaviour.

This book works on several levels. First, it shines a light on the everyday lives of real children, their practitioners and parents. While it focuses on the children aged 4–8 years who participated in the YCAR project, it acknowledges that early childhood is defined internationally as birth up to 8 years (Office of the United Nations High Commissioner for Human Rights (OHCHR), 2005: 2). Second, the book reveals how children's everyday activities enable them to construct knowledge and make sense of the world on journeys of enquiry that are important for them now and in the future. Third, the book identifies how young children's everyday activities, thinking and actions exemplify research behaviours that academics adopt and shows how research and practice are inextricably interwoven for understanding how young children construct knowledge. Finally, the book is a toolkit that practitioners and other adults who work with young children can use to reflect on – and in – their practice (Schön, 1983) to optimise young children's constructions of knowledge.

Everyday lives of real children

This book is about meanings that underpin the everyday activities of real children and the idea for it began with the everyday lives of real children, their practitioners and parents during the 20 years that I worked as an early childhood teacher. Every day, it seemed to me that the young children I was working with were engaging in enquiry to construct knowledge as a significant part of their daily activities. Anecdotally, I identified that they investigated, questioned, set problems, found solutions, tested materials and explored, among other sophisticated processes; moreover, I found that the children I worked with engaged most deeply in those activities when they decided for themselves what to do. Of course, I was aware that Piaget's constructivist theory recognised that children actively build knowledge (1972b), and that by the mid-twentieth century, he had acknowledged children as 'little scientists, constantly constructing new theories about how the world works and testing them' (Fernyhough, 2010: 158), but Piaget (1972a) regarded children's constructions of knowledge as different from those of adults: he saw them as developing incrementally as children grew older. The anecdotal evidence I found in my everyday practice as an early childhood teacher indicated that some of the ways young children and adults build knowledge may be similar, a view supported by Gopnik (1996).

Young children construct knowledge

Others have challenged Piaget's theory that children's capacity to construct knowledge to make sense of the world emerges developmentally. For example, Donaldson (1978) found that familiar contexts and materials seem to enable young children to demonstrate more sophisticated levels of understanding in their constructions of knowledge than Piaget thought (Donaldson, 1978). Children's own homes, then, may offer environments that are 'very powerful' for young children's learning (Pellegrini, Symons and Hoch, 2004; Tizard and Hughes, 1984: 249), though this is not always the case (Sylva, Melhuish, Sammons, Siraj-Blatchford and Taggart, 2010). The *Young Children As Researchers* (YCAR) project captured 4 to 8-year-old children's constructions of knowledge in environments that were familiar to them: their early childhood settings and at home.

Wood (1988) also troubles Piaget's stage theory by arguing that it was predicated on findings that relied on children's uses of verbal reasoning to explain and justify their understanding. While Piaget found young children's verbal communication to be somewhat limited, Wood (1988) proposes that this cannot be assumed to equate with the quality of their understanding. Young children express their knowledge and understanding in many different ways, including body language, talking, dancing, drawing, crafting, singing and writing (Bae, 2010; Gallas, 1994; Malaguzzi, 1998b). These – and other modalities – were adopted by young children in the YCAR project, revealing multiple ways that they built knowledge.

Although it is widely recognised that Piaget was ambivalent about social constructivism (Robson, 2012), the idea of building knowledge in social contexts has gained traction (Prawat and Floden, 1994; Rogoff, 1990). Social constructivism can be formulated in equitable 'meeting places' (Dahlberg and Lenz Taguchi, 1994: 2; Edwards, Gandini and Forman, 1998) or it may be about those with knowledge scaffolding others' understanding (Vygotsky, 1978; Wood, Bruner and Ross, 1976). In either model, parents may 'play a crucial role'

(Galinsky, 2010; Peters, Seeds, Goldstein and Coleman, 2008: 15), the influence of practitioners may be 'considerable' (Siraj-Blatchford, Sylva, Muttock, Gilden and Bell, 2002; Fumoto, Robson, Greenfield and Hargreaves, 2012: 119) or peers can affect how young children build knowledge (Corsaro, 2003; Bulotsky-Shearer, Bell, Romero and Carter, 2012). While the YCAR project generated new data from young children's everyday activities for each of these modes of social constructivism, it also elicited many new examples of young children constructing knowledge unilaterally.

Young children's constructions of knowledge have been recognised in many different ways (Robson, 2012). For example, self-regulation and metacognition are regarded as important tools for young children's constructions of knowledge (Carr, 2011; Whitebread *et al.*, 2009) and while both emerged as important elements in the YCAR project, they were just two elements among many. Equally, Hedges (2014) has worked on the notion of young children's working theories: 'creative links between existing and new experiences and thinking in children's knowledge building to strengthen their understandings of the world... facilitated by opportunities for children to share, test or explore ideas' (p. 37). There are similarities between working theories and YCAR findings but working theories occur 'when parents' and children's interests and understandings coincide' (Hedges, 2014: 37), whereas YCAR puts emphasis on children leading. YCAR findings also show how young children's constructions of knowledge can constitute research behaviour, whereas this is not a primary focus for working theories.

Piaget's (1972b) view of children's abilities to build knowledge as emergent is dissonant with the view of children as competent social actors from birth, an idea that has gained increasing popularity in the twenty-first century in the fields of children's rights and 'new' sociology (Corsaro, 2005: 3; OHCHR, 2005). Piaget was not alone: prior to the YCAR study there had been little recognition that the ways young children construct knowledge in their everyday activities could align with research behaviour on the academy's terms. Even Gopnik (1996), who subscribes to congruence between young children's mental activity and aspects of scientific theorising, sees children's understanding as 'developing' (p. 485). However, it is worth noting that Isaacs (1944) observed that the 'factor of epistemic interest and inquiry...is in every respect the same in the child as in the adult' (p. 322).

Young children are researchers

After 20 years as a teacher working in early childhood settings, I moved on to higher education to teach adults and to research in the field of early childhood education. Higher education – or the academy – is characterised as a privileged space where knowledge is produced and where knowledge producers and learners meet (Warren and Boxall, 2009). It is also a 'score-keeping world' which has a tendency to distance itself from those outside (Bridges, 1998; Lees, 1999: 382). Within the academy, I found that young children's own enquiries were not taken seriously in the ways I knew they were in early childhood settings; instead, the academy's 'rarefied world' of jargon, methodological rubrics and privileged means of communication tended to exclude children (Redmond, 2008: 17).

For some time now, there has been growing recognition that when educational research and education practice are separate, educational research may be less useful to education practice than it could be if they worked in symbiosis, for example, as doctors engage with medical research (Hargreaves, 1996; Goldacre, 2013). In the wider field of education,

Edwards, Sebba and Rickinson (2007) suggest that engagement with users 'strengthens the warrants of research' (p. 647) and indeed, older children and young people have been framed as co-researchers and researchers in educational research projects for which they have been trained to implement the academy's recognised research methods (Fielding, 2001; Michail and Kellett, 2013). Both educational research and early childhood research include enquiry focused on numerous disciplines (Alexander, 2009; Bridges, 2006; Gammage, 2006) and the YCAR project was located at the intersection of educational research and early childhood research: early childhood education research. Our field of early childhood education has also begun to find ways to bring research and practice closer: new models of research have been conceptualised that contest traditional power relationships (Formosinho and Oliveira Formosinho, 2012; Pascal and Bertram, 2012) and value young children as 'experts' in their own lives from birth (Alderson, Hawthorne and Killen, 2006; Langsted, 1994: 29). This is important if we are to build authentic accounts of young children's experiences. It is also important if we are to find ways to encourage young children to seek and construct knowledge in the short term and if we are to give them the messages now that lead to them wanting to go on building knowledge throughout their lives. Since the turn of the twenty-first century, young children's perspectives have received more attention (Harcourt, Perry and Waller, 2011) and there has been increased recognition of young children's positioning as active participants in research (Einarsdóttir, 2011) and as co-researchers (Clark and Moss, 2001). The YCAR project found that young children aged 4–8 years build knowledge in their everyday activity in ways that are congruent with academics' research behaviour. For adults to recognise such engagements, skilful observation, sensitivity, reciprocity and reflexivity, combined with robust theoretical knowledge of the field of early childhood education are crucial.

How to make this book work for you

This book reveals some of the sophisticated ways that young children build knowledge but it is also a toolkit to help early childhood leaders, tutors, practitioners, parents and students to recognise, understand, interpret and articulate young children's constructions of knowledge. These are important activities for adults who want to provide young children with the resources they need to continue to build knowledge in ways that young children value and know to be valued. They are also useful tools for helping adults to recognise if we are doing a good job in supporting young children's early education. Finally, they constitute a valuable means for informing our field of early childhood.

How the book is structured

Because the book is about ways that young children construct knowledge, different views of knowledge and how knowledge links with other related areas are a key focus for the second chapter, which also explains *epistemology*, the study of knowledge, or how we know we know. As a whole, the book draws on evidence from the *Young Children As Researchers* (YCAR) project, in particular, how young children build knowledge when they are engaging in four research behaviours that academics identified as important: exploring, finding solutions, conceptualising and basing decisions on evidence. Therefore, the second chapter also sets out how the YCAR project was designed, who participated and what the outcomes were.

The four chapters that follow on from the second chapter are about ways the young children who took part in the YCAR project behaved as researchers when they were constructing knowledge in their everyday activities at home and in their settings. Each of these chapters focuses on one of the four research behaviours that academics in the YCAR project identified as important: exploration, finding solutions, conceptualisation and basing decisions on evidence. Each links practical examples of the children's everyday activities with relevant literature, forms of knowledge, consideration of the adult's role, reflection points and corresponding, free photocopiables. These elements come together as a valuable framework that practitioners and others can use to identify and interpret some of the highly sophisticated thinking and actions that young children adopt to construct knowledge.

Ways you can choose to use the book

Based on research evidence, this is a book about the practical ways that adults who spend time with young children can recognise, value and share some of the sophisticated ways young children construct their knowledge about the world and how they can help children in that endeavour.

You know best the children you work with so you are in the best position to decide how the book will be most useful for you and, importantly, why that might be. Some of these suggestions may help you to decide.

If you are a practitioner, you may find it useful to...

- Print sets of all the photocopiables for each of your key children and use them for snapshot observations. The data you gather can show you how provision in your setting helps the children to construct knowledge. Your snapshots will also be good evidence for developing new aspects of your provision.
- Focus on how your key children engage in one research behaviour (Chapters 3–6). For example, you might use the photocopiables for 'Finding Solutions' if problem-solving is a required aspect of your early childhood curriculum. Print the relevant photocopiable for each of your key children.
- Use one of the epistemological categories (Chapters 3–6) as a focus for observing and assessing the achievements of one or more of your key children. For instance, 'experiment' or 'exploring properties' would be useful for early scientific processes, while 'deductive reasoning' or 'theory of mind' would give you evidence about your children's thinking skills. The vignettes will help you to get started.
- Select one epistemological factor (Chapters 3–6) and use the vignettes as a springboard to support your observation and assessment of one or more of your key children in regard to your selected factor. For example, 'social domains' might be a good focus if you wanted to encourage children to work together more to build knowledge. Repeat for other epistemological factors.
- Use the Research Behaviour Framework (Chapter 2) to identify research behaviours in addition to those outlined in Chapters 3–6 in your children's everyday activities.
- Focus a series of child observations for one or more children on a selected **'form of knowledge'** (Chapters 2–6). Examples from the book will be useful to build an

understanding of what it can look like in children's everyday activities. Repeat for other forms of knowledge.

- Share aspects of the book with parents, then ask parents to use selected photocopiables to observe ways their children build knowledge at home, while you do the same in the setting. Invite parents in for a discussion so you can share what you both found out about the ways their child has constructed knowledge.
- Focus on **'The adult's role'**, outlined in boxes in Chapters 3–6. Consider how your practice fits with selected descriptions and reflect on how these might help you to develop your practice in regard to supporting young children to build knowledge.
- Use the **'Reflection points'**, outlined in boxes in Chapters 3–6 to critically reflect on (i) selected aspects of your practice, (ii) how young children construct knowledge in your setting and (iii) the relationship between (i) and (ii).
- Identify one or more of the epistemological categories or factors, forms of knowledge or research behaviours (see Chapters 2–6) that you would like to encourage children to engage in. Develop an **action research project** to reflect, plan, act and observe this new aspect of your practice (see, for example, Roberts-Holmes, 2014: 78–84 or McNiff, 2010).

If you are an early childhood student, you may find it useful to…

- Critically discuss with your tutor or mentor one or more of the tasks outlined above for practitioners.
- Identify one or more of the tasks to work on when you are on placement. Critically reflect on what you have learned and feed back to your tutor or mentor.
- Follow up the reading for one or more of the examples (Chapters 3–6) and reflect critically on how the information you find out could be used to enhance practice in early childhood settings.

If you are a setting leader, you may find it useful to…

- Consider which aspects of this book can enhance the early childhood curriculum your setting uses.
- Consider which aspects of this book can enhance the dominant early childhood pedagogy in your setting.
- Develop a CPD session or programme for your practitioners, drawing on one or more of the practitioner activities suggested above.
- Select books for your staff room from the references list in the book that will encourage your practitioners to develop their practice in ways to support young children's constructions of knowledge.

If you are an early childhood studies tutor, you may find it useful to…

- Develop a module, part of a module or a single session focused on *Young Children Are Researchers*.
- Provide some or all of the references as a useful reading list for early childhood students.
- Set one or more of the practitioner activities suggested above as practicum tasks.

- Select one or more of the **'Reflection points'** outlined in boxes in Chapters 3–6 as the starting point for a student assignment or debate.

If you are a parent, you may find it useful to…

- See how your child's natural everyday activities match ways that children in the *Young Children Are Researchers* vignettes construct knowledge and behave as researchers (Chapters 3–6).
- Share the book with your child's teacher or practitioner and ask (i) how your child constructs knowledge in his or her setting and (ii) what research behaviours she or he engages in at the setting.
- Focus on **'The adult's role'**, outlined in boxes (Chapters 3–6). Consider how you support your child to build knowledge and engage in research behaviour.

Conclusion

This book suggests new ways for practitioners, parents and others who are interested in early childhood education to recognise how young children construct knowledge, often in highly sophisticated ways. It links research and practice in the field of early childhood in two ways. First, it is based on research evidence derived from the *Young Children As Researchers* project, a participatory study co-constructed with 138 young children aged 4–8 years, their parents and practitioners. Second, the book reveals how young children's constructions of knowledge can have congruence with research behaviours recognised and adopted by adult academics. Before we go further, it is important that I thank the young children and adults who generously engaged in the *Young Children As Researchers* project and indeed all the children and adults it has been my privilege to work with over many years. In myriad ways, each has co-constructed this book with me.

2

WHAT DOES IT MEAN TO KNOW?

In many different ways, those of us who work in the field of early childhood education and care help young children to know more about the world they are growing up in. However, to be able to recognise what knowledge young children are building and how they are doing so, we need to know what knowledge is. Much has been written on what counts as knowledge and it is a complex and contested area (Aguerrondo, 2009), so this short chapter cannot provide an exhaustive account. Rather, it provides enough information about the nature of knowledge to enable the reader to get the most out of this book about how young children build knowledge and how we can help them to do so. This accessible overview defines knowledge, explains and acknowledges diverse perspectives on knowledge and makes links between knowledge and other related areas, including understanding, learning and research.

The chapter has two sections. The first is concerned with the nature of knowledge in a general sense, while the second section focuses on how the *Young Children As Researchers* project produced trustworthy knowledge about the ways that young children behave as researchers in their everyday activities.

What is knowledge?

What counts as knowledge? What do we mean when we say we know? How do we know we know? The section addresses these questions by discussing some of the philosophical ideas that underpin how knowledge is defined. It goes on to deal with the issue of multiple subjective realities that constitute knowledge and its provisional nature, and draws on theoretical perspectives concerned with different forms of knowledge. Links are made between knowledge, understanding, learning and research, and these terms are defined in ways that acknowledge diverse perspectives on each and their provisional nature.

Philosophical ideas on the nature of knowledge

The ancient Greek philosophers left us a significant legacy concerning our understanding of knowledge (Thomas, 2007), for example, Aristotle (350 BC) claimed that it is part of the

human condition to want to know: 'all men by nature desire to know' (p. 1). Dew and Foreman (2014) endorse this view in the context of the world today, observing that 'human beings long for knowledge and depend on it for all aspects of life' (p. 10); they note that this is no less the case for children who 'have an unquenchable thirst for understanding about their world' (p. 10). Laevers (2005) proposes that an exploratory attitude is important for knowledge acquisition, which he exemplifies as 'openness for, and alertness to the wide variety of stimuli that form our surroundings'; he suggests that an attitude such as this is likely to lead to intrinsic motivation which means a person, 'will never stop developing', whatever their age (p. 2). *Epistêmê* was identified by the Greeks as 'a form of thinking that requires a reason for why something is the case' (Thomas, 2007: 149). *Epistêmê* is the etymological basis for 'epistemology', which is a branch of philosophy concerned with 'what counts as knowledge and truth' (Strega, 2005: 201). Luper (2004) defines epistemology as 'the theory of knowledge, the study of the nature, sources, and limitations of knowledge and justification' (p. 1): it is the study of how we know we know (Dew and Foreman, 2014) and it is also concerned with defining knowledge (Turri, 2012).

In recent decades, child development researchers have observed that children are able to engage epistemologically. According to Lovatt and Hedges (2015) this means that children

> ponder, learn, think, inquire, theorise, reason, problem solve, wonder, listen to other views, build knowledge, and, in general, make sense of the world as children themselves experience it. Children develop working theories to move through and from everyday concepts to scientific concepts in their knowledge development.
>
> *(p. 911)*

Piaget (1972a) took a relatively conservative view in his proposition that young children build incrementally on 'genetic epistemology…the origins of the various kinds of knowledge…starting with their most elementary forms…up to and including scientific thought' (p. 15), while Wimmer and Perner (1983) deduced that epistemic thinking emerges in children between the ages of 4 and 6 years. However, working with nursery aged children from 2.7 years, Isaacs (1944) observed that 'epistemic interest and inquiry…is in every respect the same in the child as in the adult' (p. 322) and in their work with children from 6 weeks to 5 years old, Hutt, Tyler, Hutt and Christopherson (1989) argue that young children present with epistemic behaviour, comprising exploration, problem-solving and acquisition of knowledge.

Plato (369 BC) established a definition of knowledge with three elements: 'justified true belief', described by Fumerton (2010) as the 'foundationalist' view of knowledge. Defining knowledge in three short words may seem simple at first glance, but there are significant challenges in deconstructing this definition and its constituent parts. Plato saw **knowledge** as superior to belief: he argued that knowing is more than believing and that knowledge without truth can be no more than belief (Audi, 1998). **Justification** is regarded as more than just a 'lucky guess': it happens when a person bases a judgement they make on the information they have (Kelley, 1991: 165). **Belief** is based on a reason for thinking something is the case because of experiences we have had (Ayer, 1940). This is inferential belief, sometimes described as inductive reasoning. While the 'truth of the premises need not guarantee the truth of the conclusion' for inductive reasoning (Johnson-Laird and Byrne,

1991) judgements derived from inductive reasoning are based on logic (Ayer, 1940), which is, in turn, regarded as a category of justification (Samelson, 2008). Nevertheless, *inductive reasoning* has been regarded as less robust than *deductive reasoning* which is based on 'externalised, objective truth' (Williams, 2002). Johnson-Laird and Byrne (1991) note that 'By definition, a valid deduction yields a conclusion that must be true given that its premises are true' (p. 2). This argument has traditionally been exemplified by syllogism, for example:

> All M are P,
> All S are M
> Therefore, all S are P.
> For example,
> All men are mortal.
> All Greeks are men
> Therefore all Greeks are mortal
>
> *(BonJour, 1998: 39)*

It is suggested that justification is based on evidence (Kelley, 1991), but this can be problematic, since definitions of evidence vary: examples of evidence may include information that we receive through our senses combined with an explanation, precedents such as those used by barristers to argue cases, philosophical arguments, documents or personal accounts (Oancea and Pring, 2009). The ways we define evidence depend on the contexts in which we are using it, but the strength of that evidence depends on the level of confidence we can have in it: evidence and proof are rarely the same thing (Oancea and Pring, 2009).

On the other hand, justification and truth do tend to have strong links (Audi, 1998). In his 'principle of verification' Hume (1748) recognised that justification may emerge from two types of reasoning (Thomas, 2007): 'abstract reasoning concerning number or quantity' or 'experimental reasoning concerning matter of fact and existence' (Hume, 1748: 123). Audi (1998) argues that when a belief is based on 'matter of fact and existence' (Hume, 1748: 123), it may be realism, which is a form of truth (p. 239). However, Popper (1965) argues that truth is not verification; he suggests that truth can only be one of two things: (i) an idea that has been proposed or (ii) an idea that is shown to be false. Audi (1998) argues that if we can provide justification for a belief that we have, just the process of providing the justification can be the basis for regarding the belief to be true.

Plato's definition of knowledge as 'justified true belief' was upheld for many centuries but in 1963 it was challenged by Gettier. Nevertheless, despite Gettier's challenge, no new definition has been agreed regarding what constitutes knowing a fact or truth, so Plato's definition has continued to prevail (Hetherington, 2009). However, this is just one type of knowledge.

Different forms of knowledge

This section defines some different categories of knowledge, introduces diverse perspectives concerning knowledge and considers the provisional nature of knowledge. The forms of knowledge that are presented here are not exhaustive; they are just a few examples, sufficient to indicate that different kinds of knowledge are valued in diverse ways and in varied contexts.

Knowing that

Plato's definition of knowledge – 'justified true belief' (369 BC), as outlined above, is propositional knowledge. Propositional knowledge is concerned with facts: knowing *that* something is the case and understanding the reasoning behind it (Ryle, 1949). 'Knowing that' is the focus for epistemology – from the ancient Greek *epistêmê* – thinking concerned with reasoning (Thomas, 2007: 149). Luper (2004) explains that a proposition is a description of an aspect of the world; if we believe the premise to be true, we also believe the proposition to be true (Luper, 2004). Such a proposition may be presented as a syllogism, as outlined above.

Knowing how

Ryle (1949) identifies procedural knowledge – 'knowing how' – as a distinct category of knowledge. He argues that a person can know 'how' to do something without knowledge of the meaning or theory underpinning the action. 'Knowing how' requires 'skills, strategies, productions and interiorized actions' (Byrnes and Wasik, 1991: 777) but does not require understanding. For example, a young child may be able to sing the nursery rhyme 'Old King Cole' without understanding what all the words mean. The ancient Greeks termed 'knowing how' as '*technê*': 'a craft or skill, distinguished from *epistêmê* by the absence of underlying principles of understanding' (Thomas, 2007: 150). There may be a relationship between propositional and procedural knowledge, but neither is necessarily contingent on the other (Ryle, 1949).

A priori knowledge

A priori (analytic) knowledge is derived from pure reasoning, and does not rely on first-hand experience (Kant, 1787). Bridges (2003) describes a priori concepts as 'philosophical' (p. 21) and a priori knowledge is acquired through a process of deduction. If a teacher asked a child to imagine there are two spacemen in a rocket and one jumps out and the child could identify that one spaceman is left in the rocket, the child would have used a priori knowledge to deduce the answer.

A posteriori knowledge

A posteriori (synthetic) reasoning combines first-hand sensory experience with mental activity to derive a conclusion (Kant, 1787). Bridges (2003) describes a posteriori reasoning as 'empirical/scientific' (p. 21); Scruton (2001) describes it as 'the joint operation of sensibility and understanding' (p. 35). A posteriori knowledge aligns with the aspect of Hume's 'principle of verification' (1748) for which judgement is derived from 'experimental reasoning concerning matter of fact and existence' (Hume, 1748: 123). Gaut and Gaut (2012) give an example of a posteriori reasoning: they showed young children a teddy bear with a handkerchief and said to the children 'Teddy is feeling very sad. He is crying and using his hankie to dry his tears. Why do you think he's sad?' A child's response – 'He's fallen over and hurt himself' – is based on the sensory experiences the child has had of falling over and the accompanying pain, coupled with her reasoning that Teddy might have had a similar experience and this might have upset Teddy.

Explicit knowledge

Explicit knowledge is knowledge that is overtly shared. Ways to share explicit knowledge may include 'documents, drawings, standard operating procedures, manuals of best practice' as well as information communication systems (Sanchez, 2005: 6). A text book is an example of explicit knowledge.

Tacit knowledge

It may not be possible to transmit some forms of knowledge in explicit ways, such as oral or written language; Polanyi (1967) observed that 'we can know more than we can tell' (p. 4). He suggests that while we may be able to acquire some knowledge by using a template provided to us by someone who knows more than us, other kinds of knowledge depend on an individual's personality, inner resources and personal experiences. They might include practices, values, traditions and judgements that we have inherited (Polanyi, 1958; 1967). Examples of tacit knowledge might include learning to ride a bike or painting a beautiful picture.

Mode 1 knowledge

'Traditional' knowledge is described by Gibbons, Limoges, Nowotny, Schwartzman, Scott and Trow (1994) as 'Mode 1' knowledge. That is, knowledge that is 'disciplinary', primarily cognitive' (p. 1), 'hierarchical', 'characterised by homogenity' and knowledge for which 'problems are set and solved in a context governed by the largely academic interests of a specific community' (p. 3). To be accomplished in producing Mode 1 knowledge requires training by more knowledgeable others in a given field and adherence to the rules of engagement of that field.

Mode 2 knowledge

Gibbons *et al.* (1994) propose Mode 2 knowledge as an alternative to Mode 1 Knowledge, particularly in regard to knowledge production. They describe Mode 2 Knowledge as applied, 'transdisciplinary', 'heterarchical and transient', suggesting it is 'more socially accountable and reflexive' (p. 3). They also indicate that Mode 2 Knowledge is likely to attract engagement by an eclectic range of practitioners working on a particular project together before going their separate ways to work on something different.

The literature suggests then, that knowledge is categorised in different ways; it is regarded through varied lenses adopted for diverse purposes. These forms of knowledge are revisited throughout the book, linked to examples of young children's research behaviour that emerged in the YCAR project.

Knowledge, research, understanding and learning

The pluralistic view of knowledge is mirrored in research as research is also defined in different ways: there exists 'no single objective definition of what actually constitutes "good quality" research' (Hillage, Pearson, Anderson and Tamkin, 1998: 25). Some definitions of research focus on the need to be systematic, for example, Kerlinger (1973) defines research as 'systematic, controlled, empirical and critical investigation of hypothetical propositions about the presumed relations among natural phenomena' (p. 1), Stenhouse's (1975) definition is simply 'systematic enquiry made public' (p .142) and Payton (1979) defines it as 'the process of looking for a specific answer to a specific question in an organized objective reliable way' (p. 4). Other definitions of research maintain the requirement for a systematic approach but also argue for a strong relationship between research and knowledge. Bassey (1990) suggests that 'provided it is carried out systematically, critically and self-critically, the search for knowledge is research' (p. 35), while Drew (1980) argues that 'Research is conducted to solve problems and to expand knowledge…it is a systematic way of asking questions, a systematic method of enquiry' (p. 4). In a UK context, the Research Excellence Framework (REF) 2014 defined research as 'a process of investigation leading to new insights, effectively shared'.

Kuhn (1970) proposes that research is legitimate when researchers adopt a single specified paradigm, with its own particular 'esoteric vocabulary and skills' (p. 64) and set of 'ontological and epistemological presuppositions' (Thomas, 2007: 151). Schostak (2002) suggests that at the heart of the argument for Kuhn's claim lies 'the status of eternal truth, the final guarantee of there being some sense in life' (p. 137). However, Feyerabend (1993) challenges this view, claiming that 'the only principle that does not inhibit progress is: "anything goes"' (p. 14). Harlen (1994) also adopts an open stance. She sees research as:

> A way of generating understanding and knowledge, yielding ideas and theories which are accepted for as long as they help our understanding of evidence but which are constantly superseded and changed when new evidence is obtained which conflicts with them. There is no end to this process; no ultimate truth or understanding.
>
> *(p. 5)*

Others endorse Harlen's view: Popper (1965) regards all knowledge as provisional, while Hargraves (2014) describes knowledge as 'constantly adapting' (p. 35). Equally, Foreman-Peck and Murray (2008) propose that 'knowledge develops by a process of active construction and reconstruction of theory and practice by those involved', implying that knowledge is not only provisional, but is also contextual. Foreman-Peck and Murray's work is concerned with educational research and their proposition aligns with a view that knowledge in the social sciences is not only theoretical but is also bound into *praxis*, defined as practice, action, or 'a wise and prudent practical judgement about how to act in *this* situation' (Carr and Kemmis, 1986: 190; Giddens, 1984; Pascal and Bertram, 2012).

While some regard knowledge as complex (Aguerrondo, 2009; Lovatt and Hedges, 2015), Bloom (1956) classifies knowledge – or knowledge acquisition – as the lowest level of learning within the cognitive domain, which, with affective and psycho-motor domains, constitutes the three domains of learning that he established. Bloom defines knowledge as the ability to 'recall or recognise information, ideas, and principles in the approximate form in which they were learned'. He regards understanding, for which the actor 'comprehends, or interprets information based on prior learning' and application, for which the actor 'selects, transfers, and uses data and principles to complete a problem or task' more highly than 'knowledge', which he presents only as 'remembering' information (Anderson and Krathwohl, 2001).

Summary

This section has considered some of the ideas that underpin knowledge: how it is defined, what may constitute knowledge, the provisional nature of knowledge and how we can know we know. Links between knowledge, understanding, learning and research have been discussed and it has been established that knowledge is regarded and valued in different ways. Despite wide acceptance of Gettier's argument (1963), consensus has not yet been able to move beyond Plato's definition of knowledge as 'justified, true belief' to create a new, universally accepted definition of knowledge. Nevertheless, justifications, truths and beliefs underpinning knowledge – the ways we can know we know – epistemology – seem to be affected by the multiple contexts, purposes and subjective realities of the people who create and use the knowledge. The *Young Children As Researchers* project began from the premise that some of those people are young children.

How do we know that young children can be researchers?

Building on Chapter 1 which explains *why* the *Young Children As Researchers* project was developed, this section of Chapter 2 explains *how* the *Young Children As Researchers* (YCAR) project was developed, to provide a foundation for the chapters that follow. This discussion is important for the reader because the book makes the claim that young children are researchers who build knowledge. That claim is warranted by knowledge derived from the YCAR project. For this book to be useful for your valuable work in early childhood, you need to have confidence that the claim is based on knowledge that is authentic and trustworthy; in other words, justified true belief. This section explains how you can have such confidence.

This second section is divided into two main parts: the first part outlines how the YCAR project was designed, while the second part focuses on introducing four important research behaviours that emerged from YCAR as key ways that young children construct knowledge.

YCAR aim and research questions

YCAR set out to conceptualise ways that young children aged 4–8 years are researchers, could develop as researchers and, importantly, may be recognised as researchers. There were four research questions:

- What might research be like in early childhood education?
- How can a study be conducted to establish young children as researchers?
- What enquiries are important to young children and how can they engage in them?
- What support structures might encourage young children to participate in research? What barriers might prevent this?

Designing YCAR

I initiated the YCAR project and I brought to it a set of assumptions (Hatch, 1995), formed through my career in early childhood education spanning quarter of a century in practice and in research. These assumptions included:

- Children have rights (OHCHR, 1989).
- Children are competent social actors (James, Jenks and Prout, 1998).
- Children may engage in research (Punch, 2002).
- Children's ways of communicating may be different from – but not inferior to – those of adults (Shevlin and Rose, 2003).
- Children are excluded from the academy which privileges its adult members and particular protocols (Redmond, 2008).

Alongside the YCAR project aim and research questions, these assumptions shaped a *value orientation* for the project that was reflected in three principled approaches adopted throughout: induction, participation and emancipation. Using an *inductive approach* meant that the project emerged from data that the participants provided (Charmaz, 2006). The project's *participatory approach* ensured that YCAR adopted a democratic stance and focused on participants' rights, particularly children's rights (Freire, 1972; Kemmis and McTaggart, 2005), while the *emancipatory approach* underpinned a critical position regarding power inequalities (Habermas, 1987): YCAR was about challenging inequalities and as such, it was about adopting an ethical stance. It followed BERA guidelines (2011) and its ethical conduct was approved by a university ethics committee.

The YCAR project was also about exploring and interpreting young children's everyday activities to capture and highlight research behaviours within them so YCAR was a qualitative study conducted in children's settings and their homes (Edwards, 2010). Participants' perspectives were prioritised, rather than methodological rubric, so in establishing the research design, flexibility was important. Research is usually conducted within a paradigm – a way of working that recognises knowledge in a particular way (Creswell, 2013): disciplines tend to adopt their own paradigms. Taking into account the YCAR research aim, objectives and questions, along with its value orientation and three approaches, YCAR rejected 'that there is only one way that knowledge can be constituted' (Hekman, 1990: 9), and a Plural Paradigm Model was adopted (Figure 2.1): a range of carefully selected paradigms, each fulfilling a specific purpose, while creating a coherent framework for recognising the knowledge that YCAR produced.

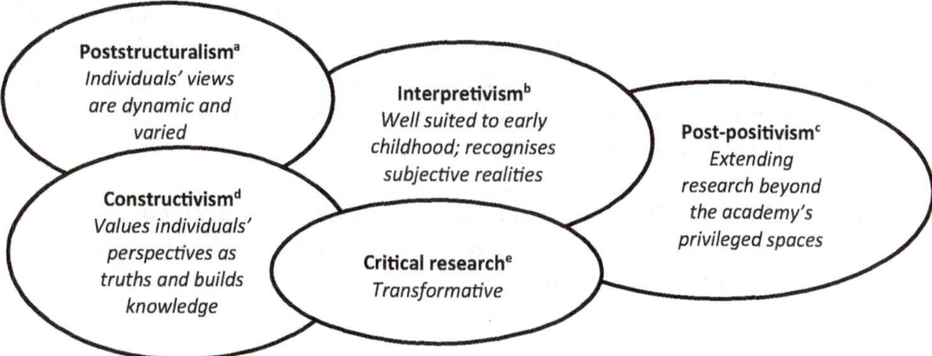

FIGURE 2.1 Plural paradigm model (Murray, 2015a)

a Hatch, 2007; Strega, 2005; Bae, 2010; b Dahlberg, Moss and Pence, 1999; Ritchie, Lewis, McNaughton Nicholls and Ormston, 2003; Lee, 2009; Hughes, 2010; c Creswell, 2013; d Ackermann, 2001; Lash, 2008; e Carspecken, 1996; Brown and Strega, 2005; Hatch, 2007

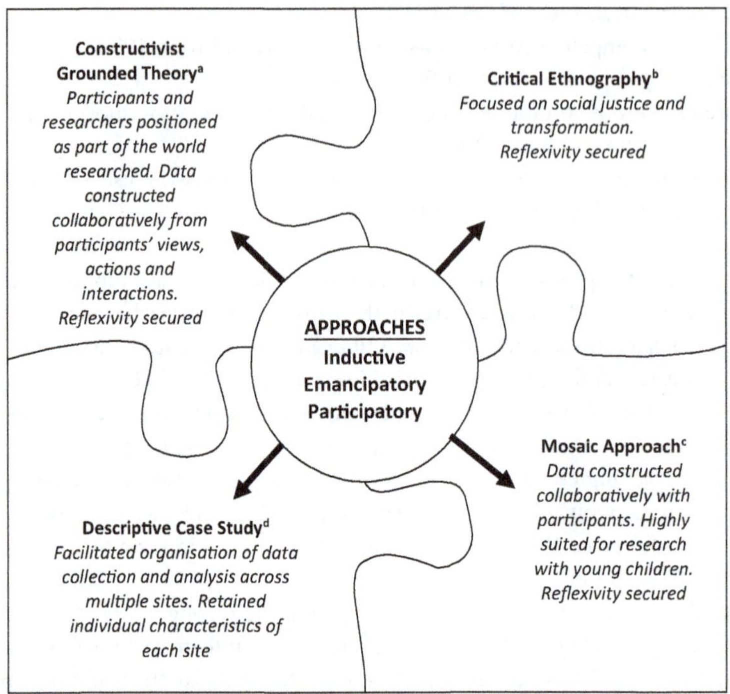

FIGURE 2.2 Jigsaw methodology (Murray, 2013, 2014, 2015a, 2016)

a Charmaz, 2006; Glaser and Strauss, 1967
b Carspecken, 1996
c Clark and Moss, 2001
d Bassey, 1999; Yin, 2012

Methodology is the academy's term for the strategy that researchers use to guide the production of knowledge in a research project. Making the methodology transparent is a key feature of knowledge production in the context of scientific method. There are many different methodologies. Jigsaw Methodology was developed for YCAR and mirrored its Plural Paradigm Model. The YCAR Jigsaw Methodology was constructed of the three approaches and four carefully selected research methodologies, each fulfilling a specific purpose, while creating a coherent strategy for producing knowledge for YCAR.

In YCAR data were co-constructed with participants in three phases:

- Phase I: Professional Early Years and Educational Researchers (PEYERs) (n=30).
- Phase II: Practitioners (n=17) and children (n=138) in early childhood settings.
- Phase III: Families (n=5) and children (n=5) in their homes.

YCAR Phase I

There is no universal definition of research (Hillage, Pearson, Anderson and Tamkin, 1998), so Phase I was about capturing definitions of research in the fields of education and early childhood education from the people who make the rules about these things: academy members (Bridges, 2006). In this way, children's everyday activities could be compared

TABLE 2.1 Research behaviour framework (RBF) (Murray, 2014, 2015a, 2016)

Researchers		
1. Seek a solution	16. Build on others' work	30. Use and apply findings in new contexts
2. Want to explore	17. Take account of context	31. Believe what they are doing is good
3. Explore with an aim	18. Plan	32. Are focused on their chosen activity
4. Explore without an aim	19. Conceptualise	33. Reflect on process
5. Explore with an aim which changes during the process	20. Question	34. Reflect on results
6. Explore with a fine focus	21. Investigate	35. Do no harm
7. Explore broadly	22. Enquire	36. Participate with others
8. Find out why things happen	23. Test and check	37. Communicate what they are doing
9. Find out how things happen	24. Are systematic	38. Can communicate what they have done
10. Examine problems	25. Are objective	39. Make links
11. Develop better understanding of the world through exploration	26. Base decisions on evidence	
12. Increase knowledge	27. Use processes that are fit for purpose	
13. Find a solution	28. Can replicate process	
14. Go beyond instinct	29. Can replicate output	
15. Gather data		

against these definitions and if children's behaviours could be shown to be congruent with the academy's perception of research, it could be argued that excluding young children from the academy could no longer be justified (Redmond, 2008). PEYERs participated in interview conversations (n=9) (Charmaz, 2006) and a focus group (n=5) (Creswell, 2008). All worked in a university and had also previously worked as practitioners in children's services. A taxonomy of 39 research behaviours emerged: A Research Behaviour Framework (RBF) (Table 2.1):

Next, in a democratic nominal grouping exercise (Delbecq and Van de Ven, 1971), PEYERs (n=23) ranked the research behaviours and identified exploration, finding solutions, conceptualisation and basing decisions as the four 'most important' research behaviours – or behaviours for scientific method – so these were the focus for the YCAR project. PEYERs proposed that participants should include young children, their early childhood practitioners and parents.

YCAR Phase II

Three multi-modal case studies (Clark and Moss, 2001; Yin, 2012) were co-constructed with children (n=138) aged 4–8 years in three early childhood settings and their practitioners, who were teachers or teaching assistants (n=17). According to the four-point scale adopted by the English inspection body, Ofsted, all three settings had most recently been judged '2 – Good'. The settings were a purposive sample, self-selected from a sampling frame of early childhood settings in a town in the Midlands that wanted to join the project and could provide rich data. All setting and participant names that appear in the book are pseudonyms.

Ash Setting was a class of 32 children aged 7–8 (20 boys and 12 girls) and 3 practitioners – in a large primary school. The statutory English National Curriculum was used (DfEE and

QCA, 1999) and the predominant pedagogic model in Ash Setting was direct instruction (Siraj-Blatchford, Sylva, Muttock, Gilden and Bell, 2002), with some opportunities for children to work independently to support their skill development and also so teachers could assess their knowledge.

Beech Setting was a reception unit in a large primary school with 46 children aged 4–5 years (23 boys and 23 girls). There were eight practitioners altogether in Beech Setting. The setting followed the statutory English Early Years Foundation Stage framework (DCSF, 2008) and its pedagogic model was an 'open framework approach' where children engaged in a combination of 'instructive learning environments in which adults support(ed) children's learning', including free play and 'group work involving direct instruction' (Siraj-Blatchford *et al.*, 2002: 56).

Cherry Setting was another reception unit in a large primary school. Here, there were 60 children aged 4–5 years (40 boys and 20 girls) as well as 6 practitioners. Again, Cherry Setting followed the statutory English Early Years Foundation Stage framework (DCSF, 2008) and its pedagogic model was similar to that adopted by Beech Setting.

During the Phase II data collection, I returned to work in early childhood settings, not as a teacher this time, but as a volunteer teaching assistant. This gave me an understanding of the culture in each of the three YCAR early childhood settings (Ryle, 1968), as well as 'insider' status in each (Griffiths, 1998); it also helped to equalise power relationships in the field, supporting the co-construction of authentic, naturalistic data (Pellegrini, Symons and Hoch, 2004).

Multiple methods were adopted to co-construct data (Clark and Moss, 2001); some were planned from the start of YCAR, while some, such as children's artefacts, were proposed by participants as YCAR progressed.

- ✓ Field notes
- ✓ Interview conversations
- ✓ Observations
- ✓ Focus groups
- ✓ Informal discussions
- ✓ Documents
- ✓ Children's artefacts
- ✓ Photographs
- ✓ Video recordings
- ✓ Audio recordings
- ✓ Research Behaviour Framework (RBF) analysis sheets

Throughout YCAR, as data emerged, participants also supported analysis. In a recursive process, they contributed to constant comparison of data against the RBF (Table 2.1); categorisation and coding of data with participants indicated 17 children for closer involvement in the project (Table 2.2). These were children who most often presented with research behaviours early in the process, but who also wanted to be part of the project and whose parents had consented to them doing so. The data co-construction continued with focus on these children. Data were collected in the summer, so as the academic year in England is September–August, most children were either 5 or 8 years old, though some were 4 or 7 years old). The home language of all 17 Phase II focus children was English, except

TABLE 2.2 Phase II setting focus children

Ash Setting	Annie (girl, aged 7), Billy (boy, aged 8), Costas (boy aged 8), Demi (girl, aged 8), Edward (boy, aged 8), Florence (girl, aged 8)
Beech Setting	Gemma (girl, aged 5), Harry (boy, aged 5), India (girl, aged 5), Johnny (boy, aged 5), Kelly (girl, aged 4), Laura (girl, aged 5)
Cherry Setting	Martin (boy, aged 5), Nora (girl, aged 5), Oscar (boy, aged 5), Pedro (boy, aged 5), Querida (girl, aged 4)

for Pedro whose home language was Turkish; Harry was bi-lingual in French and English because his father was French and his mother was English.

YCAR Phase III

Using the same filtering process, two children from each setting were identified to go on to co-construct further rich data with their families at home (Table 2.3). However, one child from Cherry Setting withdrew from Phase III of the project just before it began, so the Phase III cohort consisted of five children and their families.

All five families lived in modern, detached, four-bedroomed homes with gardens on new housing developments and all were from social class categories A or B, according to the Market Research Society scale (MRS, 2012).

In Phase III, I assumed 'outsider' status to minimise intrusion on family life and ensure families retained power (Griffiths, 1998). Initial interview conversations were arranged with each family at home when I explained and implemented ethical procedures (Alderson and Morrow, 2004; British Educational Research Association, 2011), ensured the children and their families were confident to collect data, provided resources, then left the children and families to collect the home data. A month later, in interview conversations and focus groups during second visits to each family, we shared, discussed, reviewed and analysed the multi-modal data the families had captured (Charmaz, 2006).

YCAR analysis and findings

Our analysis was guided by Charmaz's analytic model for grounded theory complemented by analytic models common to the other three methodologies. Analysis was participatory and recursive; it included memo-writing (Charmaz, 2006), child conferencing (Clark and Moss, 2001), analytic statements (Yin, 2012) and dialogic data generation (Carspecken, 1996), among other features. Eighty categories emerged from the analysis, spread across the four important research behaviours. These comprised 68 epistemological categories and 12

TABLE 2.3 Home focus children

From Ash Setting	Annie (girl, aged 7), lived with her mother and father
	Billy (boy, aged 8), lived with his mother, father and sister (aged 9)
From Beech Setting	Gemma (girl, aged 5), lived with her mother, father and brother (aged 8)
	Harry (boy, aged 5), lived with his mother, father and brother (aged 4)
From Cherry Setting	Martin (boy, aged 5), lived with his mother, father and sister (aged 4)

KEY:
FaS: Find a Solution

EPISTEMOLOGICAL BARRIERS		*FaS – Solution not shared with or witnessed by others*		
		FaS – Solution not shared with or witnessed by others (unconfirmed)		
		FaS – Denied opportunity to share solution	*FaS – Believes s/he has failed*	
		FaS – Responding to adult's semi-open questions	*FaS – Unmotivated*	
		FaS – Responding to adult's closed questions	*FaS – Has become disinterested*	
	FaS – Reproducing knowledge s/he already had	*FaS – Following adult's direction*	*FaS – Gives up*	*FaS – Solution unconfirmed*
EPISTEMOLOGICAL FACTORS	**Applications of prior experience**	**Social domains**	**Dispositions**	**Outliers**

FIGURE 2.3 YCAR epistemological barriers (Murray, 2016)

epistemological barriers. The 68 epistemological categories (Figure 2.4) were the constructs the children in the YCAR project used to build their knowledge: the provocations that enabled young children to adopt research behaviours, in other words, their building blocks for knowledge. Conversely, the 12 epistemological barriers inhibited young children's research behaviours (Figure 2.3).

Because this book is concerned with how young children build knowledge and how adults can support them in doing this, focus in the book is given to the epistemological categories, rather than to the barriers to learning.

The next step was to group the 68 categories and 12 barriers into nine epistemological factors (Table 2.4): these appear at the bottom of the epistemological barriers (Figure 2.3) and the epistemological categories displayed above (Figure 2.4) and are presented as a discrete group below.

The final element in co-constructing YCAR data was to deconstruct and evaluate each of the epistemological categories and factors through comparative critical discussion, synthesising findings with relevant extant literature for hundreds of vignettes of young children's activity that had been captured (Charmaz, 2006). This final process exposed the sophisticated processes of knowledge construction adopted by children in their everyday activities (Bae, 2010). It also revealed congruence between many of the children's natural everyday activities and the four research behaviours deemed 'most important' by academy members (Table 2.5).

These were the four research behaviours regarded by academy members as most important, from among a list of 39 research behaviours (Table 2.2). During the YCAR project, young children revealed that they used 80 epistemological categories (Figure 2.3) as building blocks during their everyday activities to construct knowledge to understand, learn and behave as researchers through exploration, finding solutions, conceptualising and basing decisions on evidence.

TABLE 2.4 YCAR epistemological factors in young children's everyday behaviours (Murray, 2014, 2015a)

Applications of prior experience	Innovation	Social domains
Autonomy	Material contexts	Cognitive domains
Dispositions	Methodological issues	Outliers

KEY:
E: Exploration
FaS: Find a Solution
C: Conceptualisation
BDoE: Base Decisions on Evidence

EPISTEMOLOGICAL CATEGORIES

Applications of prior experience	Innovation	Social domains	Autonomy	Material contexts	Cognitive domains	Dispositions	Methodological issues	Outliers
BDoE – Extrapolates								
BDoE – Applies mental model					BDoE – Applies 'Humean' reason			
BDoE – Applies prior experience					BDoE – Thinks strategically			
C – Recalling instructions		BDoE – Acts on adult opinion			BDoE – Trial and error			
C – Linking prior knowledge to new application		BDoE – Values peer perspectives			BDoE – Meta-cogniton			
C – Synthesising concepts	C – Identifies anomaly	C – Conceptualises after adult stops conceptualisation	BDoE – Enacts personal preference		C – Making links – analogy			
C – Thinking tangentially	C – Creating an imagined space / persona	C – Following adult's direction to conceptualise	C – Makes decision/s based on own criteria	BDoE – Senses provide evidence for action	C – Planning			
C – Thinking through a problem by applying concepts	C – Developing own idea[s] from external stimulus	C – Works with others to conceptualise	C – Autonomously deciding what needs to be done and doing it	C – Creates a new use for object[s]	C – Engaged in symbolic represent-tation	FaS – Excited by finding solution		
FaS – Able reader	C – Invents a process / method	FaS – Theory of mind	C – Creating a problem	FaS – Inductive reasoning	C – Language supports thinking	FaS – Motivated by finding solution		
FaS – Wants to preserve what s/he is doing	FaS – Finds own solution	FaS – Employs others to help with finding a solution	FaS – Focused on something of personal interest	FaS – Deductive reasoning	C – Using imagination	FaS – Perseveres to resolve problem		
FaS – Finds practical use for solution	FaS – Devises practical method to create solution	FaS – Shares solution	FaS – Time and freedom to explore, investigate, experiment with something of personal interest	FaS – Exploring properties	C – Involved in pursuing a train of thought	E – Seeking	BDoE – Basing Decisions on Evidence is Research	
FaS – Applying rule to create solution	FaS – Creates a problem to solve	FaS – Resolves another person's problem	FaS – Self-regulates	E – Shows interest in materials	C – Predicts	E – Curious	BDoE – Sampling issue	
E – Patterned behaviour	E – Experiment	E – Social encounter	E – Develops own agenda	E – Interested in context	E – Cause and effect	E – Focused on task	BDoE – Methodological issue	C – Applies anthropomorphism

EPISTEMOLOGICAL FACTORS

FIGURE 2.4 YCAR epistemological categories (Murray, 2016)

TABLE 2.5 Four important research behaviours

Exploration	E
Finding a solution	FaS
Conceptualisation	C
Basing decisions on evidence	BDoE

Defining the epistemological factors

Once the nine epistemological factors in the YCAR project had emerged from the data, each was defined in synthesis with extant literature to secure their trustworthiness and to promote shared understanding of their meanings in regard to *Young Children As Researchers*. These definitions are summarised below, together with tables displaying the epistemological categories that constitute each epistemological factor, alongside the research behaviours they indicate.

Applications of prior experiences resonate with a key philosophical idea that informs the academy's research activity and esteem: a posteriori conceptualisation (Scruton, 2001), discussed above. A posteriori conceptualisations were easier to identify in the YCAR project than a priori conceptualisations, because they presented more explicitly in children's actions than their a priori conceptualisations. Children's applications of prior experiences included:

TABLE 2.6 Epistemological categories and barriers: Applications of prior experience

EPISTEMOLOGICAL CATEGORIES: APPLICATIONS OF PRIOR EXPERIENCE	
Patterned behaviour	E
Applying rule to create solution	FaS
Finding practical use for solution	FaS
Wants to preserve what s/he is doing	FaS
Able reader	FaS
Thinking through a problem by applying concepts	C
Thinking tangentially	C
Synthesising concepts	C
Linking prior knowledge to new application	C
Recalling instructions	C
Applies prior experience	BDoE
Applies mental model	BDoE
Extrapolates	BDoE
EPISTEMOLOGICAL BARRIERS: APPLICATIONS OF PRIOR EXPERIENCE	
(BARRIER) Reproducing knowledge s/he already had	FaS

Innovation is regarded as the development of new ideas into something valued (Department for Business, Innovation and Skills, 2011; 2012). In the YCAR project, children developed ideas new to them that they valued for various reasons, resulting in the following epistemological categories:

TABLE 2.7 Epistemological categories: Innovation

EPISTEMOLOGICAL CATEGORIES: INNOVATION	
Experiment	E
Creates a problem to solve	FaS
Devises practical method to create solution	FaS
Finds own solution	FaS
Invents a process or method	C
Developing own ideas from external stimulus	C
Creating an imagined space or persona	C
Identifies anomaly	C

Social domains relating to children's research behaviours include children's spaces and social constructionism (Moss and Petrie, 2002), play (Gussin Paley, 2004), children problem-solving in social contexts (Ashley and Tomasello, 1998), 'ethics of an encounter' (Dahlberg and Lenz Taguchi, 1994), intersubjectivity (Göncü, 1993), social constructivism (Vygotsky, 1978), Theory of Mind (Meltzoff, 2011), children sharing decision-making (Levin and Hart, 2003; Eisele, 2003), children's peers (Löfdahl and Hägglund, 2006) and adult hegemonies (Markström and Halldén, 2009). The epistemological categories within *Social Domains* were a combination of barriers and provocations that young children encountered; these provided contexts for their research behaviours.

TABLE 2.8 Epistemological categories and barriers: Social domains

EPISTEMOLOGICAL CATEGORIES: SOCIAL DOMAINS	
Social encounter	E
Resolves another person's problem	FaS
Shares solution	FaS
Employs others to help with finding a solution	FaS
Theory of mind	FaS
Works with others to develop conceptualisation	C
Following adult's direction	C
Adult stops conceptualisation	C
Values peer perspectives	BDoE
Acts on adult opinion	BDoE
EPISTEMOLOGICAL BARRIERS: SOCIAL DOMAINS	
(BARRIER) Following adult's direction	FaS
(BARRIER) Responding to adult's closed questions	FaS
(BARRIER) Responding to adult's semi-open questions	FaS
(BARRIER) Denied opportunity to share solution	FaS
(BARRIER) Solution not shared with or witnessed by others (unconfirmed)	FaS
(BARRIER) Solution not shared with or witnessed by others	FaS

Autonomy is regarded as an 'inner endorsement of one's actions, the sense that they emanate from oneself and are one's own' (Deci and Ryan, 1987: 1025). It is congruent with intrinsic motivation, creativity, enhanced conceptualisation, empowerment and 'intentional behaviour' where choice is promoted; autonomy is oppositional to 'control behaviour' which exerts pressure to achieve extrinsically specified outcomes (Deci and Ryan, 1987: 1024; Lowrie, 2002). In the YCAR project, children's autonomy relating to their research behaviours included, among other aspects, 'senses of self' for example, agency and intentionality (Stern, 1985: 6), children's discursive and temporal spaces (Corsaro, 2003; Markström and Hallden, 2009), flow (Csíkszentmihályi, 1990), problem-setting (Pintrich and Zusho, 2002) and decision-making (Johnson-Laird and Shafir, 1993). The epistemological categories for ***autonomy*** are:

TABLE 2.9 Epistemological categories: Autonomy

EPISTEMOLOGICAL CATEGORIES: AUTONOMY	
Develops own agenda	E
Self-regulates	FaS
Time and freedom to explore, investigate, experiment with something of personal interest	FaS
Focused on something of personal interest	FaS
Creating a problem	C
Autonomously deciding what needs to be done and doing it	C
Makes decisions based on own criteria	C
Enacts personal preference	BDoE

Material contexts were an important feature for children's research behaviours. In the YCAR project, children often showed interest in the materials and objects they encountered through epistemic engagements (*i.a.* Hutt *et al.*, 1989; Morgenthaler, 2006). When children engaged with material objects, their senses seemed to give them evidence to take further action; they often engaged cognitively and physically at the same time to solve problems (Keen, 2011). Additionally, children conceptualised within their material contexts to create new uses for objects (Kant, 1787; Scruton, 2001), often as part of symbolic play (Manning-Morton and Thorp, 2003).

TABLE 2.10 Epistemological categories: Material contexts

EPISTEMOLOGICAL CATEGORIES: MATERIAL CONTEXTS	
Interested in context	E
Shows interest in materials	E
Exploring properties	FaS
Deductive reasoning	FaS
Inductive reasoning	FaS
Creates a new use for object(s)	C
Senses provide evidence for action	BDoE

Cognitive domains were revealed as aspects of children's thinking in their research behaviours. They emerged in their exploratory behaviour as causality (Stebbins, 2001) and also presented as a posteriori conceptualisation (Scruton, 2001) when they engaged in prediction (*i.a.* Klentschy, 2008), flow (Csíkszentmihályi, 1990), imagination (Kant, 1787), discourse (Habermas, 1984), symbolic representation (Bruner, 1966), planning (Cox and Smitsman, 2006) and analogy (Goswami, 1992). Additionally, children based decisions on evidence by adopting cognitive strategies including metacognition (Flavell, 1979), trial and error-elimination (Popper (1972/1979), strategic thinking (Bjorklund, 1990) and Humean reasoning (Hume, 1748).

TABLE 2.11 Epistemological categories: Cognitive domains

EPISTEMOLOGICAL CATEGORIES: COGNITIVE DOMAINS	
Cause and effect	E
Predicts	C
Involved in pursuing a train of thought	C
Using imagination	C
Using language to support thinking process	C
Engaged in symbolic representation	C
Planning	C
Making links: analogy	C
Metacognition	BDoE
Trial and error	BDoE
Thinks strategically	BDoE
Applies Hume's reason	BDoE

Dispositions are widely recognised indicators for lifelong learning, tending to be characterised as involvement, well-being, independence, resilience, creativity and self-motivation (Laevers, 1994; Carr, 2001). Particular 'dispositions' were indicated in children's research behaviours, including epistemic curiosity (Berlyne, 1954), seeking (Katz, 1994), persevering to resolve problems (McClelland, Acock, Piccinin, Rhea and Stallings, 2013), and motivated and excited by finding solutions (Gammage, 1999; Sherman and MacDonald, 2006). Children did not present with dispositions when conceptualising or basing decisions on evidence and, as indicated, some dispositions children presented with tended to present barriers to their research behaviour.

TABLE 2.12 Epistemological categories and barriers: Dispositions

EPISTEMOLOGICAL CATEGORIES: DISPOSITIONS	
Focused on task	E
Curious	E
Seeking	E
Perseveres to resolve problem	FaS
Motivated by finding solution	FaS
Excited by finding solution	FaS

(Continued)

TABLE 2.12 continued

EPISTEMOLOGICAL BARRIERS: DISPOSITIONS	
(BARRIER) Gives up	FaS
(BARRIER) Has become disinterested	FaS
(BARRIER) Unmotivated	FaS
(BARRIER) Believes s/he has failed	FaS

Methodological issues emerged in the YCAR project in regard to children's research behaviours. Just three presented within the project's primary data and the analysis and interpretation process. All linked to one research behaviour: basing decisions on evidence. They concerned uses of technology for gathering data (Shrum, Duque and Brown, 2005)and children basing decisions evidence as part of the project itself (Lansdown, 2005; 2010; Invernizzi and Williams, 2008). A sampling issue emerged but was discounted for ethical reasons.

TABLE 2.13 Epistemological categories: Methodological issues

EPISTEMOLOGICAL CATEGORIES: METHODOLOGICAL ISSUES	
Methodological issue	BDoE
Sampling issue	BDoE
Basing decisions on evidence as research activity	BDoE

Outliers formed the final epistemological factor that emerged from the YCAR project; these comprised two epistemological categories that did not fit with other epistemological factors. Children adopted anthropomorphism to support their conceptualisation (Gray, Gray and Wegner, 2007). Conversely, when solutions children devised remained unconfirmed, this presented a barrier to them finding solutions.

TABLE 2.14 Epistemological categories and barriers: Outliers

EPISTEMOLOGICAL CATEGORIES: OUTLIERS	
Applies anthropomorphism	C
EPISTEMOLOGICAL BARRIERS: OUTLIERS	
(BARRIER) Solution unconfirmed	FaS

Summary

This second section of Chapter 2 has explained how the *Young Children As Researchers* (YCAR) project was developed. It has outlined the design of the YCAR research and introduced the four research behaviours that academy members deemed 'most important'. It has also indicated ways young children indicated that they engaged in these research behaviours: *Young Children As Researchers* constructed knowledge by adopting epistemological categories in their everyday activity.

This second section has also outlined the process of scientific method that was adopted for the YCAR project. This discussion is important because transparent methodology provides a basis for trust in scientific method – a key process for knowledge production. This book makes the claim that young children are researchers who build knowledge, so for the book to be useful for your work in early childhood, you need to have confidence that this claim is warranted by knowledge that is trustworthy: justified true belief. This account of how knowledge was constructed for the YCAR project provides that warrant.

Conclusion

This chapter explains the different types of knowledge that adults and children construct and use to help them to navigate the world. Chapter 2 has considered what counts as knowledge, it has explored diverse perspectives on knowledge and it has linked knowledge with other related areas, including understanding, learning and research. It has also focused on how the *Young Children As Researchers* project produced trustworthy knowledge.

In the YCAR project, children showed they were 'experts' in their own lives (Langsted, 1994: 29) by behaving as researchers in their everyday activities. The YCAR project provides warrant for how this information can be recognised by the academy, as well as the children's families and practitioners who can use it to identify and explain how young children construct knowledge to learn about the world they are growing up in.

This chapter underpins the book as a whole, which reveals what lies at the heart of young children's learning: ways they construct knowledge. The chapters that follow show in detail how young children who participated in the YCAR project behaved as researchers in their everyday activities at home and in their settings to construct knowledge, to understand and to learn. The chapters focus on the four research behaviours that academics in the YCAR project identified as the most important: exploration, finding solutions, conceptualisation and basing decisions on evidence. For each of the 68 building blocks – or epistemological categories – that provoked young children's engagements in these research behaviours, examples are provided. The examples have been selected for the clarity with which they illustrate each epistemological category. In the following chapters, each is linked to literature concerning knowledge, research and theory; for each example, the forms of knowledge identified in this chapter are indicated and reflection points are made, as well as consideration of the adult's role, an aspect of YCAR considered further in an academic paper (Murray, 2017). Each chapter focused on one of the four research behaviours is supplemented by a practical tool that practitioners and parents can use to identify epistemological categories in their young children's everyday activities. As a package, these elements provide a valuable toolkit to identify and interpret some of the highly sophisticated thinking and actions that young children adopt in their everyday activities to construct knowledge.

3

YOUNG CHILDREN EXPLORE

This chapter is concerned with young children's exploring. Exploration was identified by academy members in the YCAR Project as one of the four most important research behaviours and is, in any case, widely considered an important behaviour for young children's development. Field (2007) suggests that denying young children opportunities to explore is likely to 'stifle curiosity, creativity and the entire learning process' (p. 243).

Some of the content concerning 'exploration' also appears in an academic paper (Murray, 2012). This third chapter is divided into two sections. The first section opens by defining exploration, then provides an overview of ways that young children's explorations have been recognised by educators. The second section features young children aged 4–8 years exploring in the YCAR Project by engaging in 10 epistemological categories; these epistemological categories acted as building blocks or strategies that enabled young children to construct knowledge through exploration in everyday activities at home and in their settings (Figure 3.1). Related forms of knowledge from other literature are also indicated for each example of young children exploring.

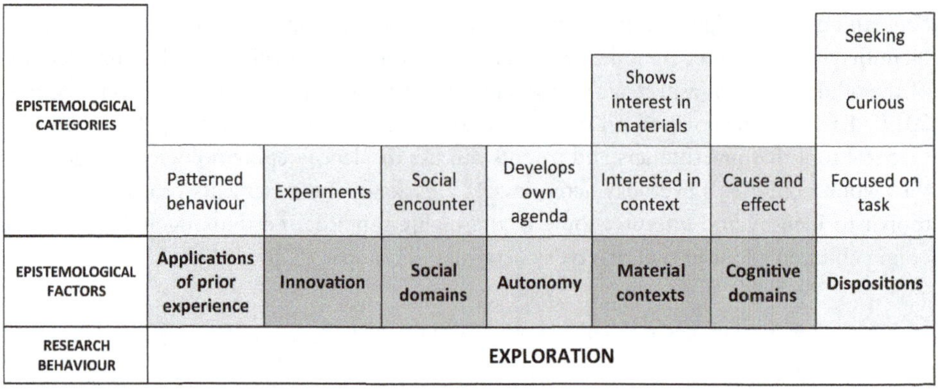

EPISTEMOLOGICAL CATEGORIES							Seeking
					Shows interest in materials		Curious
	Patterned behaviour	Experiments	Social encounter	Develops own agenda	Interested in context	Cause and effect	Focused on task
EPISTEMOLOGICAL FACTORS	**Applications of prior experience**	**Innovation**	**Social domains**	**Autonomy**	**Material contexts**	**Cognitive domains**	**Dispositions**
RESEARCH BEHAVIOUR	**EXPLORATION**						

FIGURE 3.1 Building blocks for exploration (Murray, 2015b)

Literature concerning exploration and young children

Defining exploration

The word 'explore' derives from the Latin 'to cry out' (*ex plorare*). Linking expressive communication to action is a deeply embedded feature of humanity (Burke, 1966) and Bruner and Olson (1978) suggest that 'expression and communication are *exploratory devices*'...'a point of immense importance to an understanding of the child's acquisition of knowledge' (p. 6). Young children often process and express their thoughts through action as well as words and other media (Malaguzzi, 1993; 1998a; Gallas, 1994), while our youngest children tend to 'express themselves not so much through verbal language, but primarily through various bodily cues and forms of non-verbal communication' (Bae, 2010: 208).

Exploration is recognised as research behaviour. It is particularly important in qualitative research, which focuses on exploring and interpreting contexts and processes to secure deeper understanding about people's lived experiences (Creswell, 2008; Whyte, 1949). Stebbins (2001) defines exploration in social sciences research by suggesting four 'senses' of what it means 'to explore':

1. 'to study, examine, analyse...or investigate';
2. 'to become familiar with something by testing it or experimenting with it';
3. 'to travel over or through a particular space for the purposes of discovery';
4. 'to examine a thing or idea for (specific) diagnostic purposes' (p. 2).

Humans explore from an early age

Newborn babies have well developed sensitivity to their environments which they perceive sensually (Roach, 2003), yet some of their earliest explorations are sentient, not just reflex actions (Gopnik, Mektzoff and Kuhl, 1999). Neonates initially explore through their mouths, beginning with the breast when feeding (Field, 2007) and they process and respond to sensory information for example, gentle touch such as cradling (Coon and Mitterer, 2009; Gallo, 2003). As they grow, babies continue to use their senses to explore (Moore and Meltzoff, 2008; Field, 2007) and they are able to apply what they learn from their explorations to new situations (Meltzoff and Prinz, 2002). From about three months, babies use their improving visual capability as an important tool for exploration (Atkinson, 2000), then from about six months their hands become their key tools for exploration as they gain improved visual control of what they reach and grasp (Field, 2007; Robinson, 2008). Babies' capacities for exploration develop exponentially through their first year aligning with rapid brain development (Robinson, 2008); this continues until age six (Macintyre, 2001) but is contingent on a stimulating environment that encourages infants and young children to explore, in the context of warm, nurturing relationships with familiar adults (Bowlby, 1988; Belsky, 1990; Gerhardt, 2015; Johnson, 2006; King, 1966; Rutter, 2002).

Infants appear programmed to explore objects (Garner and Bergen, 2006). Abbott and Langston (2005) describe exploration as the way babies and young children up to three years ask: 'What can and does it do?' (p. 153) and exploration has been identified as the 'precursor' to play (Field, 2007: 243). Many early childhood practitioners create and use 'treasure baskets' to encourage babies and toddlers to explore autonomously; Goldschmied and Jackson (2004) suggest that in treasure basket play, infants often use 'reach and grasp' motions and their rapidly developing hand–eye coordination to touch and bring objects towards their eyes and their mouths to explore.

Young children's curiosity and problem-solving in explorations

This section considers two features of young children's exploration that are prominent in the literature: curiosity and problem solving. Perry (2001) regards curiosity as a key factor in exploration and Berlyne (1954) suggests that 'epistemic curiosity' requires high order cognitive skills to receive and process knowledge about something that interests us. Motivation and exploration are regarded as aspects of young children's curiosity that transform their 'eagerness to know' into 'the acquisition of knowledge' (Chak, 2007: 142). Fontanesci, Gandini and Soncini (1998) regard 'enthusiasm and curiosity (as) qualities that help children to encounter new things' (p. 155) and this view resonates with a widely accepted definition of play: 'freely chosen, personally directed, intrinsically motivated behaviour that actively engages the child' (National Playing Fields Association, Children's Play Council and Playlink, 2000). Meadows (2006) agrees that exploration is an element in children's play and Hughes (2002) suggests it presents in children's symbolic play, role play and exploratory play. However, Hutt *et al.* (1989), suggest that epistemic play promotes learning, whereas ludic play may not always do so. Hutt *et al.* (1989) define epistemic behaviour as 'the acquisition of knowledge and information' (p. 222), while Hughes (1979) identifies that young children's exploration is characterised by predictable sequences, which lead to enhanced problem-solving capabilities (Hutt *et al.*, 1989; Dweck and Leggett, 1988).

Meadows (2006) distinguishes between exploration as an inductive *trial and error* process (p. 286) and deductive problem-solving that finds an answer that is already known by others, however, exploration can lead to enhanced problem-solving, particularly when it is systematic (Hutt *et al.*, 1989; Dweck and Leggett, 1988). Children are particularly likely to solve problems through exploration when they engage in open-ended activity with object play (Else, 2009; Forman, 2006; Gura, 1992). Isaacs and Isaacs (1944) observed the 'epistemic interests' of children from 2.7 years in their activity and questions: 'Why does it get lighter outside when you put the light out?' (1930: 308). Children's schemas constitute a type of exploratory problem solving. Piaget described these as 'Cognitive structures…linked together in various types of connections. The connections may be spatial, temporal, causal or implicatory…static or dynamic' (1971: 139). Schemas are 'consistent patterns of behaviour' (Nutbrown, 1999: 36) and young children will pursue their explorations of a schema repeatedly over long periods of time apparently until satiated (Athey, 2007; Arnold, 2009). Examples include finding and making circles (rotational schema), lines (vertical schema) and ways to secure objects within spaces (containing schema) (Athey, 2007). Meade and Cubey describe schemata as 'the core of developing young minds' (2008: 134).

Young children's learning and exploration

Over centuries, exploration has assumed a prominent role in the field of early childhood education. Pioneers Rousseau (1762), Pestalozzi (1810), Froebel (1826), Montessori (1916), Isaacs (1929) and Piaget (1952) all advocated exploration as a way for children to learn. In more recent literature, Moyles, Adams and Musgrove (2002) drew on empirical research evidence to link exploration and learning and Napier and Sharkey (2004) agree that 'Exploration allows children to develop their knowledge, skills and understanding' (p. 150). Children explore when they have freedom to 'propose the questions they will seek to answer through investigation', 'rather than to seek right answers to questions posed by the teacher' (Katz, 1994: 1) and Oliver and Oliver (1997) observe that children often seek information that involves them 'locating, selecting, organizing, interpreting, synthesizing, and communicating relevant information' (p. 519). However, while young children may benefit from exploration in which they construct 'with others and in democracy – her or his own epistemology' (Hoyuelos, 2004), children in western contexts seem to have decreasing opportunities to engage freely and autonomously in their own explorations (Fisher, Hirsh-Pasek, Golinkoff and Gryfe, 2008).

Summary

This section has defined exploration and has discussed babies' explorations, young children's curiosity and problem-solving as factors in exploration and the ways that young children's learning may link to their explorations. Focus now turns to the ways that children explored in the YCAR project.

Young children exploring in the YCAR project

In the YCAR project, 10 epistemological categories acted as building blocks to enable young children aged 4–8 years to construct knowledge through exploration in their everyday activities at home and in their settings (Figure 3.1). Each is discussed here with examples drawn from the YCAR study, linked to research and literature about knowledge and exploration, to provide a framework to support practitioners to observe and interpret the ways their children may construct knowledge by exploring in everyday activities.

Applications of prior experience as a factor for young children exploring

Young children in the YCAR study who were exploring sometimes applied their prior experiences to those experiences by using *'Patterned behaviour'*.

Children's patterned behaviour presented in various ways, including conforming to adult expectations, applying skills acquired from adults and engaging in exploratory behaviours used in research, such as testing, experimenting, studying or examining (Stebbins, 2001). In

(i) Patterned behaviour

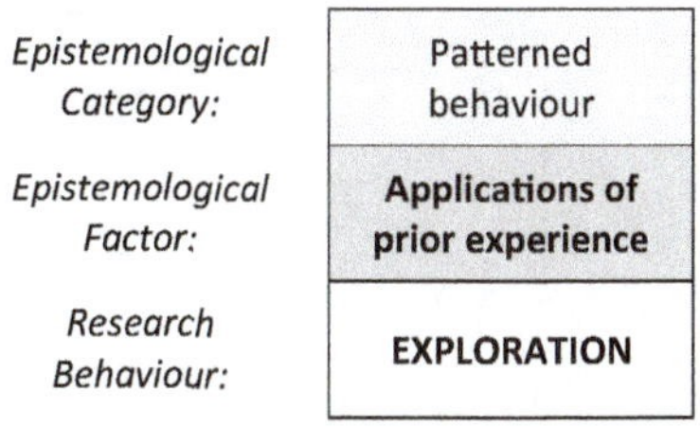

Epistemological Category:	Patterned behaviour
Epistemological Factor:	**Applications of prior experience**
Research Behaviour:	**EXPLORATION**

FIGURE 3.2 Building blocks – Patterned behaviour

the two vignettes that follow, Martin, aged 5 and Annie, aged 7, presented with patterned behaviour in the context of exploration.

Martin raises his hand

One day in Cherry Setting, during a whole class discussion session in his reception setting, 5-year-old Martin raised and lowered his hand five times in response to his teacher's questioning, but the teacher did not respond. Martin's behaviour indicated that he was enthusiastic and motivated: qualities that underpin exploration as behaviour for constructing knowledge (Chak, 2007; Fontanesci, et al., 1998). While raising his hand was expected by his teacher in this situation, its repeated use may also be regarded as an example of a trajectory schema (Nutbrown, 1999) and a dynamic physical outlet for his thinking.

Listening

In Ash Setting during a whole-class literacy session that lasted 25 minutes, 33 seconds one day, 7-year-old Annie listened repeatedly to other children and her teacher. In this context, the teacher and Annie's peers transmitted information that Annie attended to. Annie's consistent listening was a sign of her exploration as she appeared to be locating information (Oliver and Oliver, 1997: 519). Her listening over time exemplified aspects of Stebbins' definition of exploration in social sciences research (2001): she was studying and examining what the teacher and her peers were saying.

In their settings, children in the YCAR project were often required by their practitioners to follow socio-cultural conventions (Cannella, 2002). These conventions often had their basis in education policy concerned with preparation for work (Mayall, 2006), and in both vignettes here, teaching is conducted through a model of knowledge transmission. In this context, although they were in different settings, both Martin and Annie presented with patterned behaviour that had some elements of exploratory behaviour. Young children often reveal 'schemas' (Piaget, 1952; Nutbrown, 1999): 'general cognitive structures' (Athey, 2007: 48) and these may often present as 'figural thought' (Meade and Cubey, 2008: 3) or physical actions, typically:

> [placing items] next one another (proximity) or in series (order), actions of enclosing, of tightening or loosening, changing viewpoints, cutting, rotating, folding or unfolding, enlarging and reducing and so on.
>
> *(Piaget and Inhelder, 1956: 452–453)*

FORMS OF KNOWLEDGE

✓ Knowing how

THE ADULT'S ROLE

Martin's practitioner could have encouraged Martin's exploratory behaviours more strongly; she did not respond to Martin so disregarded the possibility for an 'ethics of an encounter' with him (Dahlberg and Moss, 2005) that might have led to Martin constructing more knowledge through further exploration (Napier and Sharkey, 2004: 150).

Although Annie did explore, her opportunities to do so were limited here. Had the practitioner invited her to propose her own questions which she could have then attempted to 'answer through investigation' (Katz, 1994: 1), Annie would have had greater opportunity to construct knowledge through exploration.

REFLECTION POINTS

What examples of these schemas have you noticed in young children's activities?

- Connection schema (*joining and separating*)
- Trajectory schema (*strong movement in one or more directions*)
- Rotation schema (*circles, spinning and round objects or movements*)
- Enclosure / containing schema (*being within objects or putting objects inside other objects*)
- Transporting schema (*taking self or objects from one place to another*)
- Enveloping schema (*covering self or objects*)

If you have observed some or all of these examples of patterned behaviour in young children's activities, did you notice *how* they applied prior experiences when they engaged in them?

Schemas are physical manifestations of patterns of thinking; can you recall any occasions when you have recognised that children are engaged in patterns of thinking that are not presented physically? What helped you to recognise these patterns?

Innovation as a factor for young children exploring

When children in the YCAR project were exploring, sometimes they combined '*Experimenting*' with innovation. According to Creswell (2008: 300), key characteristics of experiments in research include:

- Assigning random individuals or objects to a group.
- Control of variables.
- Manipulating treatment conditions.

(ii) Experiments

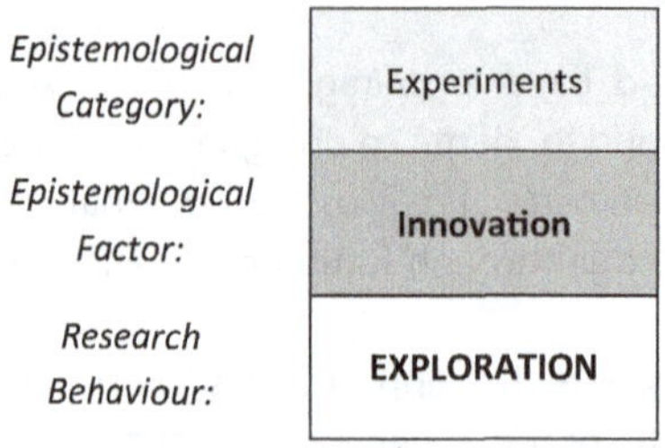

Epistemological Category:	Experiments
Epistemological Factor:	**Innovation**
Research Behaviour:	**EXPLORATION**

FIGURE 3.3 Building blocks – Experiments

The binoculars

One morning, during free-flow play in Cherry Setting, a reception class unit, 4-year-old Pedro chose to go to the Safari role play area in the outdoor area where a large mound of earth had been left by builders the previous week at the request of the practitioner. First, Pedro collected a pair of binoculars, then he used them to look at pictures of animals placed earlier by a practitioner on the fence that surrounded the outdoor area. Pedro then lowered the binoculars to survey a rock within the mound of earth. He lifted the rock and studied it closely through the binoculars.

In this vignette, Pedro engaged in exploration, innovation (epistemological factor) and experimentation (epistemological category). Pedro indicated his intention to look through the binoculars by going deliberately to collect them first of all; Robson (1993) suggests that a 'central feature (of an experiment) is that you need to know what you are doing before you do it' (p. 78). He engaged in exploratory behaviour used in research (Stebbins, 2001): he tested his binoculars by looking at the animal pictures, then he travelled to the rock and studied, examined, tested and investigated it by observing its physical properties through the binoculars. This was a procedure that Pedro developed himself to examine how to use binoculars to test the physical properties of the rock; he extended the procedure in incremental stages, indicating that he was engaged in 'experimental reasoning concerning matter of fact and existence' (Hume, 1748: 123). Pedro applied Creswell's (2008) key characteristics of experiments to his activity. By using his binoculars to examine different objects, Pedro assigned random objects to the group of objects he observed. He controlled variables by always using his binoculars to observe the objects and he manipulated treatment conditions by observing the rock on the ground then lifting it towards his binoculars. By developing his own process and pursuing it, Pedro constructed a new idea and showed that he valued what he was doing; his actions were congruent with innovation, defined as the development of new ideas into something valued (Department for Business, Innovation and Skills, 2011; 2012).

FORMS OF KNOWLEDGE

✓ A posteriori reasoning

THE ADULT'S ROLE

In this vignette, the light touch adopted by Pedro's practitioner enabled him to explore, experiment and to innovate. No practitioner intervened directly in Pedro's activity, which he chose to undertake himself. His practitioner afforded Pedro freedom, time and resources to engage in exploration, innovation and experimentation; he devised his own plan and implemented it. A model of free-flow play operating in the setting meant that Pedro could choose to go outdoors. The practitioner had ensured resources were available but did not place limitations on how he should use them, so Pedro was able to invent his own way to deploy the binoculars, animal pictures and the rock that was in the mound of earth.

REFLECTION POINTS

How can practitioners know the extent to which they should interact with children to support every child to construct knowledge?

Can you think of some resources that might encourage young children to experiment according to Creswell's (2008) key characteristics of experiments?

Social domains as a factor for young children exploring

There is much literature to suggest that social encounters can be important contexts for children's exploratory behaviour (Vygotsky, 1978; Corsaro, 2003; Lash, 2008). This is borne out by the YCAR project: as part of their exploratory behaviour, participating children sometimes engaged in *'Social encounters'*, an epistemological category within the factor 'social domains'.

(iii) Social Encounter

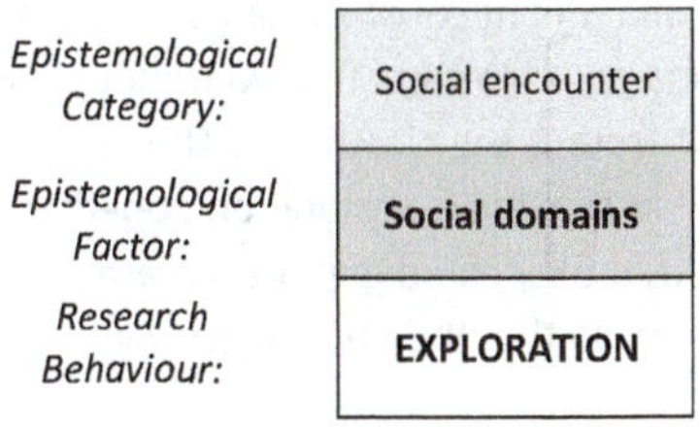

Epistemological Category:	Social encounter
Epistemological Factor:	**Social domains**
Research Behaviour:	**EXPLORATION**

FIGURE 3.4 Building blocks – Social encounter

Pierced ears?

One day in a literacy lesson in Ash Setting, the teacher had set the children a writing task with the learning objective '*To be able to understand character behaviour*'. They worked individually to write a description of a character, while seated at tables of four or more children. 7-year-old Emily and 8-year-old Florence were sitting together. A teaching assistant was supporting them and other children on their table with their task. After 25 minutes Emily asked the teaching assistant if her ears were pierced. She got up to come to look for herself and Florence joined her.

Through social encounter with Emily, Florence was moved to 'examine' the teaching assistant's ears for a 'specific diagnostic purpose'; this is behaviour congruent with exploration in social sciences research (Stebbins, 2001). Their behaviour resonates with a view that infants and young children are 'programmed' to explore (*i.a.* Gopnik *et al.*, 1999; Athey, 2007) and that they may be particularly drawn to exploring objects (Garner and Bergen, 2006). Equally, by mirroring Emily's actions, Florence expressed a wish to be aligned socially with her (Corsaro, 2003). Florence communicated this wish using non-verbal means (Malaguzzi, 1993; 1998b; Gallas, 1994; Bae 2010); she followed her friend and she adopted that means of non-verbal communication as a tool for exploratory activity (Bruner and Olson, 1978). Florence and Emily were interested in a prosaic issue – whether or not my ears were pierced – but their action had a deeper meaning: by exploring an issue they were both interested in that was not about the teacher's agenda, Florence and Emily began to develop their own epistemology (Hoyuelos, 2004), nested within their social encounter.

FORMS OF KNOWLEDGE

✓ A posteriori reasoning

THE ADULT'S ROLE

Although Florence and Emily's teacher had set all the children in the class individual tasks, she had done so within a context of social construction which afforded sufficient freedom to children to engage in interests that were not always related to the task they had been set and to move around the classroom. The teaching assistant afforded Emily and Florence freedom to pursue their exploration together. The freedom afforded to Florence and Emily meant that they could explore a matter of interest to them within the context of a social encounter, so that they had agency in the construction of knowledge that mattered to them.

REFLECTION POINTS

Can you recall any occasions when you have regretted intervening in children's activity? Why?

Consider some ways you have encouraged young children to construct knowledge by learning from each other.

What worked well and why?

Were there any challenges in doing this? Did you overcome them? How?

Autonomy as a factor for young children exploring

When they engaged in autonomous exploratory behaviour, children in the YCAR project *'Developed (their) own agenda'*.

(iv) Develops own agenda

Epistemological Category:	Develops own agenda
Epistemological Factor:	**Autonomy**
Research Behaviour:	**EXPLORATION**

FIGURE 3.5 Building blocks – Develops own agenda

Measuring stick

One day at home, 5-year-old Gemma developed her own agenda when she explored autonomously how to make a measuring stick from two wrapping paper card tubes. At the outset, she asked her mother if she could use two tubes and sticky tape. She then taped the tubes together to make the measuring stick and used pens to add the measuring units. Gemma then tested her measuring stick by asking her 8-year-old brother to stand next to the tube to gauge his height and finally, she told her mother what she had done.

During this experience, Gemma developed her own agenda by examining materials and combining them to construct a measuring stick, aligning with Stebbins' (2001) criteria for exploration in social sciences research. To pursue her agenda, Gemma had 'space' to have a sense of agency (Stern, 1985) while maintaining interdependence with her family (Moss and Petrie, 2002). This activity is congruent with Piaget's (1969) view of children as active agents who combine perception and activity to construct new understanding. Gemma demonstrates autonomy through intrinsic motivation, creativity, empowerment and intentional behaviour (Deci and Ryan, 1987: 1024; Lowrie, 2002).

FORMS OF KNOWLEDGE

✓ Knowing that
✓ Knowing how
✓ Explicit knowledge

THE ADULT'S ROLE

We cannot know whether Gemma's parents had given her an experience of a measuring stick or she had derived this from others, but we can infer that she had prior experience of a measuring stick from somewhere. Within the vignette her mother provided a context in which materials, time and freedom were sufficiently available to Gemma to enable her to act autonomously to plan, create and report her measuring stick. Gemma's 8-year-old brother also supported her autonomy by complying with her request to stand next to the tube to be measured so she could test it.

It can also be inferred that Gemma's family had previously provided her with sufficient emotional resources to give her intrinsic motivation and empowerment to plan, create, test and report her measuring stick. These emotional resources included self-esteem, confidence and resilience.

REFLECTION POINTS

Can you recall some agenda that children you know have developed themselves to learn new things?

What are the best ways that adults can help children to construct knowledge for themselves?

What are some of the challenges in ensuring that young children construct knowledge while pursuing their own agenda?

Material contexts as a factor for young children exploring

When young children in the YCAR project explored by engaging with material contexts they indicated that they were '*Interested in (those) contexts*' and '*Interested in materials*'. *Inter alia*, this behaviour was congruent with social sciences research (Stebbins, 2001), physical spaces (Dudek, 2005), exploratory play (Hutt *et al.*, 1989), flow (Csíkszentmihályi, 1990) and children's global development (Garner and Bergen, 2006; Meadows, 2006).

(v) Interested in context

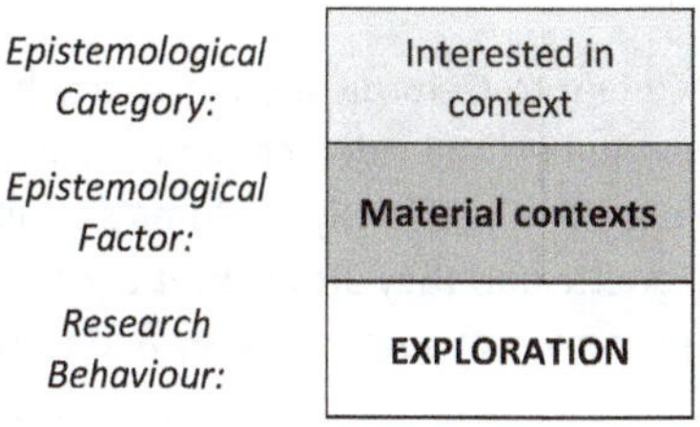

Epistemological Category:	Interested in context
Epistemological Factor:	**Material contexts**
Research Behaviour:	**EXPLORATION**

FIGURE 3.6 Building blocks – Interested in context

The guided tour

At home, 5-year-old Gemma acquired knowledge and information as she learned how to operate a camcorder to create a sequenced 'guided tour' of her home. Gemma focused the camcorder on different features she was familiar with, verbally annotating each feature. She was familiar with the names of the features, indicating she had encountered them previously, for example: 'Bin', 'Breakfast bar', 'Sun cream', 'Cooker', 'Spicy things' (spice rack), 'Sugar', 'These are the stairs', 'There's about 1, 2, 3, 4, 5, 6, 7, 8, 9, 10, 11, 12, 13 steps so you can do it whenever you want.'

Here, Gemma trialled her use of a camcorder at home, a space she knew well and to which she may have had an attachment (Spencer, 2004; Dudek, 2005): a physical context in which 'relations, options, and emotional and cognitive situations…produced (in her) a sense of well-being and security' (Malaguzzi, 1996: 40). Gemma seemed to value her home for how she could use it (Bailey and Barnes, 2009) and her interest in her context translated to her explorations of the camcorder, her home and the synthesis of the two as she explored as a researcher, travelling through the house to discover more about filming, gathering data and operating the camcorder, examining each physical object or space for the purpose of data gathering (Stebbins, 2001: 2).

Examples in the literature suggest that Gemma's behaviour is not unusual: young children aged 0–8 years do explore (Hutt *et al.*, 1989; Gopnik *et al.*, 1999; Hughes, 2002; Athey, 2007); they do so to actively construct their own epistemologies (Isaacs, 1944; Piaget, 1972a; Hoyuelos, 2004). Moreover, Gemma's 'tour' appeared to exhibit 'flow' in her thinking – an indicator for young children's optimal development (Laevers, 2000). Gemma had a goal (to use the camcorder to film her home), she was fully involved in filming her home and she personally controlled the process (Csíkszentmihályi, 1990). Gemma's opportunity to explore with a high level of autonomy was likely to be beneficial for her development across physical, cognitive, social and emotional domains (Laevers, 2000; Broadhead, 2001; Garner and Bergen, 2006; Meadows, 2006).

FORMS OF KNOWLEDGE

- ✓ Knowing that
- ✓ Knowing how
- ✓ Explicit knowledge

> **THE ADULT'S ROLE**
>
> The video camera had been lent to Gemma and her family by the researcher, affording her a medium that was new to her: the video camera enabled her to explore her home context in a way she had not done previously. Gemma's adults had provided the home that she explored in this vignette and they also contributed to this exploration by giving her time and freedom to plan and act autonomously and to report her findings.

> **REFLECTION POINTS**
>
> What are some of the ways that you have noticed young children being or becoming interested in the contexts they find themselves in?

(vi) Shows interest in materials

Epistemological Category:	Shows interest in materials
Epistemological Factor:	**Material contexts**
Research Behaviour:	**EXPLORATION**

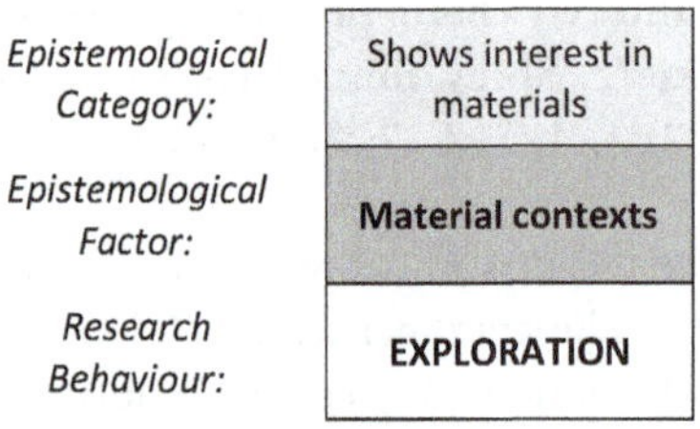

FIGURE 3.7 Building blocks – Shows interest in materials

Inasmuch as children in the YCAR project indicated interest in their contexts, they also showed interest in materials and objects as part of their exploratory behaviour.

Big cylinders

One day in Beech Setting's under-cover outdoor area, 5-year-old India showed particular interest in two hollow plastic black cylinders (2m × 0.5m) that were on the floor adjacent to each other in a large undercover area. The cylinders were offcuts from industrial water pipes. India and her friend played with the cylinders for almost 12 minutes. India walked to the cylinders, rolled a cylinder forwards while on top of it on her tummy and, with her friend, created one long 'tube'. India and her friend crawled inside one cylinder each and rolled the cylinders at the same pace several times to and fro.

Young children appear programmed to explore objects (Garner and Bergen, 2006) and during this experience, India engaged in functional, realistic object play (Morgenthaler, 2006: 65). She interacted with the cylinders inductively, constructing and problem-solving (Piaget, 1945) and travelled over and through the cylinders, indicating through her actions that she was asking herself 'What can and does it do?' (Abbott and Langston, 2005: 153). India's apparent intention to discover more about the cylinders' properties aligned with many aspects of Stebbins' (2001) definition of exploration in social sciences research: she studied, examined and investigated the cylinders, became familiar with them by testing and experimenting with them and 'travelled over (and) through a particular space for the purposes of discovery' (p. 2).

The cylinders were simple objects that seemed to prove fascinating for India and her friend, endorsing a view that children often side-line sophisticated resources in favour of everyday objects (*i.a.* Gura, 1992; Vig, 2007). Everyday objects have been shown to enhance young children's cognitive mastery (*i.a.* DeLoache, 1989; Nelissen and Tomic, 1996; Karpov, 2005; Worthington, 2010) and elements of India's cylinder play, such as creating one long 'tube' from the two cylinders may have resulted from representational thinking (Forman, 1982) or mental modelling (Craik, 1943; Johnson-Laird, 1983: x). Johnson-Laird (1983) describes a mental model as 'analogous to the structure of the corresponding state of affairs in the world' (p. 156) and Craik (1943) outlines the process of mental modeling:

> 1. 'Translation' of external processes into words, numbers or other symbols;
> 2. Arrival at other symbols through a process of "reasoning", deduction, inference, etc.
> 3. 'Retranslation' of these symbols into external processes (as in building a bridge to a design) or at least recognition of the correspondence between these symbols and external events (as in realising that a prediction is fulfilled).
>
> *(p. 50)*

Furthermore, India and her friend appeared to invest personal meanings and value in the cylinders, seeing them as contexts for socio-cultural interaction (Vygotsky, 1978; Garvey, 1991) and a locus for 'communicative power' (Gura, 1992: 43). India and her friend seemed to make both cognitive and socio-emotional connections during their object play with the cylinders (Axline, 1964; Garner and Bergen, 2006).

FORMS OF KNOWLEDGE

✓ Tacit knowledge

THE ADULT'S ROLE

In this vignette, the practitioners had provided a simple material resource: two hollow plastic black cylinders (2m × 0.5m) and the time, space and freedom to play unhindered. This enabled India and her friend to explore the material resource fully, according to their own agenda.

REFLECTION POINTS

Should the practitioner have encouraged India and her friend...

- To explore materials more deeply?
- To engage further with materials?

If not, why not?

If so, how could the practitioner have encouraged India and her friend...

- To explore materials more deeply?
- To engage further with materials?

Cognitive domains as a factor for young children exploring

'Cause and effect' was a category that emerged when young children in the YCAR project synthesised their exploratory behaviour with cognitive domains.

(vii) Cause and effect

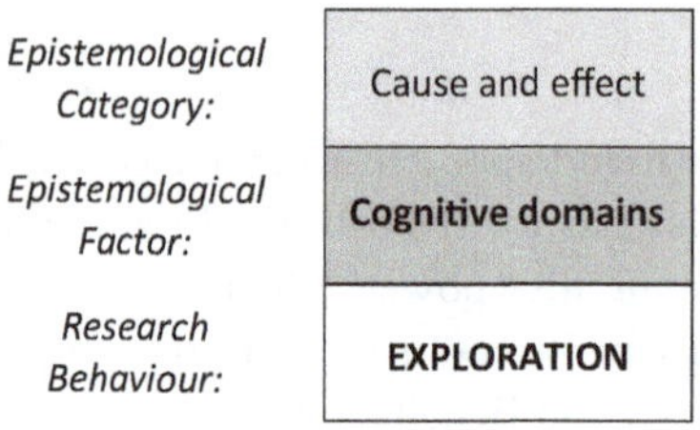

Epistemological Category:	Cause and effect
Epistemological Factor:	**Cognitive domains**
Research Behaviour:	**EXPLORATION**

FIGURE 3.8 Building blocks – Cause and effect

Cause and effect – causality – has been redefined significantly in the past century in the physical sciences (Born, 1949) but in the social sciences, Hume's original definition of causality (1739: III, xv) prevails:

> *The cause and effect must be contiguous in space and time*
> *The cause must be prior to the effect*
> *There must be a constant union betwixt the cause and effect*

Baillargeon (2004) suggests that infants as young as 11 months may be able to draw on and apply their prior knowledge to construct causal explanations.

Watch this, dudes!

One day during playtime in Cherry Setting, Martin (aged 5) stood in the middle of the playground, wearing a sunhat and two boys joined him. Martin bent over

and said: 'I'm seeing if my hat falls off! Watch this, dudes!' then he jumped up and down until his hat came off.

Here, Martin's behaviour aligns with Hume's definition of causality (1739):

- *'The cause and effect must be contiguous in space and time'*: Martin jumped and within seconds, his hat fell off.
- *'The cause must be prior to the effect'*: Martin jumped (cause) before his hat fell off (effect).
- *'There must be a constant union betwixt the cause and effect'*: First, Martin presented a causal theory (Gopnik, 2009). 'I'm seeing if my hat falls off…watch this, dudes!' Next he tested his theory by jumping up and down to see if this made his hat fall off. Last, when Martin's jumping (cause) was followed by his hat falling off (effect), the union between cause and effect was complete.

In this vignette, Martin's theorised then tested his theory of cause and effect, indicating 'intellectual understanding of physical systems and living organisms' and a capacity to explore that was congruent with scientific method (Smeyers, 2008: 64; Stebbins, 2001).

FORMS OF KNOWLEDGE

✓ A posteriori reasoning

✓ Explicit knowledge

THE ADULT'S ROLE

Here, time and freedom to engage in self-directed play, the affordance of physical space and the absence of adult instruction enabled Martin to theorise and test his theory of causality. His parents had provided him with a hat that became the key resource for his experience.

REFLECTION POINTS

Should Martin and his friends have been encouraged to develop further theorising and testing of cause and effect?

If not, why not?

If so, why?

What might practitioners need to know to support children to theorise and test cause and effect?

What other materials might support children to theorise and test cause and effect?

What adult behaviours might help children to theorise and test cause and effect?

Dispositions as a factor for young children exploring

Examples of young children's dispositions as elements in their **explorations** presented when children were 'Focused on their tasks', were 'Curious' and engaged in 'Seeking'.

(viii) Focused on task

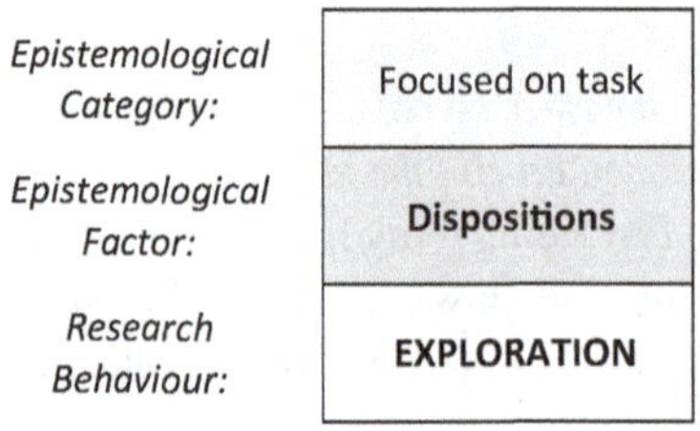

Epistemological Category:	Focused on task
Epistemological Factor:	**Dispositions**
Research Behaviour:	**EXPLORATION**

FIGURE 3.9 Building blocks – Focused on task

In the YCAR study, children were often very focused on their tasks when they engaged in epistemic behaviour.

The sandal

One day in Ash Setting, when 8-year-old Billy was sitting on the carpet listening to his teacher giving the class instructions for an art activity, he developed his own new focus. First, he looked down at his sandal and began using his fingers to manipulate it. Then he put his face almost onto his sandal while continuing to manipulate it with his fingers and observing his own actions. When the teacher had finished her exposition and said 'Let's see who's sitting beautifully then', Billy raised his head a little but continued to manipulate his sandal and observe his own actions.

Billy's behaviour exemplifies 'flow' (Csíkszentmihályi, 1990): his 'attention was completely absorbed by (his) activity' (p. 53). As he explored his sandal by observing it and fiddling with it, Billy exhibited 'concentration…strong motivation, fascination and total implication' while focusing 'attention to one limited circle' (Laevers, 2000: 24–25). Billy's close examination of his sandal is also behaviour congruent with exploration in social sciences research (Stebbins, 2001: 2).

FORMS OF KNOWLEDGE

✓ A posteriori reasoning

THE ADULT'S ROLE

In this vignette, Billy was less interested in what the practitioner said and did than he was in observing and manipulating his sandal; it was the practitioner's inability to engage Billy in what she was saying that led him to his self-chosen activity that captured his interest more strongly. At no time did the teacher stop Billy from pursuing his self-chosen activity, though we do not have sufficient evidence to know why. Billy's engagement in that activity provided evidence of significant involvement, an indicator of capacity for construction of knowledge at a deep level (Laevers, 2000).

REFLECTION POINTS

What might the reasons have been for why the teacher did not stop Billy from pursuing his self-chosen activity?

In what circumstances might it be appropriate for children to be 'off task'?

What are some of the benefits and disadvantages for children having freedom to replace tasks their practitioners have planned for them with their own self-chosen activities?

(ix) Curious

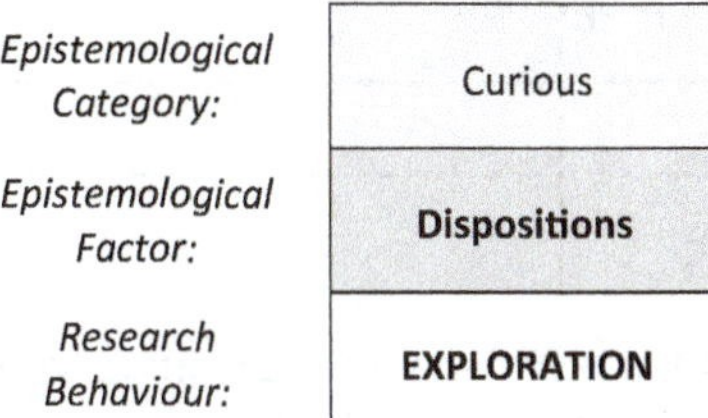

FIGURE 3.10 Building blocks – Curious

YCAR revealed many incidents of children demonstrating curiosity as part of their epistemic behaviour, a finding that is supported by other literature (Berlyne, 1954; Laevers, 2000; Perry, 2001; Chak, 2007).

The bracelet

Five-year-old Gemma's mother reported in a narrative observation she had made of Gemma's activity: '(Gemma was) playing with a bracelet. (She) tried and managed to open and close bracelet (then) decided to use (the) bracelet on her ankle as it was too big for her wrist'. Later, during a focus group with Gemma's family, her mother explained further: 'she was basically playing around with it, asking how to open the bracelet'.

In this example, Gemma's mother provided evidence that Gemma demonstrated curiosity, described as 'the exploratory drive' and categorised as a disposition (Laevers, 2000: 21). Gemma's actions also align with Chak's definition of curiosity: 'motivational force' and 'behavioural manifestation in the form of exploration' (2007: 142). Gemma 'encounter(ed) new things' (Fontanesci *et al.*, 1998: 155): 'asking how to open the bracelet…' and she 'decided to use (the) bracelet on her ankle as it was too big for her wrist'. Gemma presented with 'epistemic curiosity': 'a drive which is reduced by the reception and subsequent rehearsal of knowledge' (Berlyne, 1954: 180). Gemma's behaviour with the bracelet aligned with Stebbins' definition for exploration in social sciences research (2001): she studied, examined and investigated the bracelet, diagnosed 'it was too big for her wrist' then repurposed the bracelet as an anklet.

FORMS OF KNOWLEDGE

✓ Knowing how
✓ A posteriori reasoning
✓ Mode 2 knowledge

THE ADULT'S ROLE

By capturing data in a narrative observation and reporting her findings, Gemma's mother assumed aspects of the researcher role. Her observation indicates that she provided Gemma with an object that provoked her exploratory behaviour and encouraged her curiosity (the bracelet). She afforded Gemma time and freedom to explore the bracelet and its properties.

REFLECTION POINTS

In this example, Gemma's mother revealed Gemma's curiosity as a feature of her exploratory behaviour at home, by using a short narrative observation and contributions to a family focus group.

What are some other ways that practitioners might capture rich evidence of the ways young children construct knowledge at home or in other places that are not their settings?

How might evidence be useful?

(x) Seeking

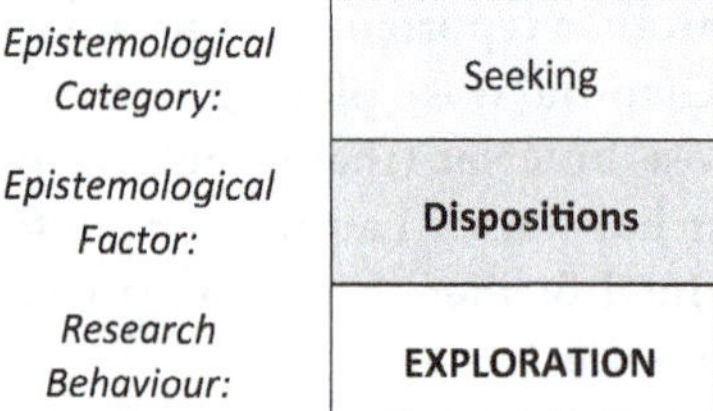

FIGURE 3.11 Building blocks – Seeking

The YCAR project featured many examples of children seeking, a disposition that tended to present when they engaged in exploratory behaviour. While this behaviour presented consistently in the activity of all five children who participated in Phase 3 at home, seeking behaviour was identified in only 11 of the 17 children closely observed in settings.

The window

During a whole class history lesson in Ash Setting, the children were all facing the white board on which the teacher had written a learning objective: 'To be able to understand what it was like for people in South Africa in the 1960s'. Billy (aged 8)

was sitting quietly on a chair at a table but while the teacher was talking he looked out of the window.

Katz (1994) suggests that children 'propose questions they will seek to answer through investigation…rather than to seek right answers to questions posed by the teacher' (p. 1). Here, Billy seemed to sideline the teacher's agenda in favour of seeking some information for himself, though there is no evidence regarding what that information was. Billy seemed to be 'locating' and possibly 'selecting' while seeking information (Oliver and Oliver, 1997: 519) and his eyes 'travelled over or through a particular space for the purposes of discovery': an indicator for exploration in the field of social sciences research (Stebbins, 2001: 2).

FORMS OF KNOWLEDGE

✓ Knowing how

✓ A posteriori reasoning

THE ADULT'S ROLE

By giving children a learning objective, the practitioner's purpose was to focus on specific learning for that lesson but it may also have limited knowledge the children could construct in the lesson. Billy rejected this limitation and he sought different ways to gather information.

REFLECTION POINTS

What are some of the ways that you have been able to encourage young children to propose questions and investigate issues that are important to them?

What has worked well and why?

What has not worked well and why?

What could you have done to make it work better?

What barriers might practitioners encounter when trying to ensure that children 'propose questions they will seek to answer through investigation…rather than to seek right answers to questions posed by the teacher' (Katz, 1994: 1).

Conclusion

This chapter has defined exploration and has then provided an overview of ways that young children's explorations have been recognised in the literature around early childhood education. It has also considered how young children engaged in exploratory behaviour in the YCAR Project by engaging in ten epistemological categories:

- Patterned behaviour.
- Experiments.
- Social encounter.
- Develops own agenda.

- Interested in context.
- Shows interest in materials.
- Cause and effect.
- Focused on task.
- Curious.
- Seeking.

These epistemological factors acted as building blocks that enabled young children to construct knowledge through their exploratory behaviour during everyday activities at home and in their settings (Figure 3.1).

For each of the building blocks concerned with young children exploring, the chapter has proposed related forms of knowledge, has identified how adults may help or hinder children to construct knowledge through exploratory behaviour, and has provided reflection points to help practitioners to consider ways they can apply the YCAR findings about young children's explorations to their own practice. The appendix (see p. 151) contains a useful tool for practitioners and parents – *Observation notes for young children's explorations*. Practitioners and parents can photocopy the tool and use it to record observations of their young children engaging in the ten epistemological categories for young children's explorations: ways we can know that young children are constructing knowledge by exploring.

4

YOUNG CHILDREN FIND SOLUTIONS

This chapter focuses on finding solutions: the second of the four research behaviours academics in the *Young Children As Researchers* (YCAR) project identified as most important. Some of the content concerning finding solutions also appears in an academic paper (Murray, 2013), which also includes a detailed literature review concerning young children finding solutions. Chapter 4 is divided into two sections. The first section defines what finding a solution may mean, particularly in the field of early childhood, and provides a brief indication of the prominent themes in the literature relating to young children finding solutions. The second section focuses on ways children in the YCAR project constructed knowledge by finding solutions in everyday activities at home and in their settings. Twenty epistemological categories acted as provocations, or building blocks, that enabled young children to find solutions, whereas 12 epistemological categories acted as barriers that prevented them from finding solutions. Each epistemological category was grouped into a relevant overarching epistemological factor. Figure 4.1 displays the epistemological categories for finding solutions according to their relevant epistemological factors; these 20 epistemological categories acted as provocations that enabled young children to find solutions. Relevant forms of knowledge from other literature are also indicated for each example of young children finding solutions.

Defining what 'finding a solution' really means in early childhood

The English word 'solution' derives from the Latin '*solvere*', meaning 'to loosen' or 'to untie'. James (1890) proposed that problems are solved by 'voluntary thinking' (I: 584) and that the processes involved are as important as the outcomes. Piaget (1972) theorised that children have innate capacity to solve problems by conceptual processing and they do so to build knowledge; he called this capacity 'genetic epistemology'.

The extant literature features numerous definitions for finding solutions – or problem solving. Tarini and White (1998) define a 'problem' as 'a challenge…a situation, a task, which in some way stimulates cognitive conflict, or a push in thinking' (p. 379); Keen (2011) describes problem-solving as a 'critical cognitive skill' (p. 18), while DeLoache, Miller and

	Able reader		Theory of mind			
	Wants to preserve what s/he is doing	Devises practical method to create solution	Employs others to help with finding a solution	Focused on something of personal interest	Inductive reasoning	Excited by finding solution
EPISTEMOLOGICAL CATEGORIES	Finds practical use for solution	Creates a problem to solve	Shares solution	Time and freedom to explore, investigate, experiment with something of personal interest	Deductive reasoning	Motivated by finding solution
	Applying rule to create solution	Finds own solution	Resolves another person's problem	Self-regulates	Exploring properties	Perseveres to resolve problem
EPISTEMOLOGICAL FACTORS	**Applications of prior experience**	**Innovation**	**Social domains**	**Autonomy**	**Material contexts**	**Dispositions**
RESEARCH BEHAVIOUR	**FIND A SOLUTION**					

FIGURE 4.1 Building blocks for finding solutions (Murray, 2015b)

Pierroutsakos (1998) characterise it as 'a goal, one or two obstacles that make the goal not immediately possible, one or typically more strategies that can be used to solve the problem, other resources that can affect which strategies are used and the evaluation of the outcome of the problem-solving process' (p. 826). Meadows (2006) defines problem-solving as 'cognitive activity' (p. 127): 'what you do when you work towards a goal but do not have a routine way to get there, or when an obstacle such as lack of skill or of knowledge interferes with a previously possible solution' (p. 126).

The relationship between finding solutions and research is well documented (Biesta, 2007; Oancea and Pring, 2008); pragmatism linked with the construction of knowledge dates back to the Ancient Greeks' concern with *praxis* – or 'practical knowledge' (Griffiths and MacLeod, 2008: 129). Finding solutions is about constructing multiple versions of 'truth' in contexts where problems present (Guba and Lincoln, 1989), so people are well placed to find solutions to problems they encounter and create themselves, including young children. Tarini and White (1998) suggest that not only teachers, but 'materials, projects and activities must pose problems to…children' (p. 379). The many ways that children solved problems in the YCAR project indicated the need to define 'finding solutions' broadly, which is also a useful approach for practitioners working with many different young children. Young children may problem-solve following adults' direction to achieve adults' pre-planned outcomes – 'scaffolding' (Wood, Bruner and Ross, 1976) 'guided participation', 'apprenticeship' (Rogoff, 1995) or 'sustained, shared thinking' (Siraj-Blatchford, Sylva, Muttock, Gilden and Bell, 2002). Alternatively, young children may find – and seek – their own solutions, when they 'learn to use tools for investigation, to experiment and observe the results and to make comparisons among objects' (Helm and

Katz, 2001: 8; Lowrie, 2002). Much has been written about children finding solutions, including its transformative potential (Dewey, 1916; Helm and Katz, 2001; Piaget, 1972), the social contexts where it presents (Ashley and Tomasello, 1998; Eisenberg, Fabes, Guthrie and Reiser, 2000), young children's problem solving with tools and gestures (Cox and Smitsman, 2006; Keen, 2011), as well as analogy (Singer-Freeman and Bauer, 2008: 332; Singer-Freeman and Goswami, 2001).

Summary

This section has considered briefly what 'finding a solution' may mean in early childhood. Different themes in the literature concerning young children's problem-solving have been introduced here but feature more prominently in the second section of the chapter which is concerned with the ways children found solutions in the YCAR project and how these findings may support practitioners in their work with young children.

Young children finding solutions in the YCAR project

This second section of Chapter 4 focuses on the 20 building blocks – or provocations – that children in the YCAR project used to construct knowledge by finding solutions in everyday activities at home and in their settings (Figure 4.1). Each is discussed here with examples from the YCAR study, linked to research and literature about knowledge and problem-solving, to provide a framework to support practitioners to observe and interpret the ways their children may construct knowledge by finding solutions in their everyday activities.

Applications of prior experience as a factor for young children finding solutions

Children in the YCAR project sometimes found solutions when they applied experiences they had had previously in new situations. Children's behaviours revealed categories for this section that included *'Applying a rule to create a solution'*, *'Finding a practical use for a solution'*, *'Wanting to preserve what they had done'* and using their *'Ability to read'*.

In the YCAR project, children sometimes applied rules to create solutions, often seeming to employ an 'idea of generality – the single, universally correct method that will work for

(i) Applying a rule to create a solution

Epistemological Category:	Applying a rule to create a solution
Epistemological Factor:	**Applications of prior experience**
Research Behaviour:	**FIND A SOLUTION**

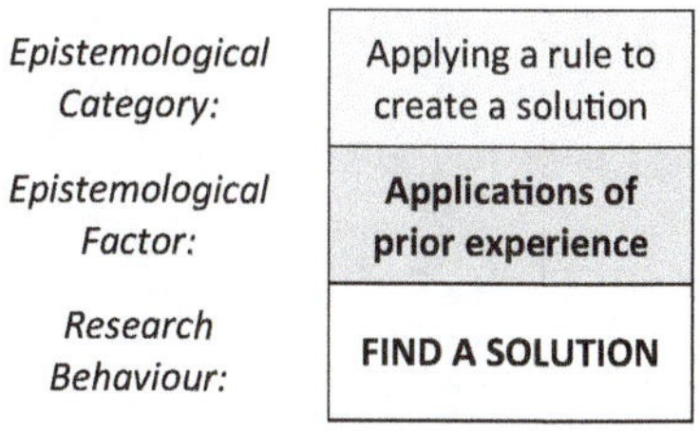

FIGURE 4.2 Building blocks – Applying a rule to create a solution

all problems and for all people' (Papert, 1993: 143–144). This tended to present as a 'what works' model: children seemed to perceive that what they had learned previously could 'be translated into rules for action…' (Biesta, 2007: 11). Many examples focused on literacy and numeracy, perhaps reflecting the English government's policy emphasis on children's attainment in literacy and numeracy at the time the YCAR data were captured (West, 2010, DfE, 2010).

Gemma's workbook

Gemma (5 years) and her brother (8 years) had been tasked by their grandmother to work through brand new, commercially produced English workbooks at their dining room table. Their grandmother was sitting at the table, helping them and their mother was also in the room. Gemma began writing in her book:

> **Gemma: *'Put…the…'***
> **Gemma's Mother: *'…b'***
> **Gemma looked at the book.**
> **Gemma's Grandma pointed at Gemma's book: *'The ball…'***
> **Gemma: *'Under'***
> **Gemma's Grandma: *'"Under" – yes'***
> **Gemma: 'U'. Gemma began writing**
> **Gemma's Grandma pointed at the book: *'Yes – "d"'.***
> **Gemma was writing, saying: *'Under…u…d…'***
> **Gemma's Grandma: *'Yes – "d"…that's "d" babes – no'.***

As Gemma attempted to spell, she used analogy to problem-solve (Goswami, 1992; Brown and Kane, 1988; Tunteler and Resing, 2007): the application of 'a relation learned in one set of materials to a new, very different, set of materials' (Singer-Freeman and Bauer, 2008: 332). She applied phonic knowledge she had learned previously to this new task. Given the emphasis on literacy in early childhood settings in England when the YCAR data were collected, it may be inferred that adult support for spelling had already been given to her.

FORMS OF KNOWLEDGE

✓ Knowing that
✓ Knowing how
✓ Explicit knowledge
✓ Mode 1 knowledge

THE ADULT'S ROLE

Gemma's grandmother and mother scaffolded her writing; they acted as more knowledgeable others (Bruner, 1966; Vygotsky, 1978), supporting Gemma to decode for reading and encode for writing. However, as noted, Gemma was also applying phonic knowledge she had already acquired to this task (Singer-Freeman and Bauer, 2008): adults may have previously supported her in gaining this knowledge.

REFLECTION POINTS

Identify ways that practitioners and parents can help young children to apply what they have learned *in their settings* to solve new problems at home.

Identify ways that practitioners and parents can help young children to apply what they have learned *at home* to solve new problems in their settings.

What are the challenges children, parents and practitioners might encounter in either case?

What can be done to help to overcome these challenges?

(ii) Finds practical use for solution

Epistemological Category:	Finds practical use for solution
Epistemological Factor:	**Applications of prior experience**
Research Behaviour:	**FIND A SOLUTION**

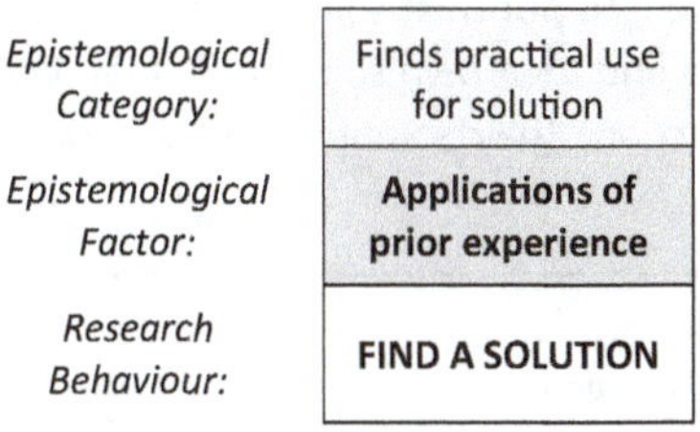

FIGURE 4.3 Building blocks – Finds practical use for solution

In their everyday activities in the YCAR study, sometimes children discovered practical uses for solutions they had found.

Sticky dough

Gemma (5 years) was baking at home one day with her grandmother. She found her cookie dough too sticky to work with and decided to apply flour to the dough, which made it less sticky, solving her problem. She then made her new, non-sticky dough into a round cookie shape, slowly slid the dough onto her hands and lifted it onto a tray ready for baking. While she slid the cookie dough onto the tray, she said to her grandmother: 'I'm doing it easily. It's easy for me'.

Here, Gemma demonstrated pragmatism: 'practical knowledge' (Griffiths and MacLeod, 2008: 129). Gemma solved the problem of her sticky dough by applying flour. Because she only applied flour to make dough less sticky and did not also try other ingredients, it may be inferred that a prior experience had taught her that flour can make dough less sticky. Griffiths and MacLeod (2008: 129) note that *praxis* is 'open to new perspectives and understandings. It is therefore open to revision'; by manoeuvring the non-sticky dough onto the baking tray, she found a new practical use for the solution she had found.

FORMS OF KNOWLEDGE

✓ A posteriori reasoning
✓ Explicit knowledge

THE ADULT'S ROLE

Gemma's grandmother avoided directing Gemma, which enabled Gemma to find and apply her own solution, then put it to a new practical use herself: a revised purpose (Griffiths and MacLeod, 2008). Gemma's grandmother also afforded her sufficient time to find her own solution, then put it to practical use. Gemma was able to report her success to her grandmother, to confirm it.

REFLECTION POINTS

Spend time observing young children during free play to see if they find solutions.

See if they are able, then, to put their solutions to new, practical uses.

What helps children to find their own solutions? Does anything hinder them?

What helps children to put their solutions to new, practical uses? Does anything hinder them?

(iii) Wants to preserve what s/he is doing

Epistemological Category:	Wants to preserve what s/he is doing
Epistemological Factor:	**Applications of prior experience**
Research Behaviour:	**FIND A SOLUTION**

FIGURE 4.4 Building blocks – Wants to preserve what s/he is doing

On occasions, children in the YCAR study wanted to preserve their solutions, which suggested they valued them. This behaviour resonates with ideas about 'functionings' and agency that are identified in the *Human Development and Capabilities Approach (HDCA)* (Sen, 1985): 'A functioning is being or doing what people value and have reason to value. A capability is a person's freedom to enjoy various functionings…Agency is a person's ability to pursue and realize goals she values and has reason to value' (Alkire and Deneulin, 2009: 22). When children want to preserve what they are doing and do so, they are respected as competent agents (Corsaro, 2005; James and James, 2008; Moss and Petrie, 2002).

Sugar cube igloo

One day in Cherry Setting, a task in continuous provision that the teachers had asked all the children aged 4–5 years to complete was to build a small igloo on a table from sugar cubes. This task was part of a topic focused on hot and cold. When Pedro (aged 4) had built his igloo from sugar cubes, his friend ran by and almost nudged the table. Pedro warned: 'That's going to break it'. By accident, his friend then did nudge the table and the igloo collapsed. Pedro sighed, then began constructing again, though this time, rather than an igloo, he designed and built a sturdy tower surrounded by a protective wall (Figure 4.5).

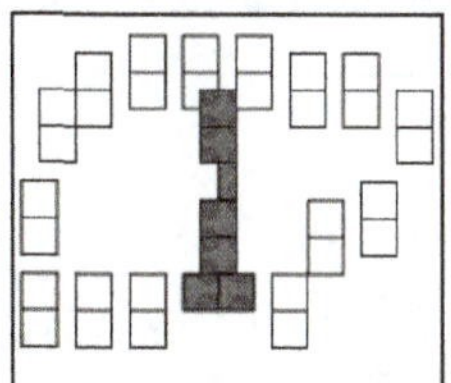

FIGURE 4.5 Pedro's sugar construction (Murray, 2012).

Pedro's initial igloo building was a solution to the problem set by the teachers. Having completed this task, Pedro demonstrated in two ways that he wanted to preserve what he was doing and therefore he valued what he was doing (Alkire and Deneulin, 2009). First, he warned his friend not to nudge the table. Second, having seen his igloo destroyed, he decided to build a tower, surrounded by a protective wall: Pedro 'acted independent(ly)', establishing his agency (James and James, 2008: 9; Moss and Petrie, 2002; Stern, 1985).

FORMS OF KNOWLEDGE

- ✓ A posteriori reasoning
- ✓ Explicit knowledge
- ✓ Mode 2 knowledge

THE ADULT'S ROLE

The ways that practitioners had organised Cherry Setting meant that Pedro had the opportunity to express his wish to preserve what he was doing. The setting organisation related to physical resources, time, culture and an ethic which empowered Pedro to value and want to preserve what he was doing and to have agency to do so.

REFLECTION POINTS

What aspects of settings you have worked in afford young children agency?

What may hinder children's agency?

Have children you have worked with wanted to preserve what they have done?

What have adults put in place to facilitate this?

Do adults sometimes stop children from preserving something they have created and value?

Why might this happen?

How might such an experience affect children's sense of agency?

(iv) Able reader

Epistemological Category:	Able reader
Epistemological Factor:	**Applications of prior experience**
Research Behaviour:	**FIND A SOLUTION**

FIGURE 4.6 Building blocks – Able reader

When the YCAR project took place there was, in England, a government policy emphasis on teaching young children to read through a combined approach of systematic synthetic phonics and reading comprehension skills (Rose, 2006; DfE, 2012). Practitioners were expected to teach children from 3 years to learn to blend letters to read words and to acquire semantic reading skills and knowledge (Goouch and Lambirth, 2011).

The reader

Martin (aged 5) had been in his reception class in Cherry Setting for two terms when one day at home he decided to read to his mother the scripts on a pack of 'Ben Ten Top Trump' cards, one after another. *Ben Ten* is a children's animation that appeared regularly on television during the YCAR project. Its main character was Ben Tennyson, a boy aged 10 who had found a magic gadget that enabled him to transform into different 'alien heroes' with exceptional powers (Cartoon Network, 2016). The animation included other characters, among them 'Waybig'. While Martin was reading the script on one card to his mother, he said: "Ben (Ten) just needs to be careful never to transform into Waybig indoors... 'Cos he's nearly one hundred feet from head to toe".

Martin's reading ability at 5 years old was characteristic of 'adultification', since literacy opens the door to aspects of the world that those who cannot read are denied (Jenks, 2005; Postman, 1994: 124). In the context of the HDCA, Martin's ability to read was a 'functioning': he was able do what he valued which was to read about *Ben Ten* (Sen, 1985; Alkire and Deneulin, 2009), enabling him to lead the agenda in the dyad between his mother and himself, in turn, giving him capability in two ways. First, to enjoy reading in that socially constructed context (Schaffer, 1992; Rogoff, 1995; Sen, 1985; Alkire and Deneulin, 2009) and second, finding a solution: advising that Ben Ten does not transform himself into the 100-foot Waybig indoors.

FORMS OF KNOWLEDGE

✓ A priori knowledge
✓ Explicit knowledge
✓ Mode 1 knowledge

THE ADULT'S ROLE

In this dyad at Martin's home, Martin's mother afforded him time and agency to lead his own agenda, which included reading the cards, then finding a solution to a potential problem that he devised.

REFLECTION POINTS

Alkire and Deneulin (2009: 22) identify that the *Human Development and Capability Approach* has three key strands: functioning, capability and agency:

'A *functioning* is being or doing what people value and have reason to value.

A *capability* is a person's freedom to enjoy various functionings – to be or do things that contribute to their well-being.

Agency is a person's ability to pursue and realise goals she values and has reason to value'.

Consider some of the practical ways that you have supported young children to achieve functionings, capability and agency.

Consider how you could build your practice further in regard to supporting young children to achieve functionings, capability and agency.

Innovation as a factor for young children finding solutions

When children in the YCAR project found their own solutions, sometimes these were innovative: they developed new ideas into something that was valued (Department for Business, Innovation and Skills, 2011; 2012). The categories for innovation as part of young children finding solutions included *'Finding their own solution'*, *'Creating a problem to solve'* and *'Devising a practical method to create a solution'*.

(v) Finds own solution

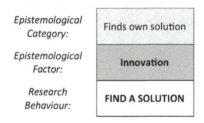

Epistemological Category:	Finds own solution
Epistemological Factor:	**Innovation**
Research Behaviour:	**FIND A SOLUTION**

FIGURE 4.7 Building blocks – Finds own solution

During the YCAR project, children often found their own solutions (Edwards, 1998; Helm and Katz, 2001) and this tended to happen in social contexts (Ashley and Tomasello, 1998; Denham, Blair, Demulder, Levitas, Sawyer and Auerbach-Major, 2003; Eisenberg *et al.*, 2000).

Dividing cookies

One day, Gemma (aged 5) and her brother (aged 8) were baking cookies at home with their grandmother. The raw cookie dough had been shaped into small balls. Gemma's grandmother began to read aloud from the recipe: 'Put the cookies on a baking tray...' Gemma interrupted: 'No – do it like this – I'll show you. Two for you, two for me. Two for you, two for me'. As she spoke, Gemma divided the raw cookie balls equally between her brother and herself. Gemma and her brother placed the balls of dough on their own baking trays.

Here, the problem was that the recipe did not account for two sets of cookies. Gemma devised a novel way to achieve the goal of preparing the cookie dough for the oven in a way that ensured her brother and she had equal amounts of dough. In doing so, Gemma engaged in 'important cognitive activity', working towards a goal but not in a 'routine way' (Meadows, 2006: 127). Gemma found a solution autonomously (Lowrie, 2002), though it emerged in a social context, widely recognised as beneficial for problem-solving (Ashley and Tomasello, 1998; Denham *et al.*, 2003).

FORMS OF KNOWLEDGE

- ✓ Knowing how
- ✓ Explicit knowledge
- ✓ Mode 2 knowledge

THE ADULT'S ROLE

Gemma's grandmother did not provide the solution to a problem: the recipe did not account for two sets of cookies. This enabled Gemma to find her own solution. The social context in which the problem arose and was solved was important: had Gemma been baking alone, she would not have needed to divide the raw cookies into two sets. It also enabled her to report her solution as she was enacting it.

> **REFLECTION POINTS**
>
> Consider the ways you have seen practitioners give young children opportunities to find their own solutions to authentic problems.
>
> What can practitioners do to help children in this regard? Why?
>
> Does anything hinder these opportunities? If so, what? What can be done to address this?

(vi) Creates a problem to solve

Epistemological Category:	Creates a problem to solve
Epistemological Factor:	**Innovation**
Research Behaviour:	**FIND A SOLUTION**

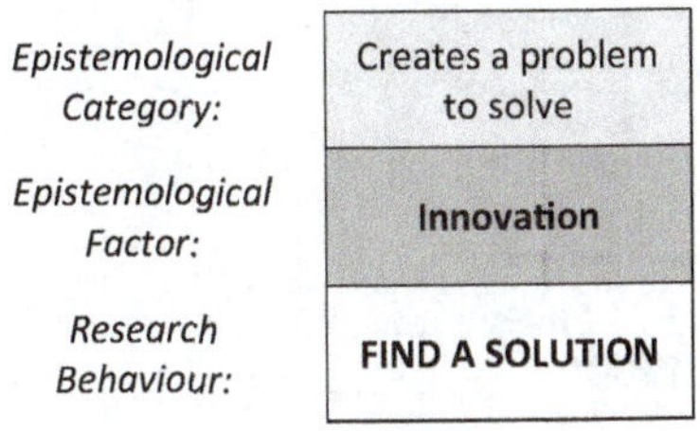

FIGURE 4.8 Building blocks – Creates a problem to solve

Sometimes, children in the YCAR study also created their own problems to solve before finding their solutions (Pintrich and Zusho, 2002; Brown and Campione, 2002; Lowrie, 2002).

Keeping score

At home, during her family's focus group, Gemma, aged 5, explained how she had created a problem which she solved. Gemma, aged 5, shared a photograph of herself and said 'That's me' (Figure 4.9).

She went on to explain: 'I was playing with that ball and that thing and I was writing down my scores...That's making the score' (Figure 4.10).

Gemma's mother asked her to tell me more:

Gemma: *'I did that ball in the thing that the ball sticks on...'*

Gemma's mother: *'So it was a chart wasn't it? Like a target wasn't it?'*

Gemma: *'Yes.'*

Gemma's mother: *'With a...sticky ball that you threw. And you decided to...'*

Gemma: *'They're all the scores that I got.'*

Gemma's father: *'So you put in all the scores.'*

FIGURE 4.9 That's me

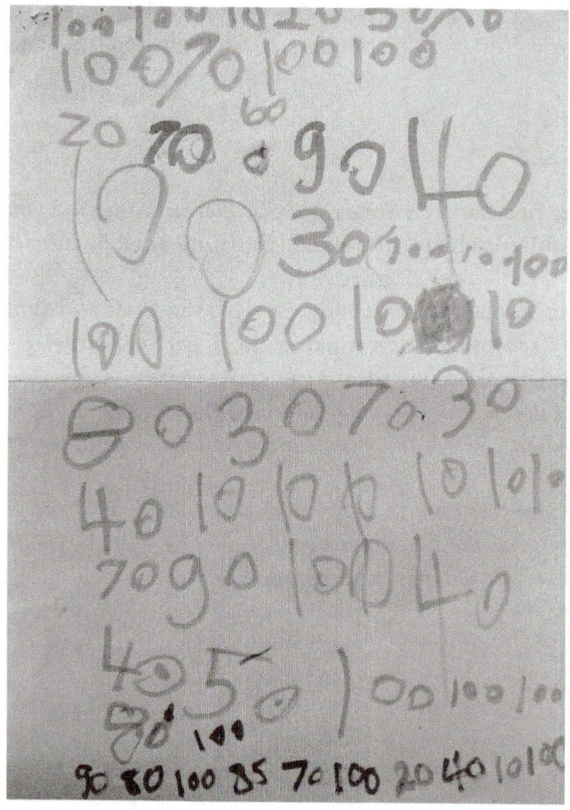

FIGURE 4.10 Making the score

When playing a game with a Velcro® ball and numbered target, Gemma decided that she needed a chart for recording her scores. Gemma's planning, her development of strategy and resources and her evaluation of this activity resonated with established definitions of problems, problem-setting and problem-solving (DeLoache, Miller and Pierroutsakos, 1998; Helm and Katz, 2001; Tarini and White, 1998). Gemma demonstrated agency by posing *and* resolving her own problem in this context that was meaningful to her (Helm and Katz, 2001; Lowrie, 2002). Aligning with the DBIS (2011; 2012) definition for innovation, she developed an idea that was new to her and it was valued by herself and her parents: first, Gemma shared a photograph of herself working on the activity, second, she retained and shared the scoring card and finally, her mother and father were eager to present what she had done as data for the YCAR project.

FORMS OF KNOWLEDGE

✓ Knowing that
✓ A posteriori reasoning
✓ Explicit knowledge

THE ADULT'S ROLE

Gemma's parents had given basic elements of the target game: the Velcro® target board with numbers and a ball. However, they did not provide her with a commercially produced scorecard, nor did they make one for her. Instead, they ensured that she had access to paper and pens, so she was able to design and make a score card for herself. Before she undertook this activity, Gemma had had experiences that had helped her to learn how to form numbers; adults may have been instrumental in helping her but this can only be inferred as the evidence is not clear.

REFLECTION POINTS

What experiences and resources might encourage young children to:

- Set their own problems.
- Solve their own problems.
- Innovate – i.e. develop new ideas into something valued (DBIS, 2011; 2012).

(vii) Devises practical method to create solution

Epistemological Category:	Devises practical method to create solution
Epistemological Factor:	**Innovation**
Research Behaviour:	**FIND A SOLUTION**

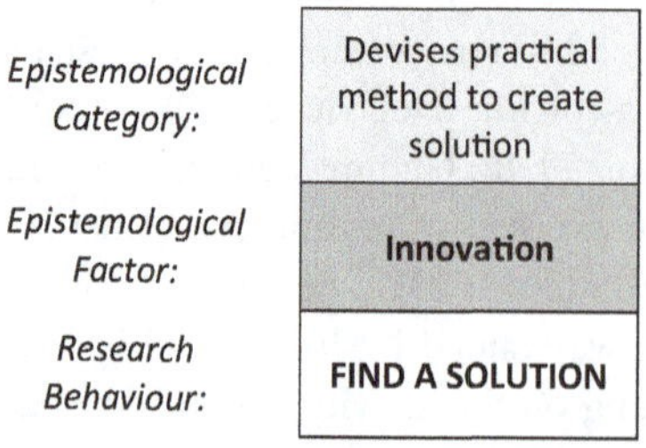

FIGURE 4.11 Building blocks – Devises practical method to create solution

Aligning with pragmatism – 'practical knowledge' (Griffiths and MacLeod, 2008: 129) – children in the YCAR study sometimes devised practical methods to create solutions.

The eraser

In the summer term in Ash Setting, the teacher had set the children in the class a literacy task. 8-year-old Demi (aged 8) was sitting with three other children when she noticed that her writing was different from theirs. She said to them: *'I thought we were supposed to…'* then stood up, went to the teaching assistant and asked her: *'Can I borrow your rubber?'* She then returned to her table and erased her work.

Turning over

During an art lesson in Ash Setting, Costas (aged 8) was working at a table with other children, as his teacher had directed him to do. He drew a pattern, similar to one that the teacher had modelled earlier, stopped, looked at it, then turned over his sheet and began again.

Both Demi and Costas devised practical methods to create solutions: Demi thought her work did not match that of her peers so she erased it and Costas indicated his dissatisfaction with his first pattern by turning over his sheet and starting again.

Demi and Costas adopted pragmatic responses (Griffiths and MacLeod, 2008: 129) that relied on understandings that they had assimilated by being in Ash Setting for almost a year. Demi's actions were interwoven with themes of peer culture and social constructivism (Vygotsky, 1978; Corsaro, 2005); both children wanted to do what they deemed the right thing (Kohlberg, 1984). In response to problems that Demi and Costas identified, they created innovative solutions (DBIS, 2011; 2012): each devised a new practical method to create and act on a solution, indicating they valued their solutions more than allowing their problems to persist.

FORMS OF KNOWLEDGE

✓ Knowing how

✓ A posteriori reasoning

THE ADULT'S ROLE

The teacher had created a culture in this setting in which both Demi and Costas wanted to complete their tasks in ways they believed they should do. It may be argued that the teacher was limiting the children's constructions of knowledge by requiring them to conform to narrow expectations. However, paradoxically, their realisation that they were not conforming and their attempts to address this resulted in them innovating by providing practical methods to create solutions.

REFLECTION POINTS

What are the features of an early childhood setting's culture that might encourage children to devise practical methods to create new solutions to problems?

What features of a setting's culture might discourage children from devising practical methods to create new solutions to problems?

Social domains as a factor for young children finding solutions

When they found solutions, children in the YCAR project often did this in social contexts. The categories within this factor included '*Resolves another person's problem*', '*Shares a solution*', '*Employs others to help with finding a solution*' and '*Theory of Mind*'.

(viii) Resolves another person's problem

Epistemological Category:	Resolves another person's problem
Epistemological Factor:	**Social domains**
Research Behaviour:	**FIND A SOLUTION**

FIGURE 4.12 Building blocks – Resolves another person's problem

Resolving other people's problems emerged from the YCAR project as an 'effect' of children finding solutions.

Use a snow machine!

One day, during a whole class carpet time in Cherry Setting, Mrs Green the teacher was discussing 'hot and cold' with the children as part of their topic. She asked the children: 'What could you use if you are hot?' Oscar (5 years) responded: 'Use a snow machine!' Mrs Green replied to Oscar's proposal: 'Great idea if you could have everything you want but if you were hot now then what would you do?' Oscar replied: 'Take my shirt off.'

Oscar initially thought that Mrs Green's first question was an open possibility problem that he could resolve. He assumed that he and his teacher shared common language and meanings and a 'joint focus of attention': key features of intersubjectivity (Göncü, 1993: 188). However, what followed indicated their perspectives were not aligned. Mrs Green's reply indicated that she was seeking a more pragmatic response than Oscar's 'snow machine' proposal. However, Oscar appeared unabashed as he provided a further solution – 'Take my shirt off' – taking account of the newly implied limitations. Oscar engaged in social interaction with his teacher as he attempted to resolve the problem she presented, yet his practitioner began to 'shut down' his solutions by adding parameters. However, even the teacher's narrower second question was semi-open, whereas most adults' questions in English early childhood settings are closed (Siraj-Blatchford and Manni, 2008).

FORMS OF KNOWLEDGE

✓ A priori knowledge

✓ Explicit knowledge (Oscar's responses)

✓ Tacit knowledge (Oscar's assumptions relating to intersubjectivity (Göncü, 1993)

THE ADULT'S ROLE

The teacher seemed to reject Oscar's attempt to resolve the first problem she presented. He then resolved a second problem she posed. The teacher might have been more specific in her questioning but because she was not, this encouraged Oscar to persist in engaging with his teacher to attempt to resolve the problems she presented.

REFLECTION POINTS

Ask a colleague to observe your practice for an hour and note down the questions you ask the children you are working with.

Tally up how many open questions and closed questions you asked.

Look at your colleague's notes. Did you present problems to the children that engaged them to think critically to resolve them?

Now swap with your colleague.

What did this activity tell you both about the ways you challenge children to find solutions?

(ix) Shares solution

Epistemological Category:	Shares solution
Epistemological Factor:	**Social domains**
Research Behaviour:	**FIND A SOLUTION**

FIGURE 4.13 Building blocks – Shares solution

Children often seemed to share their solutions in the present study.

Bear hunt subtraction

One day in Cherry Setting, during a whole class carpet time focused on the story 'We're going on a Bear Hunt' (Rosen, 1993), the teacher Miss Hunt unpacked a bag as the children watched and she took out ten items they might 'need for a bear hunt', for example, a map, hat and binoculars. A few at a time, Miss Hunt then removed objects from the children's view and asked children to tell their partners how many were left, engaging them in solving subtraction problems. At each opportunity, Querida (aged 4) shared her solutions with her partner by telling them to her.

In this context of guided participation (Rogoff, 1995), Querida's teacher required her to 'interpret, organize, and use information from the environment' (Lash, 2008: 34) and she did so. However, she did not seem to 'acquire or construct increasingly complex skills, knowledge, and intelligence' (Lash, 2008: 34) because to answer the teacher's questions, Querida already had to know how to count and subtract. Therefore, although Querida engaged in joint problem-solving with her friend, this did not enable her to construct new knowledge (Ashley and Tomasello, 1998; Topping, Miller, Murray, Henderson, Fortuna and Conlin, 2011).

FORMS OF KNOWLEDGE

✓ A posteriori reasoning
✓ Explicit knowledge
✓ Mode 1 knowledge

THE ADULT'S ROLE

To find solutions to the problems the teacher posed, children needed to be able to count and subtract. Querida and other children who could already perform these operations found solutions and shared them with their partners yet the opportunities for them to engage in problem solving that challenged them were limited. For children who were not able to count or subtract in this vignette, these skills were not scaffolded by this activity, so opportunities for them to find and share solutions were also limited.

> **REFLECTION POINTS**
>
> Identify some problems that have provided authentic challenges to children you have worked with.
>
> What processes did they go through when they were seeking solutions?
>
> Have they always found solutions? Did this matter?
>
> Are there benefits to children sharing solutions to problems they have solved? If so, what are they? If not, why not?

(x) Employs others to help with finding a solution

Epistemological Category:	Employs others to help with finding a solution
Epistemological Factor:	**Social domains**
Research Behaviour:	**FIND A SOLUTION**

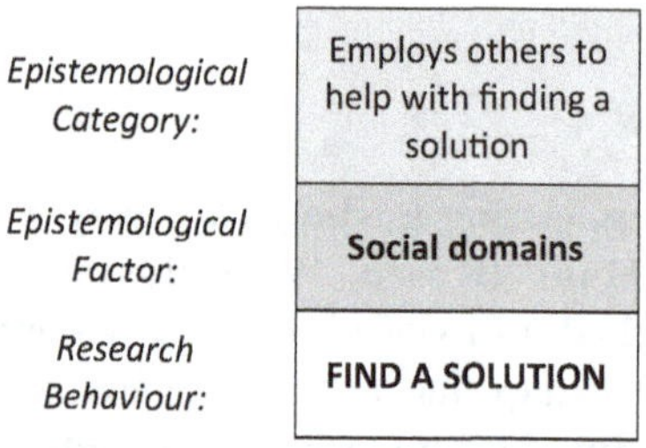

FIGURE 4.14 Building blocks – Employs others to help with finding a solution

As well as sharing their own solutions with others, children in the YCAR project sometimes employed others to help with finding solutions.

Martin's questions

One bedtime at home, Martin and his mother engaged in a question-and-answer session.

Martin: *'Mummy – I've got a question: how did babies grow in the tummy with the seed?'*

Martin's mother: *'Well, once the seed is in the mummy's tummy – yeah? Mummy's tummy is lovely and warm and safe isn't it?'*

Martin: *'Mmm...but how do they grow?'*

Martin's mother: *'How do they grow? Well – the seed attaches itself to the mummy's tummy and you know all the blood that goes round your body?'*

Martin wriggled around on the bed.

This dyad resonates with social constructivist models such as Schaffer's 'joint involvement episodes' (1992), Alexander's 'dialogic teaching' (2008) and Siraj-Blatchford *et al.*'s 'sustained, shared thinking' (2002: 8). Such models are considered conducive to problem-solving (Ashley and Tomasello, 1998; Denham *et al.*, 2003). During the exchange, Martin exercised 'power and autonomy' (Lowrie, 2002: 355) by employing his mother to provide solutions to his questions. Because they were his questions and the dyad took place at home, the context was meaningful for Martin, recognised as successful for social problem solving (Lowrie, 2002). Martin mirrored the elements that Rogoff (1990) identifies for problem-solving in social contexts: first, when he said 'Mummy – I've got a question', he verbalised a plan. When he asked: 'How did babies grow in the tummy with the seed?' he recalled how babies grow prenatally. He also sequenced his questions coherently, building each on the previous response, consciously constructing his questions to elicit solutions (his aim) and employing his mother to provide those solutions. Martin's incremental sequencing of questions also aligns with Vygotsky's idea (1978) that cognitive structures are transformed when a learner approaches a challenging task in social interaction with a more knowledgeable other.

FORMS OF KNOWLEDGE

- ✓ A priori knowledge (questions and answers)
- ✓ A posteriori reasoning (Martin wriggling to gain sensory understanding)
- ✓ Explicit knowledge
- ✓ Mode 1 knowledge

THE ADULT'S ROLE

Martin's mother was a resource for Martin here; she allowed herself to be employed to help him find solutions to problems he posed. She provided him with the information he requested in a meaningful way and in the context of a secure, trusting relationship.

REFLECTION POINTS

What can settings do to create contexts in which children pose challenging questions to adults?

(xi) Theory of mind

Epistemological Category:	Theory of mind
Epistemological Factor:	**Social domains**
Research Behaviour:	**FIND A SOLUTION**

FIGURE 4.15 Building blocks – Theory of mind

Theory of mind (TOM) – 'the understanding of others as psychological beings having mental states such as beliefs, desires, emotions and intentions' – is discussed extensively in psychology and neuroscience fields (*i.a.* Astington, Harris and Olson, 1988; Davies and Stone, 1995; Meltzoff, 1995: 838; 2011). Links have been made between children's ability to talk about such mental states and their 'developing capacities for representing and reasoning with them' (Meins, Fernyhough, Johnson, and Lidstone, 2006: 181). Young children are recognised as 'far more capable…than was thought even two or three decades ago' (Whitebread, 2012: 137) regarding their ability to 'attribute perception and consequent beliefs to other people' (Senju, Southgate, Snape, Leonard and Csibra, 2011: 878). In the

YCAR project, TOM sometimes presented in children's everyday behaviours in social contexts.

High heels

One day in the sitting room at home, Gemma's mother was trying on new shoes at home, and said to Gemma's grandmother: 'I don't think the 5 would fit because I need the size for the width'. Gemma (aged 5) suggested: 'Why don't you put an extra heel?'

Gemma suggested that her mother adds 'an extra heel' behind each of the existing heels as she thought this would make the shoes larger, which is what her mother said she needed. Gemma empathised with her mother's discomfort when she was trying on the new shoes and her suggestion indicates an 'understanding of others as psychological beings having mental states such as beliefs, desires, emotions and intentions', congruent with theory of mind (Meltzoff, 1995: 838). Equally, Gemma's suggestion linked emotion and intention with reasoning (Meins *et al.*, 2006).

FORMS OF KNOWLEDGE

✓ Knowing that
✓ A posteriori reasoning
✓ Explicit knowledge (Gemma shared her proposition)
✓ Tacit knowledge (Gemma empathised with her mother's mental state)

THE ADULT'S ROLE

The adults begin the discussion which provides the context for Gemma to display theory of mind.

REFLECTION POINTS

With ethical guidelines in place, spend some time observing theory of mind presenting in children aged 2, 3, 4 and 5 years: capture ways they recognise 'beliefs, desires, emotions and intentions' in others' behaviours (Meltzoff, 1995: 838).

What do you notice?

How do they respond?

What helps the children to recognise 'beliefs, desires, emotions and intentions' in others' behaviours (Meltzoff, 1995: 838)?

Autonomy as a factor for young children finding solutions

During the YCAR project children often demonstrated their autonomy when they were finding solutions. Categories that supported this behaviour included *'Self-regulation'*, *'Time and freedom to explore, investigate, experiment with something of personal interest'* and *'Focused on something of personal interest'*.

(xii) Self-regulates

Epistemological Category:	Self-regulates
Epistemological Factor:	**Autonomy**
Research Behaviour:	**FIND A SOLUTION**

FIGURE 4.16 Building blocks – Self-regulates

When children in the YCAR project found solutions autonomously, they tended to self-regulate. Sometimes termed self-management, there is no clear definition of self-regulation in the literature (Bronson, 2000) but there is recognition that it features various elements: cognitive, emotional, social, metacognitive and motivational (Ramdass and Zimmerman, 2011; Whitebread, 2012). Whitebread (2012) suggests that 'emotional warmth and security… feelings of control…cognitive challenge' and 'articulation of learning' are four 'principles for a pedagogy of self-regulation' (pp. 7–13).

Annie's omelette

One day, Annie (aged 7) was cooking an omelette at home with her mother looking on, while filming, Annie was stirring the omelette mixture, but stopped and read the recipe under her breath. Then she sighed and said to herself: 'Oh right – now where?'

Annie actively and constructively set herself a goal by reading the recipe (Pintrich and Zusho, 2002: 250), part of problem-solving (Eisenberg, Farbs, Guthrie and Reiser, 2000). She experienced 'emotional warmth and security' in her mother's presence, alongside 'feelings of control' and 'cognitive challenge' when reading the recipe and considering her next steps, and she articulated her progress by engaging in meta-communication (Garvey, 1991: 134; Whitebread, 2010: 7–10): a widely recognised device that combines speech with rational thinking (Flavell, Green, Flavell and Grossman, 1997).

FORMS OF KNOWLEDGE

✓ A posteriori reasoning

✓ Tacit knowledge

THE ADULT'S ROLE

Annie's mother provided emotional warmth and security that enabled Annie to experience feelings of control and cognitive challenge and to articulate her learning: four 'principles for a pedagogy of self-regulation' (Whitebread, 2012: 7–13).

> **REFLECTION POINTS**
>
> Consider some practical ways that you have afforded young children:
>
> - Emotional warmth and security.
> - Feelings of control.
> - Cognitive challenge.
> - Articulation of learning.
>
> These are key elements for a 'pedagogy of self-regulation' (Whitebread, 2012: 7–13).
> What examples of self-management have you seen in young children linked to one or more of these principles?

(xiii) Focused on something of personal interest

Epistemological Category:	Focused on something of personal interest
Epistemological Factor:	**Autonomy**
Research Behaviour:	**FIND A SOLUTION**

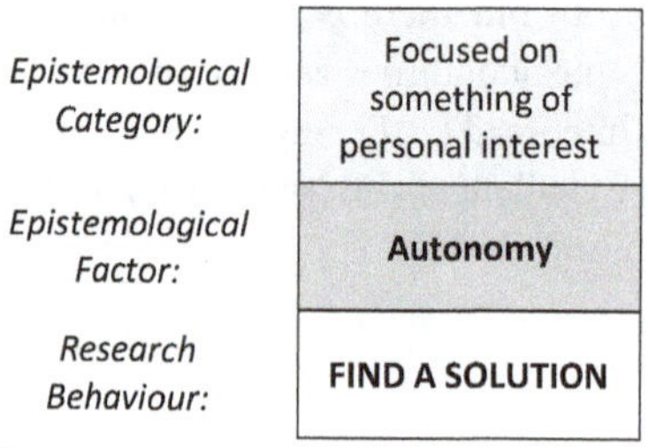

FIGURE 4.17 Building blocks – Focused on something of personal interest

In the YCAR project, when children found solutions autonomously, it sometimes happened when they had a focus of personal interest. There were more incidents of this at home (n=40) than in their settings (n=13). Focusing on something of personal interest resonates with literature concerning involvement, identified as an indicator of deep-level learning (Laevers, 2000).

Billy and the camcorder

During an analysis session for the YCAR project, Billy observed himself on video footage that had been taken of an art lesson when he and his class peers had been tasked with their creating their own pictures in the style of African art. As he watched the footage, Billy provided a commentary:

'I'm doing that thing when you have one of those ear things (cotton bud) and you do it red white and yellow and you draw the thing on a black piece of paper and we do round it in dots. I did white'.

Billy's commentary quickly moved from the art task to repeatedly focusing on the camcorder that had captured the footage:

'That's Howard looking at the camera. Now he's getting up.'

'I'm back. I'm just so interested in the camera.'

'I was giving the camera a pinch.'
'I was interested in the camera.'

Billy's repeated reference to the camera (camcorder) and his behaviour with it during the art lesson suggests he was fascinated by it and wanted to understand it better so he focused his attention in a limited way to become deeply involved in the camcorder (Laevers, 2000).

FORMS OF KNOWLEDGE

✓ A posteriori reasoning
✓ Explicit knowledge
✓ Mode 2 knowledge

THE ADULT'S ROLE

The camcorder engaged Billy's deep interest and involvement. His teacher afforded Billy autonomy to leave his art task to focus deeply on investigating the camcorder, while the researcher gave him the opportunity to focus deeply on the camcorder again during the analysis session and reflect on his involvement in it.

REFLECTION POINTS

When you have observed young children engaging with objects that capture their interest and involvement, what did they do to show they were interested and involved in each object?

(xiv) Time and freedom to explore, investigate, experiment with something of personal interest

Epistemological Category:	Time and freedom to explore, investigate, experiment with something of personal interest
Epistemological Factor:	**Autonomy**
Research Behaviour:	**FIND A SOLUTION**

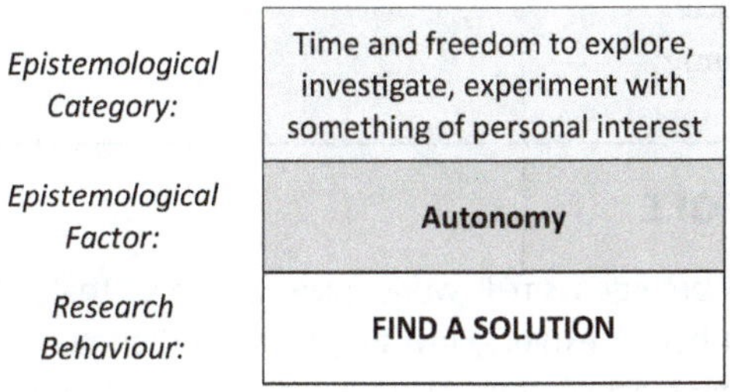

FIGURE 4.18 Building blocks – Time and freedom to explore, investigate, experiment with something of personal interest

When children found solutions autonomously during the YCAR project, it was often because they had time and freedom to explore, investigate and experiment with something of personal interest. Time has been linked with 'being' (Heidegger, 1962), 'consciousness' (Merleau-Ponty, 2002: 481) and identity (Lyotard, 1992). Markström and Halldèn (2009) suggest time guides 'the teacher's social order' in early childhood settings so that children's freedom may be diminished by the adult's agenda.

Chilly polar regions

During a free-flow play session in Cherry Setting, Nora (5 years) and her friend chose to play with the 'Chilly Polar Regions Small World Play (SWP)' which featured small world polar animals, a helicopter, a ship, and people on a table top covered with white and blue fabric to represent snow and water. Nora tried to put a SWP lifebelt over a SWP person's head so the SWP person could wear it. She tried to push it over the person's head; it would not go on. Nora took it off and tried again and it still would not go on. She repeated this three times, in the end pushing so hard that she became red in the face, indicating her effort as she tried to force on the lifebelt. After more than two minutes, Nora pushed the lifebelt onto the SWP person then she put him into the boat.

Here, Nora had time and freedom to explore, investigate and experiment with something of personal interest. She explored whether the lifebelt could be pushed over the person's head, by examining it for 'diagnostic purposes' (Stebbins, 2001: 2). In her actions, she adopted elements of scientific investigation: question, hypothesis, experiment (Penn State LeHigh Valley, 2016). She questioned, then hypothesised that she would be able to put the lifebelt on the person. She experimented by testing her hypothesis: controlling the variables, restricting them to herself, the SWP lifebelt and SWP person and manipulating the treatment conditions by exerting increased pressure in repeated tests. The solution was found: the lifebelt went on the person and Nora was able to continue her small world play (Creswell, 2008). Nora pursued her play autonomously: she planned according to a goal and operated consciously and voluntarily to enact her goal (Heidegger, 1962; Lyotard, 1992; Merleau-Ponty, 2002: 481), without time constraints imposed by her teacher (Markström and Halldèn, 2009).

FORMS OF KNOWLEDGE

✓ A posteriori reasoning

THE ADULT'S ROLE

Nora's teacher had provided small world play resources that interested her. Nora's interest encouraged her to explore, investigate and experiment with the small world play resources and her teacher afforded Nora sufficient autonomy, time and freedom to do so.

> **REFLECTION POINTS**
>
> What ***play resources*** have you provided that have encouraged children to:
>
> - **Explore:** examine for 'diagnostic purposes' (Stebbins, 2001: 2)?
> - **Investigate:** question, hypothesis, **experiment** by controlling variables and manipulating conditions (Creswell, 2008; Penn State LeHigh Valley, 2016)?
>
> What are specific ***features of these resources*** that have encouraged children you have worked with to explore, investigate and experiment?
>
> Are practitioners always able to afford young children sufficient time and freedom to explore, investigate and experiment autonomously during their play until the children find their own solutions? If not, what prevents this?

Material contexts as a factor for young children finding solutions

Sometimes children engaged with material contexts when finding solutions as part of the YCAR project. This factor included the categories 'Exploring properties', 'Deductive reasoning' and 'Inductive reasoning'

(xv) Exploring properties

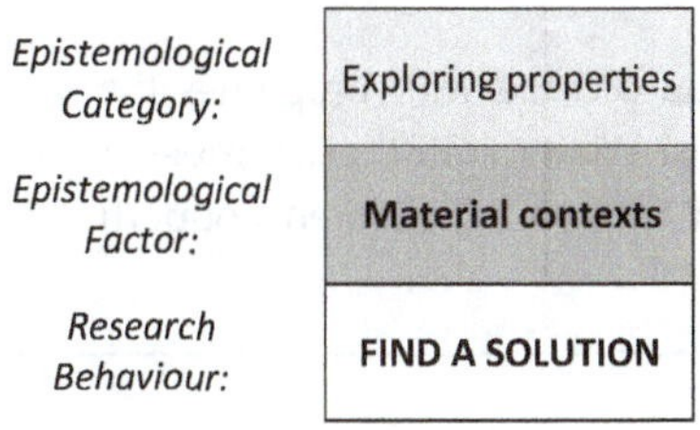

Epistemological Category:	Exploring properties
Epistemological Factor:	**Material contexts**
Research Behaviour:	**FIND A SOLUTION**

FIGURE 4.19 Building blocks – Exploring properties

Apple seeds

One day during free-flow play in Beech Setting, Kelly (aged 5) had chosen to go to the snack table. She was sitting eating an apple. She began to talk to a practitioner nearby:

Kelly: '*Do you know why I'm eating an apple?*'

Practitioner: '*Why?*'

Kelly: '*Because I'm counting the seeds.*'

Kelly finished eating the apple and she counted six seeds aloud and she said to the practitioner:

Kelly: '*1, 2, 3, 4, 5, 6 – six seeds.*'

This vignette aligns with the definition of problem solving proposed by DeLoache *et al.* (1998): 'a goal, one or two obstacles that make the goal not immediately possible, one or typically more strategies that can be used to solve the problem...and the evaluation of the outcome of the problem-solving process' (p. 826). Kelly identified that her goal for eating the apple was to count how many seeds it contained. She identified the apple's flesh as an obstacle and eating the apple as a strategy and she evaluated the process by confirming aloud the number of seeds at the end. The seeds were one of the apple's properties and Kelly explored that property by examining it for a specific 'diagnostic purpose' (Stebbins, 2001: 2): to see how many seeds it contained.

FORMS OF KNOWLEDGE

- Knowing that
- A posteriori reasoning
- Explicit knowledge

THE ADULT'S ROLE

In this vignette, the practitioner's questioning was open – 'Why?' – and she allowed Kelly to lead all aspects of the problem solving process, rather than imposing an adult agenda.

REFLECTION POINTS

What resources could you provide with properties that are likely to provoke young children to solve problems? What might those 'problems' be?

What resources might limit young children's opportunities for exploring properties to find solutions? Why?

(xvi) Deductive reasoning

Epistemological Category:	Deductive reasoning
Epistemological Factor:	**Material contexts**
Research Behaviour:	**FIND A SOLUTION**

FIGURE 4.20 Building blocks – Deductive reasoning

'Valid deduction' which 'yields a conclusion that must be true given that its premises are true' (Johnson-Laird and Byrne, 1991: 2) is regarded as a 'reliable cognitive process' (Schechter, 2013: 229) and has traditionally been favoured by the academy and policymakers as a robust basis for research claims (Bridges, Smeyers and Smith, 2009). Evidence that supports premises for deductive reasoning must be 'formally demonstrable' (Ayer, 1940:

191). YCAR children engaged in deductive reasoning, usually in practical and material contexts.

Pushing the tricycle

During a free-flow play session in Cherry Setting, as part of continuous provision, Querida (aged 4) joined peers Iris and Tilly outside on the wheeled toys. Iris and Tilly were sitting on a tricycle and Querida tried to push them but could not move the tricycle initially. Querida pushed again and moved the tricycle forwards, then pushed them around the outdoor area.

Querida tried immediately to push the tricycle, indicating that she had already had experience of pushing resulting in forward motion. She based her reasoning on praxis – 'practical knowledge' derived from experience (Griffiths and MacLeod, 2008: 129). She also reasoned deductively, basing her conclusion on premises that were true (BonJour, 1998; Hume, 1739; Johnson-Laird and Byrne, 1991):

- Pushing results in forward movement (major premise).
- Querida pushed the tricycle (minor premise).
- The tricycle moved forward (conclusion).

FORMS OF KNOWLEDGE

✓ Knowing that

✓ A posteriori reasoning

THE ADULT'S ROLE

Cherry Setting practitioners afforded Querida resources and opportunity to facilitate her activity and the sophisticated deductive reasoning that underpinned it. Both were included as YCAR research data, but Cherry Setting practitioners did not capture either because they were focused on adult led activities with other children.

REFLECTION POINTS

What balance of time should practitioners give to supporting and assessing young children's constructions of knowledge in adult-led or child-led learning contexts? Why?

Do practitioners always recognise the qualities of children's thinking that inform children's actions?

If not, what factors might help them to do so?

(xvii) Inductive reasoning

Epistemological Category:	Inductive reasoning
Epistemological Factor:	**Material contexts**
Research Behaviour:	**FIND A SOLUTION**

FIGURE 4.21 Building blocks – Inductive reasoning

Sometimes children in the YCAR study engaged in inductive reasoning, usually in practical contexts. To create a logical argument through inductive reasoning, a premise need not be 'formally demonstrable' as it has to be for deductive reasoning but should 'accord with our past experience' to provide 'evidential support' for the argument's conclusion (Ayer, 1940: 190–191; Schechter, 2013: 226).

Camcorder tripod

Harry's father captured video footage of Harry (aged 5) setting up the camcorder tripod; the footage showed that this lasted 5.06 minutes. Later, during a focus group with Harry's family at home, Harry explained how he solved the problem of erecting the camcorder tripod to capture video footage for the YCAR project. He said: '*I know why we use the tripod...so we can stand the camera up. And we can get the legs higher. We can get the tripod up so you can see it. It took one or two years to get it up*'.

When Harry inferred that the time for setting up the tripod was 'one or two years', he indicated that he believed the tripod took time to set up. He wanted to communicate that it had taken a long time but he could not identify precisely how long, so his solution was estimating it had taken 'years'. Harry reasoned logically by drawing on evidence from his past experience to infer a 'best estimate' of the time (Ayer, 1940: 190–191). Harry reasoned inductively but he did not know that the video footage showed that the time spent was 5.06 minutes, providing a more 'formally demonstrable' premise than Harry's (Ayer, 1940: 191).

FORMS OF KNOWLEDGE

✓ Knowing that
✓ Explicit knowledge

THE ADULT'S ROLE

Harry's father captured a second perspective of Harry setting up the camcorder tripod; that video footage provided evidence may be regarded as more 'reliable' than Harry's report (Schechter, 2013: 229). Nevertheless, recalling this event for the researchers provided Harry with an opportunity to think logically by reasoning inductively (Ayer, 1940).

REFLECTION POINTS

Deductive reasoning has to be based on 'formally demonstrable' evidence, whereas inductive reasoning must only be based on premises based on 'our past experience' (Ayer, 1940: 190–191).

Think of examples when you have used deductive reasoning to make judgements in your work with young children.

Think of examples when you have used inductive reasoning to make judgements in your work with young children.

On reflection, what is your view of the strength of evidence and quality of logic for those judgements?

Reflect on your work with young children and think of examples when they have reasoned deductively and inductively. How did they use these different types of reasoning to find solutions?

Dispositions as a factor for young children finding solutions

When children were finding solutions in the YCAR project, they adopted dispositions. Sometimes children engaged with material contexts when finding solutions as part of the YCAR project. The categories *'Perseveres to resolve a problem'*, *'Motivated by finding a solution'* and *'Excited by finding solution'* were included in this factor.

(xviii) Perseveres to resolve problem

Epistemological Category:	Perseveres to resolve problem
Epistemological Factor:	**Dispositions**
Research Behaviour:	**FIND A SOLUTION**

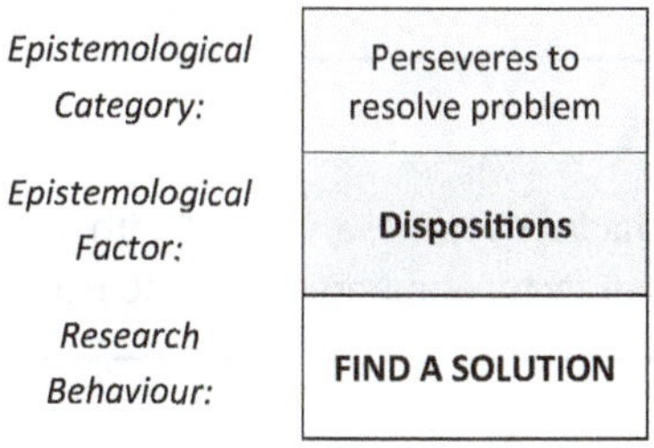

FIGURE 4.22 Building blocks – Perseveres to resolve problem

The YCAR project included several examples of children persevering to solve problems; these examples tended to present more readily in children's homes than in their settings. However, this example of Querida persevering took place in Cherry Setting.

Looking for shoes

One day in Cherry Setting home base, during free-flow play Querida (aged 4) was playing with her friend Siobhan (aged 5) in the igloo role play that had been set up by practitioners as part of a topic on *Hot and Cold*. The role play centred on a white tent and the teachers had asked children to remove their shoes when playing in there. The teacher played the tambourine which the children in the setting knew

to be a signal for tidying up ahead of lunchtime. Querida came out of the igloo and looked around her on the floor. She picked up some shoes and said: 'These aren't my shoes!' She put the shoes down and looked all around the igloo. She went into the igloo and came out. She moved away from the igloo and looked behind a nearby book box. She found her shoes, sat down and put them on.

Querida persevered to resolve the problem she set herself which was to put on her shoes. She completed the task (McClelland, Acock, Piccinin, Rhea and Stallings, 2013) which included problem-solving features: a goal (put on her shoes) obstacles (she could not find her shoes), strategies (she looked around the tent, in the tent then nearby the tent) and resources (the shoes) (DeLoache *et al.*, 1998).

FORMS OF KNOWLEDGE

✓ A posteriori reasoning
✓ Explicit knowledge

THE ADULT'S ROLE

The adult's rule that children should remove their shoes when playing in the igloo led to the problem that Querida encountered. The adults in the setting also set up the timetable – tidy up time and lunchtime – that led to the imperative that motivated Querida to want to find her shoes and put them on. No adult supported Querida to find or put on her shoes – she did this herself, and in doing so, persevered to find a solution to her problem.

REFLECTION POINTS

Reflect on examples of children you have worked with who have persevered to find solutions to problems. What factors supported them to persevere?

(xix) Motivated by finding solution

Epistemological Category:	Motivated by finding solution
Epistemological Factor:	**Dispositions**
Research Behaviour:	**FIND A SOLUTION**

FIGURE 4.23 Building blocks – Motivated by finding solution

Deci and Ryan (1987) suggest that when learners experience threats, deadlines, evaluation and surveillance, their intrinsic motivation for learning is diminished, whereas when learners are given choices and positive feedback their intrinsic motivation for learning increases. Most

young children in pre-school settings seem motivated to learn (Cordova and Lepper, 1996); in the literature motivation is linked to curiosity (Berlyne, 1954; Gammage, 1999; Chak, 2007). In the YCAR project, finding a solution sometimes motivated children to want to construct further knowledge.

Billy asks questions

During an interview at home, Billy's mother shared a discussion that she had had with Billy in Covent Garden on a family daytrip to London. Billy had asked her why one of the street entertainers had put out a hat. His mother had responded: 'They're collecting money for their performance'. Billy then asked another question: 'Is that all that they get to live on?'.

Dahlberg and Lenz Taguchi (1994: 2) suggest that knowledge is best constructed in a 'meeting place' in which the learner participates in the creation of their knowledge. In the discussion that Billy's mother reports, she and Billy are in such a space and Billy's questioning indicates his accumulating knowledge in a context of 'observation…curiosity…stimulation' and 'attachment' (Gammage, 1999: 107). Billy was intrinsically motivated to ask his first question; when his mother provided 'positive feedback' (Deci and Ryan, 1987: 1027), he was able to ask his second question because he was intrinsically motivated and involved in that context of 'reflexive "co-construction"' (Siraj-Blatchford, *et al.*, 2002: 10).

FORMS OF KNOWLEDGE

✓ Knowing that
✓ Explicit knowledge
✓ Mode 2 knowledge

THE ADULT'S ROLE

Billy's mother co-constructed a space with Billy in which Billy was able to participate in the creation of his own knowledge by questioning his mother. Her response to his first question gave him one solution and this motivated him to ask a second question.

REFLECTION POINTS

Reflect on your practice to identify occasions when your provision for young children has included choices and positive feedback that have motivated children to construct further knowledge.

(xx) Excited by finding solution

Epistemological Category:	Excited by finding solution
Epistemological Factor:	**Dispositions**
Research Behaviour:	**FIND A SOLUTION**

FIGURE 4.24 Building blocks – Excited by finding solution

The etymology of 'excite' derives from the Latin *'ex'* (out) and *'citare'* (to move) so *'ex citare'* means 'to set in motion'. Children's excitement is correlated with happiness (Tsai, Louie, Chen and Uchida, 2007). Nelson (2012) suggests that children may be excited by finding solutions to problems; sometimes this was the case for children in the YCAR project.

Annie's homework

One evening Annie (aged 7) was sitting at her kitchen table with a dictionary, turning its pages. She was part-way through a homework task which required her to find words beginning with each letter of the alphabet. Her mother was with her in the kitchen and this dyad followed:

Annie's mother: *'What [are] you looking for? A verb that begins with "I"?'*
Annie: *'Yes.'*
Annie's mother: *'Go on then ...how are you doing it?'*
Annie: *'An adjective'*
Annie's mother: *'Sweetheart – how are you doing it?'*
Annie: *'I'm going to start from the beginning. Oh, oh! I already found one!'*

This vignette exemplifies 'scholarisation' of English childhoods (Mayall, 2006); the expression that Annie brought to her statement – 'Oh – found one!' indicates her excitement at finding a solution in the context of her school work (Sherman and MacDonald, 2006; Nelson (2012).

FORMS OF KNOWLEDGE

✓ Knowing that
✓ Explicit knowledge
✓ Mode 1 knowledge

THE ADULT'S ROLE

Clore and Palmer (2009) note that cognitive tasks can be influenced by others' affective reactions because the latter communicate information about value. Here, Annie's mother seems to enable Annie to focus on her task by providing guided participation that is demanding yet emotionally warm (Rogoff, 1995).

REFLECTION POINTS

Can you recall times when children you have worked with have been excited by finding solutions?

What were the antecedents?
What happened next?
Did this help them to construct knowledge? How?

Conclusion

This fourth chapter in the book has defined what finding a solution may mean, particularly in the field of early childhood, and has briefly indicated prominent themes in the literature relating to young children finding solutions. It has also considered how young children engaged in finding solutions in the YCAR Project through 20 epistemological categories:

- Applying a rule to create a solution.
- Finds practical use for solution.
- Wants to preserve what s/he is doing.
- Able reader.
- Finds own solution.
- Creates a problem to solve.
- Devises practical method to create solution.
- Resolves another person's problem.
- Shares solution.
- Employs others to help with finding a solution.
- Theory of mind.
- Self-regulates.
- Focused on something of personal interest.
- Time and freedom to explore, investigate, experiment with something of personal interest.
- Exploring properties.
- Deductive reasoning.
- Inductive reasoning.
- Perseveres to resolve a problem.
- Motivated by finding a solution.
- Excited by finding a solution.

These epistemological categories acted as building blocks that enabled young children to construct knowledge by finding solutions during everyday activities at home and in their settings (Figure 4.1).

For each of the building blocks concerned with young children finding solutions, the chapter has indicated related forms of knowledge, has discussed ways that adults may influence children to construct knowledge through problem-solving, and has provided reflection points to help practitioners to consider ways they can apply the YCAR findings about young children's problem-solving to their own practice. A useful tool for practitioners and parents – *Observation notes for young children finding solutions* may be found in the appendices (see p. 153). Practitioners and parents can photocopy the tool and use it to record observations of their young children engaging in the 20 epistemological categories for young children's problem-solving: ways we can know that young children are constructing knowledge by finding solutions.

5

YOUNG CHILDREN CONCEPTUALISE

Children are often excluded from social participation because adults assume they are less capable than adults of conceptualisation so less equipped than adults to make rational decisions (Van Beers, Invernizzi and Milne, 2006). The YCAR project challenged that assumption by providing evidence that young children engage in 'a process of thinking about a problem situation through particular "concepts"' (Metcalfe, 2007: 149). This chapter is about the ways young children in the YCAR project engaged in conceptualisation. In Phase I, participating academy members identified conceptualisation as one of the four most important research behaviours.

This chapter has two sections. The first defines conceptualisation and briefly discusses some ways that extant literature suggests young children conceptualise. The second section is concerned with ways that young children in the YCAR project engaged in 24 epistemological categories that acted as provocations – or building blocks – that enabled them to conceptualise at home and in their settings. Each epistemological category was grouped into a germane overarching epistemological factor. Figure 5.1 displays the epistemological categories for children's conceptualisations, grouped according to their relevant epistemological factors. Relevant forms of knowledge indicated in other literature are connected to each example of young children conceptualising and the second section considers how the YCAR findings about young children's conceptualisation may support practitioners and other adults in their work with young children.

Concepts, conceptualising and early childhood

The etymology of 'concept' is derived from the Latin '*conceptus*', meaning something received or captured. Silverman defines 'concepts' as 'clearly specified ideas deriving from a particular *model*' (2006: 400), yet definitions of concepts have long been a focus for philosophical debate. Much of our current understanding about concepts has come from Enlightenment philosophers, particularly Kant.

Kant (1787) suggested that judgement must include mental activity to be robust and he proposed that we reason according to two types of concept: a priori concepts which emerge

						Making links – ANALOGY	
						Planning	
	Recalling instructions					Engaged in symbolic represent-tation	
EPISTEMOLOGICAL CATEGORIES	Linking prior knowledge to new application	Identifies anomaly				Language supports thinking	
	Synthesising concepts	Creating an imagined space or persona	Conceptualises after adult stops conceptualisation	Makes decision/s based on own criteria		Using imagination	
	Thinking tangentially	Developing own idea/s from external stimulus	Following adult's direction to conceptualise	Autonomously deciding what needs to be done and doing it		Involved in pursuing a train of thought	
	Thinking through a problem by applying concepts	Invents a process or method	Works with others to conceptualise	Creating a problem	Creates a new use for object/s	Predicts	Applies anthropo-morphism
EPISTEMOLOGICAL FACTORS	**Applications of prior experience**	**Innovation**	**Social domains**	**Autonomy**	**Material contexts**	**Cognitive domains**	**Outliers**
RESEARCH BEHAVIOUR	**CONCEPTUALISATION**						

FIGURE 5.1 Building blocks for conceptualisation

from purely mental activity senses or a posteriori concepts which combine sensory experience with mental activity. Bridges (2003) describes a priori concepts as 'philosophical' and a posteriori concepts as 'empirical/scientific' (p. 21), and he proposes that 'philosophising in educational research' includes both. In the YCAR project, more examples of a posteriori conceptualisations were identified in children's behaviours than a priori conceptualisations, probably because a posteriori conceptualisations tended to include actions, whereas a priori conceptualisations are, by their nature, concerned with internal mental activity. Scruton (2001) suggests a 'faculty of concepts' should be actively applied to establish judgements as 'truth' (p. 35). He contrasts this with a 'faculty of intuitions', favoured by empiricists, who regard information derived through the senses as the only verifiable source of knowledge (*i.a.* Hume, 1748). Kant (1787) saw concepts as active ways to think but regarded intuitions, mediated by our senses, as a more passive way of establishing knowledge (Mensch, 2011).

According to Scruton (2001), synthesis was an important consideration for (Kant, 1787): he regarded judgement as a synthesis of induction and concept and in contemporary research, Thomas (2007) sees 'theories' emerging in practical ways from 'experience and intuition'.

Some concepts are commonly seen in young children's daily activities. In the literature, conceptualisation is linked to **representation,** widely recognised as underpinning human knowledge (Bruner, 1966; Durkheim, 1915): Norris (2000) notes that Kant (1787) thought judgement derived from concepts affects **imagination**, 'the very condition of possibility for all knowledge and experience' (p. 384). From 12 months, young children may engage in pretend play (Leslie, 1987), supporting the development of conceptualisation in 'emotional, intellectual, creative and social areas' (Smilansky and Shefatya, 1990: 131). Schemas are an externalisation of internal conceptualisations (Athey, 2007) and while theory of mind (Meltzoff, 1995), cause and effect (Baillargeon, 2004) and deductive reasoning (Johnson-Laird and Byrne, 1991) have all been considered in the book in respect of other research behaviours in the YCAR project, they are also expressions of young children's conceptualisation, alongside the specific epistemological categories of conceptualisation considered in this chapter.

Summary

This section has defined conceptualisation and has discussed briefly some ways that children conceptualise. The second section of Chapter 5 is concerned with the ways that children conceptualised in the YCAR project and how these findings may support practitioners in their work with young children.

Young children conceptualising in the YCAR project

Each of the 24 epistemological categories – building blocks – that supported young children to conceptualise in the YCAR project is now discussed and exemplified. Each is discussed here with examples drawn from the YCAR study, linked to research and literature about knowledge and conceptualisation. Together with consideration of the adult's role (Murray, 2017) and reflection points, they form a framework that practitioners can use to identify ways the children they work with may construct knowledge by conceptualising in everyday activities in their settings and at home.

Applications of prior experience as a factor for young children conceptualising

In the YCAR project, children sometimes revealed that they conceptualised when they applied prior experiences to new situations. When they did so, their behaviours indicated that they were *'Thinking through problems by applying concepts'*, *'Thinking tangentially'*, *'Synthesising concepts'*, *'Linking their prior knowledge to new applications'* and *'Recalling instructions'*.

(i) Thinking through a problem by applying concepts

Epistemological Category:	Thinking through a problem by applying concepts
Epistemological Factor:	**Applications of prior experience**
Research Behaviour:	**CONCEPTUALISE**

FIGURE 5.2 Building blocks – Thinking through a problem by applying concepts

Leaning tower

During a free-flow play session in Cherry Setting, Oscar (aged 5) piled up large wooden blocks. He shouted: 'The leaning tower of tyres!', applying prior experience of 'The Leaning Tower of Pisa' to this new context:

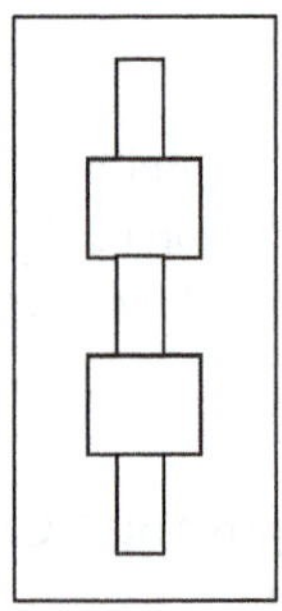

FIGURE 5.3 The leaning tower of tyres

Here, Oscar thought through what he wanted to build and what it was by developing and applying 'clearly specified ideas deriving from a particular *model*': Silverman's definition of concepts (2006: 400), Once built, Oscar gave meaning to his first construction: 'The leaning tower of tyres!', applying a prior experience of the leaning tower of Pisa to this new context. He may have been there or he may have learned of it from books or other media. Oscar used blocks to represent the tower; representation is strongly linked to conceptualisation and the construction of knowledge (Bruner, 1966; Durkheim, 1915). He applied a posteriori conceptualisation by combining past and present sensory experiences with mental activity (Kant, 1787; Bridges, 2003).

FORMS OF KNOWLEDGE

✓ Knowing that
✓ A posteriori reasoning
✓ Explicit knowledge

THE ADULT'S ROLE

The practitioner had afforded Oscar freedom to choose to build with the blocks and to choose what to build without limits. This enabled Oscar to engage in a posteriori conceptualisation: he used mental activity to link his past and present sensory experiences.

REFLECTION POINTS

Consider how children you have worked with have combined sensory experience with mental activity in block play, and by so doing have applied a posteriori conceptualisation.

(ii) Thinking tangentially

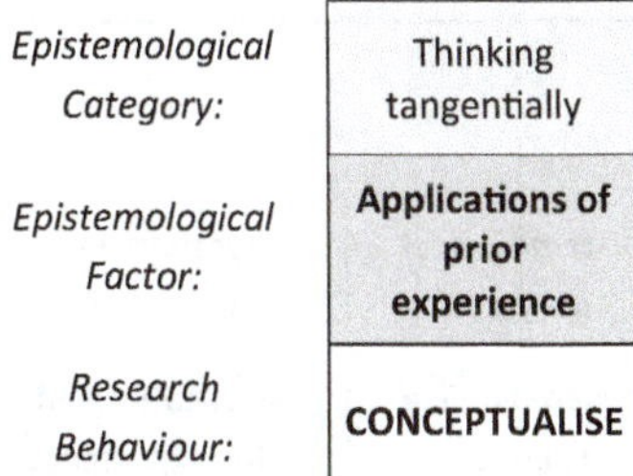

FIGURE 5.4 Building blocks – Thinking tangentially

Sometimes the YCAR children thought tangentially, and sometimes this included them linking imagination into their conceptualisations (Kant, 1787; Leslie, 1987; Smilansky and Shefatya, 1990).

Goat mask

Harry (aged 5) was playing with his brother in the sitting room at home in the early evening. He put on a goat mask and looked over at a blanket, announcing: 'I'm being a goat and I'm going to sleep with this blanket on'. He picked up the blanket, lay down and put it over himself.

Harry engaged in a posteriori conceptualisation to think tangentially: he conceived one 'clearly specified idea' by juxtaposing two disparate '*models*' (Silverman, 2006: 400). Harry considered his experiences of goats and his own bedtime and combined these separate premises through mental activity to elicit 'a goat going to sleep with a blanket on'. Although based partly on his experiences of goats and bedtime, Harry's new concept was imagined – 'the very condition of possibility for all knowledge and experience' (Kant, 1787; Norris, 2000: 384) – in the context of pretend play with his brother (Leslie, 1987; Smilansky and Shefatya, 1990).

FORMS OF KNOWLEDGE

✓ A posteriori reasoning

✓ Explicit knowledge

THE ADULT'S ROLE

Harry's mother filmed this vignette; she had created an environment, with simple resources, in which Harry and his brother engaged in free pretend play.

REFLECTION POINTS

Make a list of resources that might be useful for helping young children to think tangentially in free pretend play?

What are some of the characteristics of those resources?

(iii) Synthesising concepts

Epistemological Category:	Synthesising Concepts
Epistemological Factor:	**Applications of prior experience**
Research Behaviour:	**CONCEPTUALISE**

FIGURE 5.5 Building blocks – Synthesising concepts

Children in the YCAR project sometimes synthesised two or more concepts. Bloom (1956) regards synthesis as a higher order cognitive skill for constructing knowledge.

Annie reflects

During an interview for the YCAR project in Ash Setting, Annie (aged 7) analysed and interpreted her own actions in a literacy lesson that had been captured earlier on video. On the video, Annie frequently put up her hand to respond to her teacher's questions but other children, not Annie, were invited by the teacher to respond. I asked Annie how she felt about not being chosen and she answered: 'Well I feel I'm kind of happy because somebody else gets a chance but I'm a bit disappointed that I don't get a chance because I know it'.

Here, Annie engages in a priori conceptualisation – pure mental reasoning (Scruton, 2001; Bridges, 2003). Her response juxtaposed several concepts. Her comment 'somebody else gets a chance' indicates a *code of morality* (Kohlberg, 1984; Johansson, 2009), yet this is balanced with her *justification* that she should 'get a chance because I know it'. Annie acknowledged her own awareness of two emotional states: happiness and disappointment, while also articulating an ethical encounter: a 'conjuncture of the same and other' (Levinas, 1980: 80).

FORMS OF KNOWLEDGE

✓ Knowing that
✓ A priori knowledge
✓ Explicit knowledge

THE ADULT'S ROLE

With the consent of Annie's parents, the researcher provided an opportunity, context and a question which led to Annie articulating her a priori conceptualisation, so it became apparent.

REFLECTION POINTS

Have you used video footage with children to reveal their motivations, thoughts and ideas? What did you find out?

If you have not used video in this way, try it and consider what it tells you about young children's a priori and a posteriori conceptualisation.

(iv) Linking prior knowledge to new application

Epistemological Category:	Linking prior knowledge to new application
Epistemological Factor:	**Applications of prior experience**
Research Behaviour:	**CONCEPTUALISE**

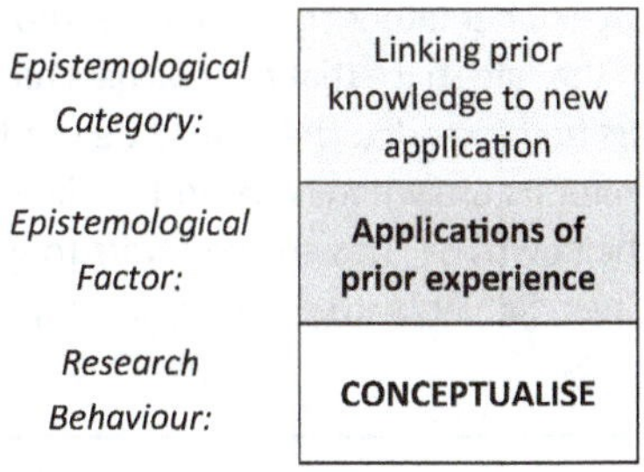

FIGURE 5.6 Building blocks – Linking prior knowledge to new application

Linking prior knowledge to a new application is an epistemological category that lies at the very heart of those grouped within the epistemological factor 'applications of prior experience'. As part of a topic on Hot and Cold, the Cherry Setting teachers had set up a white tent indoors and told the children it was an igloo. One day Nora (aged 5) and her friend Sadie (aged 5) chose to play in the tent where they developed a narrative within which Nora linked prior knowledge to a new application.

In the tent

Nora > Sadie: *'Shall we play Mum and Dad in our little flat and that's our flat?'* (pointing to the igloo)

Nora and Sadie went into the igloo.

Nora > Sadie: *'And we were scared of dogs weren't we?'*

Nora > Sadie: *'In real life my Dad actually cried. Pretend I was the mum and I was kissing him.'*

In socio-dramatic play young children often revisit and develop prior experiences to create and recreate their own meanings and discourses in new situations (Cobb-Moore, Danby and Farrell, 2010; Gussin Paley, 2004). Here, Nora linked prior knowledge of her family to a new application: her narrative. She synthesised her prior experiences of seeing and hearing her family with mental activity to develop a posteriori conceptualisation within socio-dramatic role play (Scruton, 2001; Smilansky and Shefatya, 1990). Interwoven in Nora's conceptualisation is theory of mind – 'the understanding of others'...beliefs, desires, emotions and intentions' (Meltzoff, 1995: 838) – *'in real life my Dad actually cried. Pretend I was the mum and I was kissing him'*.

FORMS OF KNOWLEDGE

✓ A posteriori reasoning
✓ Explicit knowledge

THE ADULT'S ROLE

Nora drew on her experience of her father crying and her mother's reaction to him. She revisited that experience in the safe space that her teachers had created by providing the tent. Although the teachers had intended the tent to be used in socio-dramatic play as an igloo, they did not monitor its use when Nora and Sadie were playing in it, affording them freedom to choose their own use. This enabled Nora to synthesise prior experiences of seeing and hearing her family with mental activity to develop a posteriori conceptualisation.

REFLECTION POINTS

Consider how children you have worked with have combined sensory experience with mental activity in socio-dramatic play, and by doing so have applied a posteriori conceptualisation.

(v) Recalling instructions

Epistemological Category:	Recalling instructions
Epistemological Factor:	**Applications of prior experience**
Research Behaviour:	CONCEPTUALISE

FIGURE 5.7 Building blocks – Recalling instructions

Children sometimes recalled instructions during the YCAR project, drawing on memory to support their conceptualisation.

Harry films

One day I visited Harry and his family at home and demonstrated how the camcorder worked so that they could capture data for the YCAR project at home. After I had left, Harry filmed alone, whispering: 'What next? Hmm – "Power".' He pressed the button and filmed.

Recall of instructions requires us to draw on memory, processed in different parts of the brain for different purposes (Ashcraft, 2006). Long-term memory is 'connected to existing knowledge' (Woolfolk and Perry, 2012: 46), short term memory relates to information in the long-term memory that is activated through cognitive processing (Cowan, 1988) and 'working memory' (Baddeley, 1992) is an executive function that facilitates recall and planning (Whitebread, 2012: 145). Prior to this event, Harry had been given a 'particular model' – strategies for reading – from which he derived his own 'clearly specified idea' (Silverman 2006: 400) during the event: reading the 'Power' sign on the camcorder. Harry used his working memory to store and manipulate information he had been given for operating the camcorder (Baddeley, 1992). He then recalled information about the camcorder's operation as well as how to read 'Power'. In this way, Harry used his memory to engage in 'a process of thinking about a problem situation through particular "concepts"' (Metcalfe, 2007: 149).

FORMS OF KNOWLEDGE

✓ A posteriori reasoning
✓ Explicit knowledge
✓ Mode 2 knowledge

THE ADULT'S ROLE

The adult had provided the explanation for operating the camera that Harry watched, listened to and stored in his memory. He later drew on this sensory memory and combined it with mental activity – a posteriori conceptualisation – to work out how to operate the camcorder himself.

REFLECTION POINTS

What is the most successful way you have found to help children to gain new skills?

- Listening to instructions?
- Watching a demonstration?
- Doing it for themselves?
- Other?

How does the way you have identified that children tend to learn new skills best align with the idea of a posteriori conceptualisation – the combination of sensory experience with mental activity?

Innovation as a factor for young children conceptualising

Examples of children conceptualising while engaging in innovative behaviour presented in the YCAR project when the children *'Invented processes or methods', 'Developed their own ideas from external stimuli', 'Created imagined spaces or personae'* and *'Identified anomalies'*.

(vi) Invents a process or method

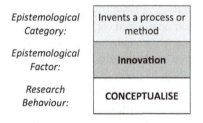

Epistemological Category:	Invents a process or method
Epistemological Factor:	**Innovation**
Research Behaviour:	**CONCEPTUALISE**

FIGURE 5.8 Building blocks – Invents a process or method

Johnny's watch

One day in Beech Setting, Johnny (5 years) invented a method to create a representation of a wristwatch. Johnny took some strips of paper, measured one strip around his wrist and cut a section off the end. He then scrunched another paper strip and stuck it on the first strip. He wrapped the strip around his arm, then unwrapped it, glued it, then readjusted it four times until he was happy that his creation resembled a wristwatch that fitted his wrist. He showed his wristwatch to a friend, saying: 'Look at this!'

Here, Johnny adopted a 'concept': a 'clearly specified idea deriving from a particular *model*' (Silverman, 2006: 400). His model was a watch he had seen previously and his idea was to make a watch. Johnny then engaged in 'a process of thinking about a problem situation through a particular "concept"' (Metcalfe, 2007: 149). His problem situation was how to make his own watch and he innovated to create his own version, developing his new ideas into something he valued (DBIS, 2011; 2012). By creating his watch then showing it to his friend, Johnny indicated that he valued it.

FORMS OF KNOWLEDGE

✓ Knowing that
✓ A posteriori reasoning
✓ Explicit knowledge

THE ADULT'S ROLE

Johnny's practitioners had provided materials from which he could choose freely to make what he wished. This enabled him to invent his own method for conceptualising a representation of a watch.

REFLECTION POINTS

Had Johnny's practitioner used his wristwatch as a basis for teaching him number recognition or telling the time, how might this have enhanced or detracted from his experience of inventing a method?

(vii) Developing own idea/s from external stimulus

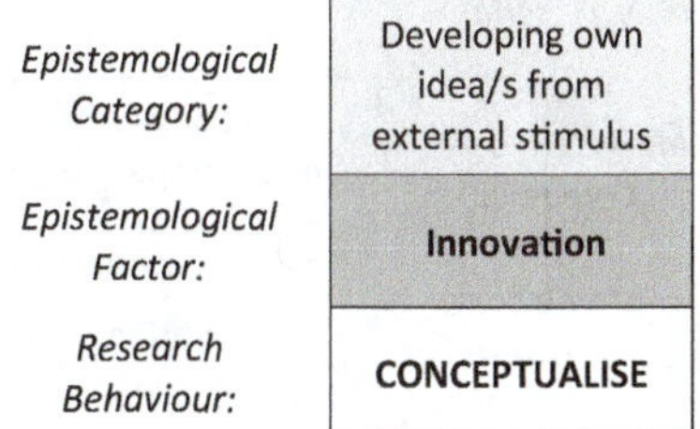

FIGURE 5.9 Building blocks – Developing own idea/s from external stimulus

Children in the YCAR project sometimes conceptualised when developing their own ideas from external stimuli (Scruton, 2001).

Dog

One day in an art lesson in Ash Setting, the teacher's objective was 'To be able to understand features of African designs'. At the start of the lesson the teacher modelled African designs for the class. Edward (aged 8) and his class were then tasked with making African designs on paper. Edward began his task but after a few minutes, moved 'off task': he mimed being a dog, including scratching.

Here, Edward sidelined the task he had been set by his teacher and invented a new task that engaged him. In doing so, he used a posteriori conceptualisation (Kant, 1787; Bridges, 2003):

he drew on his prior sensory experience of seeing and hearing a dog and thought about how to translate this into a dog mime in class. Edward's behaviour was innovative: miming a dog was a new idea in the art class and his decision to do this instead of focusing on the teacher's task indicated that he valued his mime more than his set task (DBIS, 2011; 2012).

FORMS OF KNOWLEDGE

✓ A posteriori reasoning

✓ Explicit knowledge

THE ADULT'S ROLE

Despite giving Edward and his peers a narrowly defined objective, the teacher did not intervene when Edward moved off task. This enabled him to pursue his own agenda and by doing so develop a posteriori conceptualisation (Kant, 1787; Bridges, 2003).

REFLECTION POINTS

What would Edward have learned had he pursued only the teacher's set task? In what ways was the quality of his learning different because he pursued his own agenda in this context?

(viii) Creating an imagined space or persona

Epistemological Category:	Creating an imagined space or persona
Epistemological Factor:	**Innovation**
Research Behaviour:	**CONCEPTUALISE**

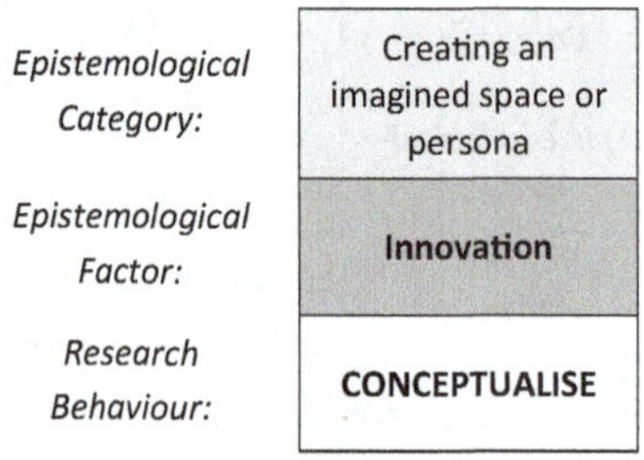

FIGURE 5.10 Building blocks – Creating an imagined space or persona

Sometimes in the YCAR study, children innovated by conceptualising imagined spaces and people (DBIS, 2011; 2012; Scruton, 2001; Silverman, 2006).

Secret spies

One day at home, Gemma (aged 5) told me about a game of 'Secret Spies' she said she had played with her friend in a stately home they visited with their parents. 'We had to have nobody seeing us and we made a little den....When we had to go home that's when we had a game of spies and we came upstairs and... it was like a...bit where you could go through – the secret door'.

Gemma and her friend developed a 'clearly specified idea deriving from a particular model' (Silverman, 2006: 400): a little den for spies accessed through a secret door. This idea was the interplay of their conceptualisation with their imagination: 'the very condition of possibility for all knowledge and experience' (Norris, 2000: 384). Children's 'secret spaces' feature in the literature (*i.a.* Clark, 2010; Kyrönlampi-Kylmänen and Määttä, 2011): they are often places where young children create and recreate their own meanings and discourses in socio-dramatic play (*i.a.* Cobb-Moore *et al.*, 2010; Gussin Paley, 2004).

FORMS OF KNOWLEDGE

✓ A posteriori reasoning

✓ Explicit knowledge

THE ADULT'S ROLE

Gemma's parents took her to the stately home, arranged a peer for her to play with and gave them freedom to play without adults. This enabled them to use available resources to develop an imaginative game together that drew on their past experiences.

REFLECTION POINTS

How might the 'clearly specified idea deriving from a particular model' (Silverman, 2006: 400), have been different if Gemma's friend had not been with her?

How might it have been different had their parents played as well?

(ix) Identifies anomaly

Epistemological Category:	Identifies anomaly
Epistemological Factor:	**Innovation**
Research Behaviour:	**CONCEPTUALISE**

FIGURE 5.11 Building blocks – Identifies anomaly

Kuhn (1970) suggests that 'discovery commences with the awareness of anomaly' (p. 52). In the YCAR study, children sometimes identified anomalies in their everyday activities.

Cogs and gears

One day in their sitting room, Martin and his sister were playing with a construction game – 'Cogs and Gears' – as Martin's mother filmed them. As he was constructing, Martin repeatedly referred to the picture on the 'Cogs and Gears' box. He pointed

to a component in the picture on the box and noted: 'There's none of these'. Next, Martin picked up a piece that was not pictured on the box and he continued making his model with other pieces that were different from the image on the box.

Martin identified a 'particular *model*' – the picture on the box – and from this he derived a 'clearly specified idea' (Silverman, 2006: 400): to build an exact facsimile of that image. However, he observed an anomaly which led him to adapting his original 'clearly specified idea' (Silverman, 2006: 400), to discover a different construction that did not require the missing piece (Kuhn, 1970). Martin's action was innovative: he developed a new idea by engaging in 'a process of thinking about a problem situation through particular "concepts"' (Metcalfe, 2007: 149) and his persistence indicated that he valued what he was doing (DBIS, 2011; 2012).

FORMS OF KNOWLEDGE

✓ Knowing that
✓ A posteriori reasoning

THE ADULT'S ROLE

Had Martin's mother supplied all the components that were in the image on the box, Martin would not have been able to identify an anomaly or conceptualise his own new design.

REFLECTION POINTS

Martin might have become frustrated by the lack of components, causing him to leave his construction but instead he persisted, and conceived a new idea. What factors might have helped him to do this?

Social domains as a factor for young children conceptualising

Young children conceptualised in social contexts in the YCAR project when they *'Worked with others to develop conceptualisation'*, *'Followed adults' direction'* and when they *'Conceptualised after adults stopped their conceptualisation'*.

(x) Works with others to conceptualise

Epistemological Category:	Works with others to conceptualise
Epistemological Factor:	**Social domains**
Research Behaviour:	**CONCEPTUALISE**

FIGURE 5.12 Building blocks – Works with others to conceptualise

Space rocket

In Beech Setting during free-flow play Laura had chosen to go into the 'space rocket' role play area with a friend. Inside, she held up a silver rectangle (1m. × 0.5m) and said to her friend: 'Pretend this was our door...pretend we are taking off'. Laura and her friend got under the table in the 'space rocket' and pretended to take off.

Laura imagined a 'particular model' (Silverman, 2006: 400) – that the old cardboard box covered in aluminium foil was a space rocket and that she and her friend were astronauts. She then developed a 'clearly specified idea' from this (Silverman, 2006: 400): that she and her friend were 'taking off'. By using the phrase 'taking off', Laura indicates she has had some experience of rockets, probably on film or in books, which she synthesised through mental activity with the resources in the role play area; in this way, she demonstrates a posteriori conceptualisation (Kant, 1787; Scruton, 2001). To support her conceptualisation, Laura engaged with her friend in socio-dramatic thematic-fantasy play and symbolic representation through which they created and recreated their own meanings and discourses (Cobb-Moore *et al.*, 2010; Gussin Paley, 2004; Smilansky and Sheftaya, 1990).

FORMS OF KNOWLEDGE

✓ A posteriori reasoning
✓ Explicit knowledge

THE ADULT'S ROLE

Leading play in this social context gave Laura 'agency' (Edmiston, 2008; James and James, 2008: 9), which enabled her to develop a posteriori conceptualisation (Kant, 1787; Scruton, 2001).

REFLECTION POINTS

What topics and resources for socio-dramatic thematic fantasy play might encourage young children to engage in a posteriori conceptualisation by helping them to combine sensory experience with mental activity?

(xi) Following adult's direction to conceptualise

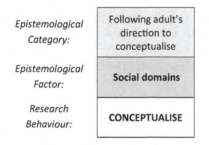

Epistemological Category:	Following adult's direction to conceptualise
Epistemological Factor:	**Social domains**
Research Behaviour:	**CONCEPTUALISE**

FIGURE 5.13 Building blocks – Following adult's direction to conceptualise

It is noteworthy that children in the YCAR project only followed adults' directions to conceptualise in their settings (n=10), not at home.

Mathematics lesson

One day, during a whole class mathematics lesson in Ash Setting, the teacher Mrs Adjoki had provided an exposition, then asked the children to work through some mathematical problems she had written on the board. All the children were sitting on chairs or the carpet facing the board and each had a whiteboard and pen. Mrs Adjoki asked Florence (aged 8) and Jolyon (aged 7) to sit together at a table; they did so. Florence copied the teacher's writing from the board onto her own small whiteboard and mouthed the numbers as she did so. She then spoke to Jolyon, saying '10': the answer.

Here, the teacher directed Florence and her peers, by organising and 'scaffolding' their development of an aspect of mathematical conceptualisation (Wood, Bruner and Ross, 1976). Florence followed 'a process of thinking about a problem situation through particular "concepts"' (Metcalfe, 2007: 149), pursuing 'clearly specified ideas deriving from (the teacher's) particular *model*' (Silverman, 2006: 400), leading her to make a posteriori proposition through experience combined with mental activity (Kant, 1787; Scruton, 2001).

FORMS OF KNOWLEDGE

✓ A posteriori reasoning
✓ Explicit knowledge
✓ Mode 1 knowledge

THE ADULT'S ROLE

The teacher adopted a knowledge transmission model followed by a session in which children trialled the method they had been taught, which would give the teacher the opportunity to assess their understanding. Under the teacher's guidance, Florence engaged in a posteriori conceptualisation: she combined sensory experience with mental activity. She watched and listened to the teacher's exposition then recalled it while using mental activity to answer the set problem.

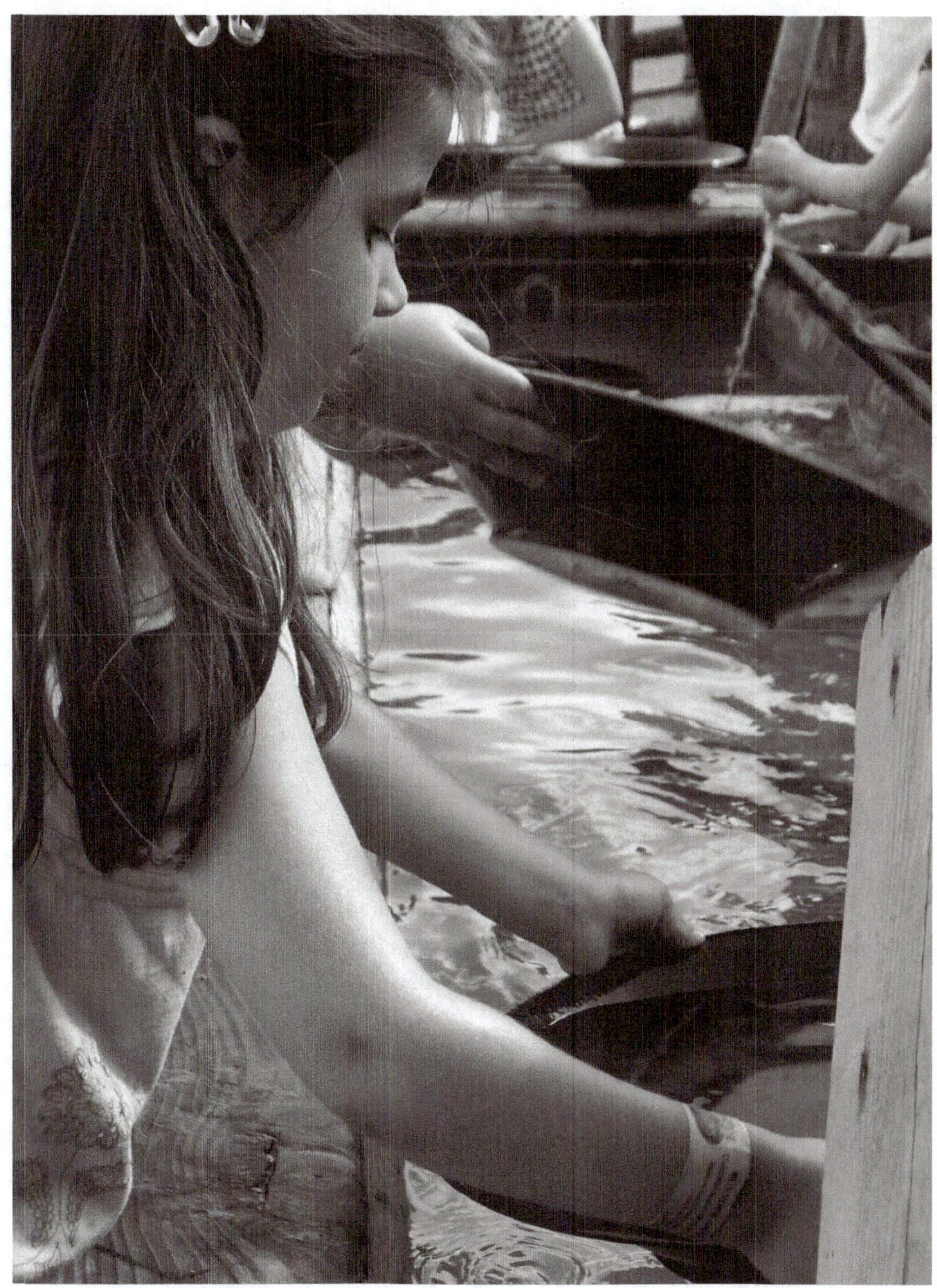

FIGURE 5.21 Gemma at the open farm

THE ADULT'S ROLE

Gemma's parents provided her with the stimulus of the experience of visiting the open farm which resulted in her having the fool's gold. Her mother encouraged her to conceptualise how she would use the fool's gold by providing it during the discussion so that she could revisit its properties through her senses.

REFLECTION POINTS

What are some of the most successful ways that you have used objects as stimuli to support young children to construct knowledge

What made them successful?

(xviii) Involved in pursuing a train of thought

Epistemological Category:	Involved in pursuing a train of thought
Epistemological Factor:	**Cognitive domains**
Research Behaviour:	**CONCEPTUALISE**

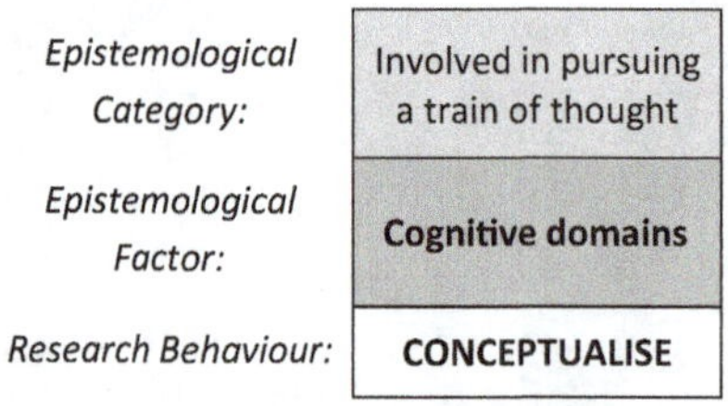

FIGURE 5.22 Building blocks – Involved in pursuing a train of thought

Sometimes, as part of the process of conceptualising, children in the YCAR project became involved in pursuing a train of thought, resonating with literature addressing 'flow' and 'involvement' (Csíkszentmihályi, 1990; Laevers, 2000; Pascal *et al.*, 1996).

Saving the polar bear

During a free-flow play session in Cherry Setting, for nine minutes, Martin (aged 5) played in the *Chilly Polar Regions Small World Play* area which featured a table top covered with white and blue fabric to represent snow and water, small world play polar animals, a helicopter, a ship, and small world play people. Martin picked up a polar bear and put it in the boat then on the helicopter. Martin walked the polar bear along the table top with his hand, put the polar bear in the boat hull and put the lid on. He put the polar bear down on the boat with a lifebelt around it. In role as the polar bear, Martin said in a squeaky voice: 'I'm in a boat. Eh, eh, eh'. He put the polar bear against the steering wheel and said: 'I never sit him on a seat…the boat is sinking!' Then he said to the polar bear: 'There you are – get in the helicopter'.

In his narrative, Martin developed a series of 'clearly specified ideas deriving from a particular *model*' (Silverman, 2006: 400): concepts. His models were his own prior experiences – real, or media representations – of a boat and a helicopter, which he applied to his small world play. His focused attention on the small world play over time exemplified 'flow' (Csíkszentmihályi, 1990) – 'concentration…attention to one limited circle…strong motivation (and) fascination' (Laevers, 2000: 24) – a condition correlated with cognitive mastery (Laevers, 2000; Pascal, Bertram, Ramsden, Georgeson, Saunders and Mould, 1996).

FORMS OF KNOWLEDGE

✓ Knowing that
✓ A posteriori reasoning
✓ Explicit knowledge

THE ADULT'S ROLE

The small world play resources set out by the practitioners engaged Martin's interest and encouraged him to become involved in developing a narrative and maintain it for nine minutes.

REFLECTION POINTS

Laevers (2000) identifies that high levels of involvement and well-being are indications of 'deep-level learning'. He characterises optimal involvement in young children as 'total concentration and absolute implication. Any disturbance or interruption would be experienced as a frustrating rupture of a smoothly running activity' (p. 25).

Identify some innovative ways that practitioners could help young children to increase their involvement in activities.

(xix) Using imagination

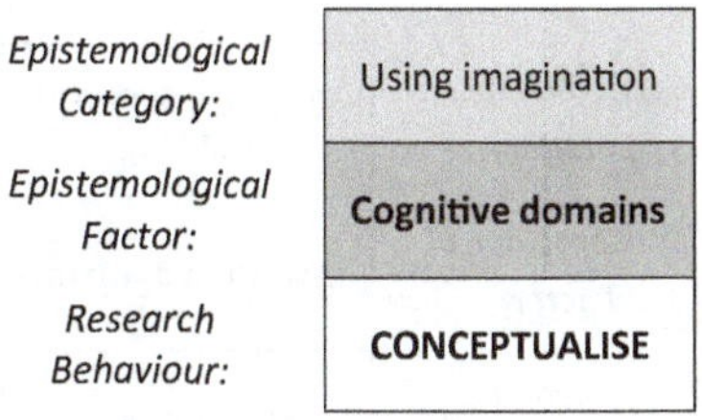

Epistemological Category:	Using imagination
Epistemological Factor:	**Cognitive domains**
Research Behaviour:	**CONCEPTUALISE**

FIGURE 5.23 Building blocks – Using imagination

While children's imagination emerged as a subsidiary behaviour within other epistemological categories, 'using imagination' was identified as a distinct epistemological category.

The train

During an interview at home, Billy (aged 8) recounted: 'we had crafting and I made a train bank…it's like you make a train, you put a little thing there and…

you have to pull it a little bit like the bit like that and then you pull the thing like that and then it opens'.

Billy used his experiences of real trains and representations of trains as a 'particular model' on which to base his 'clearly specified idea' – the model train that he conceptualised (Silverman, 2006: 400). The moving elements Billy had added suggest he used his imagination as part of his conceptualisation. As indicated, Norris (2000) suggested that Kant saw imagination as 'the very condition of possibility for all knowledge and experience' (p. 384); it is also described as 'extensive and complex' (Newson and Newson, 1979: 12), and the 'fruit of the harmony of ideas' (Malaguzzi, cited in Kaufman, 1998: 288).

FORMS OF KNOWLEDGE

✓ A posteriori reasoning
✓ Explicit knowledge

THE ADULT'S ROLE

Billy's parents had provided him with experiences of trains, physical resources for him to make his train, as well as time, freedom and opportunity to do so.

REFLECTION POINTS

Consider some practical ways that practitioners might support parents to help young children to develop and use their imagination in ways that engage them in higher order thinking: critical thinking, problem solving and the application of knowledge (Brookhart, 2010).

(xx) Language supports thinking

Epistemological Category:	Language supports thinking
Epistemological Factor:	**Cognitive domains**
Research Behaviour:	**CONCEPTUALISE**

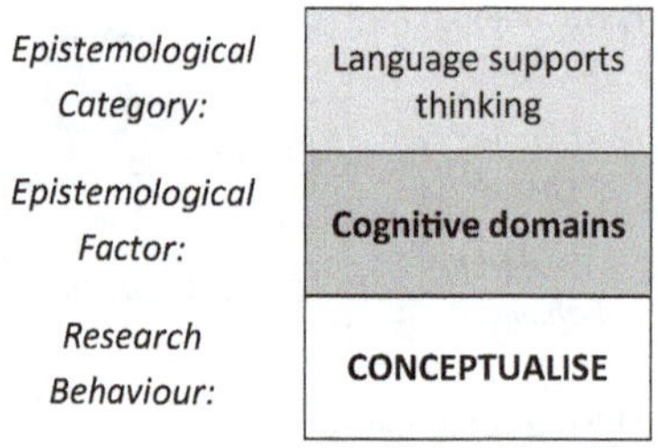

FIGURE 5.24 Building blocks – Language supports thinking

Children often used language to support their thinking processes in the YCAR project (Vygotsky, 1962).

Spelling 'bath'

In Beech Setting one day during a free-flow play session, Harry (aged 5) and his friend Sam (aged 5) had chosen to do a writing activity on the computer. Harry had called over his teacher Mrs Evans and had showed her his work so far. Mrs Evans said: '"Bath" – you did "bath"'. Harry responded: 'I want "Barf"...I want "barf"'. Harry had spelt 'b-a-r-f' on the computer.

Harry used oral language to express his thinking (Vygotsky, 1962); he engaged in discourse with his teacher; Habermas (1984) defines discourse as dialogue combined with rational thinking. Harry articulated the phonemes in 'bath' as he had heard them, but this did not translate to accurate spelling; the lack of phonic regularity in English is an issue for young children who are learning to be literate in English (Suggate, 2011). Nevertheless, Harry's use of language supported and demonstrated his understanding of a number of reading strategies: complex decoding skills phonological knowledge and grapho-phonic cues (Goouch and Lambirth, 2011). Harry linked the reading strategies he had learned in previous experiences with mental activity in this context, and by doing so, engaged in the process of a posteriori conceptualisation (Kant, 1787; Scruton, 2001).

FORMS OF KNOWLEDGE

✓ Knowing that
✓ A posteriori reasoning
✓ Explicit knowledge
✓ Mode 1 knowledge

THE ADULT'S ROLE

Prior to this vignette, adults had helped Harry learn a range of reading strategies which he attempted to use for spelling in this context. Harry's teacher supported his attempts by helping him to segment to spell and by articulating orally the word 'bath' with a short vowel.

REFLECTION POINTS

Is there a 'best way' for all children to learn to read? Why?
Is there a 'best age' for all children to learn to read? Why?
Who should decide? Why?

(xxi) Engaged in symbolic representation

Epistemological Category:	Engaged in symbolic representation
Epistemological Factor:	**Cognitive domains**
Research Behaviour:	**CONCEPTUALISE**

FIGURE 5.25 Building blocks – Engaged in symbolic representation

As indicated earlier in the book, children in the YCAR project often used representation, regarded as important for human cognition (Bruner, 1966; Vygotsky, 1976). Symbolic representation, 'a symbolic system…governed by rules or laws forming and transforming propositions' (Bruner, 1966: 45) may occur when children 'separate the meaning of an object from the object itself and to give identities to objects other than their actual ones (Boyzatis and Watson, 1993: 729).

Bears

In her bedroom at home one day, Annie (aged 7) fiddled with some small pottery bear ornaments on the windowsill and said to her mother: 'They're usually in twos'. Annie's mother asked: 'Why do they need to be in twos?' Annie said: 'I was – it's just I saw them and thought – ohh…' and her mother said: 'Mmm? Pardon?' and Annie responded: 'I just saw them and thought – ohh…'. Later, during her family focus group at home, Annie watched the video footage of this vignette with her mother and father and Annie explained the reason why 'They're usually in twos'; she said 'Because they're dance partners.'

Annie was able 'to separate the meaning of an object from the object itself' (Boyzatis and Watson, 1993: 729): she created her own meaning for her pottery ornaments as 'dance partners' (Bruner, 1966). Annie ruled that her bear ornaments had to be in pairs, symbolising a desire for order and her understanding of a mathematical concept as well as a social convention. In this activity, Annie created a concept – a 'clearly specified idea' that her bears had to be 'in twos', 'deriving from a particular model': that they were 'dance partners' (Silverman, 2006: 400).

FORMS OF KNOWLEDGE

✓ Knowing that
✓ A posteriori reasoning
✓ Explicit knowledge
✓ Mode 1 knowledge

THE ADULT'S ROLE

Annie's mother's question 'Why do they need to be in twos?' followed by 'Mmm? Pardon?' indicated irritation. Annie's reticence to answer her mother indicated she realised that her mother did not share her own understanding regarding the bear ornaments. Later discussion around the video gave Annie an opportunity to explain her actions and intentions to her mother and father.

REFLECTION POINTS

What examples have you seen of young children separating 'the meaning of an object from the object itself and (giving) identities to objects other than their actual ones' (Boyzatis and Watson, 1993: 729).

For some of those examples, suggest how the children conceptualised: what were their 'clearly specified ideas' and the 'particular models' from which their ideas were derived (Silverman, 2006: 400)?

(xxii) Planning

Epistemological Category:	Planning
Epistemological Factor:	**Cognitive domains**
Research Behaviour:	**CONCEPTUALISE**

FIGURE 5.26 Building blocks – Planning

Children's planning was sometimes evident in the YCAR project.

Waiting to be elephants

One day during free-flow play in Cherry Setting, Pedro (aged 5) chose to go outside. The children in the setting had limited access to the field, controlled by the use of eight coloured bands. The field was set up as a safari park following a setting visit the previous week to a safari park. Pedro approached one of his peers, then another, and said: 'Come and play'. He put on an elephant mask and his two friends did the same. Pedro got a chair and moved it to other chairs in a row. He said to his friends: 'I'm going to wait'. He sat down on a chair facing the field where other children were playing and his two friends joined him. Pedro sat with his elephant mask on, watching children playing in the field and waiting his turn to play in the 'safari park'. After several minutes, children moved from the field and Pedro and his friends went onto the field.

Pedro developed a concept: a 'clearly specified idea' that he wanted to play elephants outside with his friends, 'deriving from a particular model' that was the visit the week before to the safari park (Silverman, 2006: 400). Because of the rule in the setting that no more than eight children could play on the grass, he had to wait until other children had finished their game there. While he waited, Pedro prepared for his game by gathering friends, securing an elephant mask and ensuring he was in a prime position to see when his opportunity to play on the field arose. Pedro's plan involved him identifying a goal and a strategy for pursuing and realising it and he valued the idea of playing elephants with his friends on the field so much that he was prepared to wait. Pedro's planning indicated his agency (Alkire and Deneulin, 2009).

FORMS OF KNOWLEDGE

✓ A posteriori reasoning

THE ADULT'S ROLE

The system that adults had set up to control numbers of children going onto the field may have been a catalyst for some of Pedro's planning. He used the waiting time to gather his friends, organise a waiting place and secure his elephant mask.

REFLECTION POINTS

The High/Scope pedagogic model includes children's planning as a key feature of its methodology in which young children plan, do and review their own daily activities (Schweinhart, Barnes and Weikart, 1993). In what ways might young children's constructions of knowledge be supported when they plan their own activities? Do you have some examples from your own practice?

(xxiii) Making links – analogy

Epistemological Category:	Making links – analogy
Epistemological Factor:	**Cognitive domains**
Research Behaviour:	**CONCEPTUALISE**

FIGURE 5.27 Building blocks – Making links – analogy

Children often made links in their activities in the YCAR project, providing numerous examples of analogy. Reasoning by analogy is regarded as a 'core component of human cognition…important for learning and classification, and for thought and explanation' (Goswami, 2007: 55); Goswami (2007) highlights Holyoak and Thagard's (1995) definition of analogy as 'mental leaps'.

The academy members who participated in the YCAR project – termed PEYERs (Professional Early Years and Educational Researchers) – contributed to analysis and interpretation of data, providing 'guiding ideals' (Blumer, 1969: 2) and verification. Following their video observation of Annie reading a recipe and cooking an omelette at home, PEYERs Robert, Diane and Enid reflected that Annie made links between these different activities; in other words, Annie used analogy.

The recipe

Robert: ***'She's using text for information, she was asking questions, she was observing what was happening and making observations on that – like – "Should this white bit of shell be in here?"'***

Diane: ***'Kind of applying theory to practice.'***

Enid: ***'And she was able to read at the same time as watching (the omelette cooking).'***

The PEYERs' remarks indicate they recognised that Annie made 'mental leaps' between reading the recipe and cooking the omelette (Holyoak and Thagard, 1995). In doing so, Annie synthesised the recipe with the information her senses gave her in a process of mental activity as she cooked the omelette; by doing so, she engaged in a posteriori conceptualisation (Kant, 1787; Scruton, 2001).

FORMS OF KNOWLEDGE

✓ Knowing that
✓ A posteriori reasoning
✓ Mode 2 knowledge

THE ADULT'S ROLE

Here, the adults interpreted Annie's actions. Annie also had opportunities to interpret her video footage of this vignette actions and, similarly to the adults, she highlighted that she was reading the recipe and cooking at the same time:

'I'm just reading it [the recipe]...It just says "season with salt and freshly milled black pepper"...Now I'd like to add a tiny bit of pepper – yes – OK'.

REFLECTION POINTS

What are the challenges for parents and practitioners in identifying the 'mental leaps' young children make between different activities (Holyoak and Thagard, 1995)?

Outliers as a factor for young children conceptualising

There was one outlier that linked to young children's conceptualisations in the YCAR project: *'Applying anthropomorphism'*.

(xxiv) Applies anthropomorphism

Epistemological Category:	Applies anthropomorphism
Epistemological Factor:	**Outliers**
Research Behaviour:	**CONCEPTUALISE**

FIGURE 5.28 Building blocks – Making links – Applies anthropomorphism

Anthropomorphism is linked with analogy in the literature, though there is acknowledgement that it is not the same (Melion, Rothstein and Weemans, 2014). Anthropomorphism is the attribution of human traits to non-human objects or animals and seems to present commonly in various cultures across the human life course (Epley, Waytz, Akalis and Cacioppo, 2008; Melion, Rothstein and Weemans, 2014), though it has been recognised that it presents particularly among children aged 2–7 years (Lane, Wellman and Evans, 2010; Piaget, 1929). Reasons that are proposed for anthropomorphism include loneliness and desire for control (Epley, *et al.*, 2008).

Thirsty camcorder

One day in Ash Setting, Billy commented on video footage of everyday activities as part of the YCAR analysis. In the footage, a water bottle appeared in the bottom of the camcorder shot: one of Billy's classmates had reached for it from behind the camcorder to take a drink, but only the bottle, not the classmate, was visible. Billy observed: 'The camera is drinking!'

Billy attributed human behaviour – drinking – to the camcorder (Epley, *et al.*, 2008). His comment exemplified anthropomorphism and to make it he adopted a posteriori conceptualisation (Kant, 1787; Scruton, 2001): he used mental activity to synthesise his own sensory experience of himself and others drinking with what he saw on the video.

FORMS OF KNOWLEDGE

✓ A posteriori reasoning
✓ Explicit knowledge

THE ADULT'S ROLE

The role of the adult in this vignette was to film in Ash Setting, then to replay the video so that Billy could analyse his behaviour, affording him possibilities of metacognition and agency. Billy assumed agency by focusing attention on his own agenda: anthropomorphism

REFLECTION POINTS

Consider examples of anthropomorphism that you have seen young children present. How did it present?

Reasons that are proposed for anthropomorphism include loneliness and desire for control (Epley, *et al.*, 2008). What were the reasons for the example of anthropomorphism that you have seen in young children?

Conclusion

This chapter has defined and addressed concepts and conceptualisation and it has considered how the YCAR project revealed 24 epistemological categories that acted as building blocks to enable young children to construct knowledge by conceptualising during everyday activities at home and in their settings. These included:

- Thinking through a problem by applying concepts.
- Thinking tangentially.
- Synthesising concepts.
- Linking prior knowledge to new application.
- Recalling instructions.
- Invents a process or method.
- Developing own idea/s from external stimulus.
- Creating an imagined space or persona.
- Identifies anomaly.
- Works with others to conceptualise.
- Following adult's direction to conceptualise.
- Conceptualises after adult stops conceptualisation.
- Creating a problem.
- Autonomously deciding what needs to be done and doing it.
- Makes decisions based on own criteria.
- Creates a new use for object/s.
- Predicts.
- Involved in pursuing a train of thought.
- Using imagination.
- Language supports thinking.
- Engaged in symbolic representation.
- Planning.
- Making links – analogy.
- Applies anthropomorphism.

These epistemological categories acted as building blocks that supported young children to construct knowledge by conceptualising during everyday activities at home and in their settings (Figure 5.1).

Each of the building blocks concerned with young children conceptualising has been linked to related forms of knowledge, and the chapter has discussed ways that adults in the YCAR project supported children to construct knowledge through conceptualisation. Reflection points have been provided to help practitioners to consider ways they can apply the YCAR findings about young children's conceptualisation to their own practice. A useful tool for practitioners and parents – *Observation notes for young children's conceptualisations* may be found in the appendices (see p. 157). Practitioners and parents can photocopy the tool and use it to record observations of young children engaging in the 24 epistemological categories for young children's conceptualising: ways we can know that young children conceptualise to construct knowledge.

6

YOUNG CHILDREN BASE DECISIONS ON EVIDENCE

This chapter is about the ways young children in the YCAR project based decisions on evidence during their everyday activities at home and in their early childhood settings and by doing so, engaged in research behaviour identified as important by academics. Some of the content of this chapter also appears in Murray (2016).

There are two sections in this chapter. The first defines what basing decisions on evidence means, and how this relates to children. The second section focuses on ways young children in the YCAR project engaged in 14 epistemological categories that acted as provocations – or building blocks – to enable them to base decisions on evidence at home and in their settings. Each epistemological category was grouped into one of the nine epistemological factors. Figure 6.1 displays the epistemological categories for children basing decisions on evidence, grouped according to its related epistemological factor. Links are made between examples of young children basing decisions on evidence and relevant forms of knowledge identified in other literature. The second section also considers how the YCAR findings about young children basing decisions on evidence may help practitioners and other adults in their work with young children.

What does it mean to base decisions on evidence?

This first section of Chapter 6 considers other literature concerned with decisions, evidence and 'basing decisions on evidence' as well as discussing children as decision-makers.

Defining decision-making

The etymology for the word 'decision' is in the Latin verb '*decidere*', from '*caedere*' meaning 'to cut' and 'de-', meaning 'off', so that its literal meaning is 'to cut off'. This may be implied to refer to debate. Lehmann (1950; 1957) first identified 'decision theory', the interdisciplinary study of how decisions are made: 'goal-directed behaviour in the presence of options' (Anand, 1993; Kahneman and Tversky, 1979; Kahneman, Slovic and Tversky, 1982; Hansson, 1994: 6).

EPISTEMOLOGICAL CATEGORIES					Metacognition	
	Applies prior experience				Trial and error	Methodological issue
	Applies mental model	Values peer perspectives			Thinks strategically	Sampling issue
	Extrapolates	Acts on adult opinion	Enacts personal preference	Senses provide evidence for action	Applies 'Humean' reason	BDoE is research
EPISTEMOLOGICAL FACTORS	**Applications of prior experience**	**Social domains**	**Autonomy**	**Material contexts**	**Cognitive domains**	**Methodological issues**
RESEARCH BEHAVIOUR	**BASE DECISIONS ON EVIDENCE**					

FIGURE 6.1 Building blocks for basing decisions on evidence

Decision-making and reasoning are correlated mental processes and decisions are made through a combination of 'complex and unobservable mental processes' (Johnson-Laird and Shafir, 1993: 1). Damasio (2006) proposes that humans make many decisions with no 'conscious knowledge nor a conscious reasoning strategy' (p. 167) and he hypothesises that decisions are made by body and mind working in symbiosis. While the brain may consciously reason to make decisions in new situations, this process leaves a 'somatic marker' that makes decision-making more automatic in subsequent similar situations (p. 173). This view may be particularly relevant to young children who tend to express their preferences using many different modalities (Norwegian Ministry of Education and Research, 2006; Bae, 2009).

Defining evidence

The word 'evidence' derives from the Latin '*evidens*', a conflation of 'ex-' ('out of') and '*videre*' ('to see'), meaning 'apparent'. Defining evidence seems fraught with difficulty. Oancea and Pring (2008) suggest it has various meanings, dependent on 'the nature of the question' and 'given situations' and they provide a helpful typology of 'what counts as evidence': 'observable data …previous judgements…documents…arguments that have survived critical scrutiny…personal accounts…identification of implicit social rules and norms…and expert judgements' (p. 20).

Evidence is interwoven with knowledge when it is used as a warrant to justify what constitutes knowledge (Foreman-Peck and Murray, 2008). For example, as indicated in Chapter 2, Hume's *principle of verification* proposes 'learned work' should include 'abstract reasoning concerning number or quantity' or 'experimental reasoning concerning matter of fact and existence' (Hume, 1748: 123). The idea of verification was developed further in the 1920s by *The Vienna Circle*, a group of philosophers who coined the term 'logical positivism' (Ayer, 1959): 'the verification of meaningfulness through observation', which in turn became the dominant rubric for research, not least twentieth-century behaviourist psychological studies (Thomas, 2007: 3). Although these views have been counterbalanced by qualitative approaches that frame evidence as subjective meanings and multiple realities, a persistent focus remains in educational research on securing evidence that demonstrates 'what works' (Biesta, 2007; Feuer, Towne and Shavelson, 2002). This focus has been fuelled by policymakers seeking proof, rather than evidence (Oancea and Pring, 2008).

What might it mean to 'base decisions on evidence'?

The Greeks used the term *epistêmê* when they 'require(d) that reasons are given as to why something is the case' (Thomas, 2007: 149); evidentialism is the 'moral duty to proportion one's beliefs to evidence' (Wood, 2008: 7). Hume (1748) advocated scepticism when he argued that 'A wise man…proportions his belief to the evidence' (p. 83); he suggested that evidence amounts to universally observable events coupled with uniformity of experience – in other words, generalisability. Hume's view opposes Descartes' (1637) rationalist premise that knowledge emerges from reflecting and thinking. These ideas continue to challenge contemporary philosophers (*i.a.* BonJour, 1985; Bridges, Smeyers and Smith, 2009; Sosa, 2003). Definitions for evidence are as diverse as the purposes to which that evidence may be put so that it can be argued that those who make decisions are in the best position to define what constitutes evidence for their own contexts.

Do children base decisions on evidence?

We have known for many years that infants are able to indicate their preferences and apply criteria as evidence for making choices, for example, they choose faces rather than plain circles (Bruner, Olver and Greenfield, 1967; Fantz, 1961; 1965). Article 12 of the United Nations Convention on the Rights of the Child gives international legal status to children as decision-makers in matters affecting them (OHCHR, 1989):

> 1. States Parties shall assure to the child who is capable of forming his or her own views the right to express those views freely in all matters affecting the child, the views of the child being given due weight in accordance with the age and maturity of the child.
> 2. For this purpose, the child shall in particular be provided the opportunity to be heard in any judicial and administrative proceedings affecting the child, either directly, or through a representative or an appropriate body, in a manner consistent with the procedural rules of national law.

However, translating the Convention's policy into practice has been 'fraught with difficulties' (Ennew, 2008; Shevlin and Rose, 2008: 423). Part of the problem is the Convention's focus on giving children's views 'due weight in accordance with the age and maturity of the child' (Lansdown, 2005); this point conflicts with views of children as competent (Qvortrup, 1994) and was addressed in regard to children up to eight years in a later document which advocates 'recognition of young children as social actors from the beginning of life' (OHCHR, 2005: 2). Children can engage with decision-making and want to do so (Morrow, 2008; Van Deth, Abendschön and Vollmar, 2011; Cox and Robinson-Pant, 2010).

Children's decision-making is seen as a democratic practice (Fielding and Moss, 2011) and social inclusion seems manifest in communities that engage children in decision-making (Pells, 2010; McGinley and Grieve, 2010). However, many communities, including schools, tend to sideline children's decision-making (Jones and Welch, 2010; Lewars, 2010; Rudduck and McIntyre, 2007) and schools, in particular, are seen as 'places of unfreedoms' (Cox, Dyer, Robinson-Pant and Schweisfurth, 2010: 174).

Summary

This first section of Chapter 6 has briefly discussed literature concerned with defining decisions, evidence and 'basing decisions on evidence' and has considered perspectives on children as decision-makers. The second section addresses the ways that children based decisions on evidence in the YCAR project and how practitioners can use these findings to support practitioners in their work with young children.

Young children basing decisions on evidence in the YCAR project

Each of the 14 epistemological categories – building blocks – that supported young children to base decisions on evidence in the YCAR project is discussed here, together with examples linked to research and literature about knowledge and basing decisions on evidence, reflection points and consideration of the adult's role (Murray, 2017). This forms a framework that practitioners can use to identify ways the children they work with may construct knowledge by basing decisions on evidence in everyday activities in their settings and at home.

Applications of prior experience as a factor for young children basing decisions on evidence

Children in the YCAR project sometimes based decisions on evidence in the context of applying their prior experiences to new situations. Children's behaviours indicated that they extrapolated from their prior experiences, adopted mental models as well as simply applying their prior experiences.

(i) Extrapolates

Epistemological Category:	Extrapolates
Epistemological Factor:	**Applications of prior experience**
Research Behaviour:	**BASE DECISIONS ON EVIDENCE**

FIGURE 6.2 Building blocks – Extrapolates

Extrapolation from prior experience constitutes a 'means to extend data' (Magnussen and Palinscar, 2006: 41). It is recognised as a higher order cognitive process (Gray, Goldstein and

Thomas, 2004; Schleicher, 2007), yet also as a 'natural tendency' (Stavy and Tirosh, 2000: 87) and a functioning of infants as young as six months (von Hofsten, Fenq and Spelke, 2000).

Sore eyes

One lunch-time in Cherry Setting playground, Oscar told the teaching assistant that his eyes were hurting; they appeared red and sore. The teaching assistant asked Oscar: 'Do you have medicine?' He replied: 'No my Mum's skint at the moment. Well she's not skint but she doesn't want to spend money on that.'

Oscar extrapolated in his response: he moved beyond answering the teaching assistant's question, extending the information he had about his mother's financial affairs to suggest that she did not sufficiently value medicine for his poorly eye to 'want to spend money on that' (Magnussen and Palinscar, 2006).

FORMS OF KNOWLEDGE

✓ Knowing that
✓ A priori knowledge
✓ Explicit knowledge

THE ADULT'S ROLE

The practitioner's question provided the provocation for Oscar to answer, then extend beyond the information requested, and so extrapolate.

REFLECTION POINTS

What skills, attributes and opportunities might help young children to extrapolate?

(ii) Applies mental model

Epistemological Category:	Applies mental model
Epistemological Factor:	**Applications of prior experience**
Research Behaviour:	**BASE DECISIONS ON EVIDENCE**

FIGURE 6.3 Building blocks – Applies mental model

Children's behaviours sometimes indicated their uses of evidence from prior experiences to develop and apply mental models. As indicated in Chapter 3, mental models are cognitive representations of the tangible world (Forrester, 1975; Johnson-Laird, 1983; Klein and

D'Esposito, 2007) that are manifested in three stages: translating external processes into symbols, reasoning to elicit new symbols and retranslating the new symbols into external processes (Craik, 1943). Mental modelling may support the inductive reasoning required to manage 'ill-defined, complex strategic situations' (Klein and D'Esposito, 2007: 163): the 'messy' 'real world' (Robson, 1993: 3).

Making lunch

One day at home, Gemma (aged 5) completed an analysis sheet focused on her making lunch. On the sheet, she wrote:

> ***'I made lunch'***
> **First: *'I cut the bread'***
> **Next: *'I buttered it'***
> **Then: *'I put on ham, cheese and tomato'***
> **I did it: *'With a grown-up'***
> **It was good because: *'It was fun'***
> **I will change how I do things from now on: *'I would do it more often.'***

Gemma's analysis exemplified mental modelling: it was 'analogous to the structure of the corresponding state of affairs in the world (making lunch)' (Johnson-Laird, 1983: 156), so representative of fact (making lunch) (Craik, 1943; Forrester, 1975; Johnson-Laird, 1983). Furthermore, Gemma's analysis indicated a 'dynamic' creative process and represented 'a sequence of events' (Johnson-Laird, 1983: 156); it translated external processes (making lunch) into words…through a process of 'reasoning' (Craik, 1943: 50).

FORMS OF KNOWLEDGE

✓ A posteriori reasoning
✓ Explicit knowledge
✓ Mode 2 knowledge

THE ADULT'S ROLE

Gemma had engaged in this activity with an adult who may have helped her to make lunch by scaffolding the experience (Wood *et al.*, 1976) and helped her to complete the analysis form. However, there is not sufficient evidence to know for sure the precise actions of the adult.

REFLECTION POINTS

Consider practical ways that practitioners might support young children's reasoning skills through the mental modelling process (Craik, 1943):

> (1) "Translation" of external processes into words, numbers or other symbols; (2) Arrival at other symbols through a process of "reasoning", deduction, inference, etc. (3) "Retranslation" of these symbols into external processes (as in building a bridge to a design) or at least recognition of the correspondence between these symbols and external events (as in realising that a prediction is fulfilled).
>
> *(p. 50)*

(iii) Applies prior experience

Epistemological Category:	Applies prior experience
Epistemological Factor:	**Applications of prior experience**
Research Behaviour:	**BASE DECISIONS ON EVIDENCE**

FIGURE 6.4 Building blocks – Applies prior experience

When children in the YCAR project used their prior experiences as a building block for decision-making, this seemed to require them to use their memories (Cowan, 1988; Baddeley, 1992; Conway, 2010) as well as deductive reasoning (Johnson-Laird and Byrne, 1991). Knauff (2007) describes deductive reasoning as:

> an inference in which one or more propositions are true, given that other propositions are true. The propositions that are taken for granted are called premises. The propositions that are deducted from the premises are referred to as conclusions.
>
> *(p. 21)*

Scientific, mathematical and linguistic rubrics may amount to 'premises' and during the YCAR project, children sometimes drew on their experiences to recall these, then use them for new decision making, or drawing conclusions (Knauff, 2007).

Gemma subtracts

During free-flow play in Beech Setting one day, Gemma (aged 5) adopted a mathematical rubric to write on a whiteboard:

5 – 5 = 1

then she counted, using her fingers and erased the first '5' and wrote '6' instead:

6 – 5 = 1

Gemma applied prior experience of subtraction rules to a problem she devised for herself and she used deductive reasoning to achieve her conclusion (Knauff, 2007), self-correcting from 5 to 6 for the first number as she did so:

- *Major Premise:* Subtracting one number from another results in a number that is left when the second number is subtracted from the first number.
- *Minor Premise:* Gemma subtracts the second number from the first number.
- *Conclusion:* The resulting number is that which is left when the second number is subtracted from the first number.

Gemma counted on her fingers to work out and check her conclusion and the evidence of counting her fingers informed her that her first number sentence was inaccurate. Based on that evidence, she decided to count again to conclude with the correct number sentence.

FORMS OF KNOWLEDGE

✓ Knowing that
✓ A posteriori reasoning
✓ Explicit knowledge
✓ Mode 1 knowledge

THE ADULT'S ROLE

Gemma's practitioners had provided a whiteboard and pen as a resource that was available for her to choose. We can infer that an adult had taught her subtraction rules and had done so in such a way that Gemma was confident to make the decision to self-correct, based on the evidence of counting her fingers.

REFLECTION POINTS

Reflect on your practice to identify examples of young children applying their prior experiences of mathematics rules adults have taught them to their self-chosen activities.

Did they use deductive reasoning?
If so, were they accurate in their premises and conclusions?
If not, did they self-correct?

Social domains as a factor for young children basing decisions on evidence

As part of their everyday social interactions, children in the YCAR project engaged in basing decisions on evidence and this presented in two ways: children sometimes acted on adult opinions and sometimes appeared to value their peers' perspectives.

(iv) Acts on adult opinion

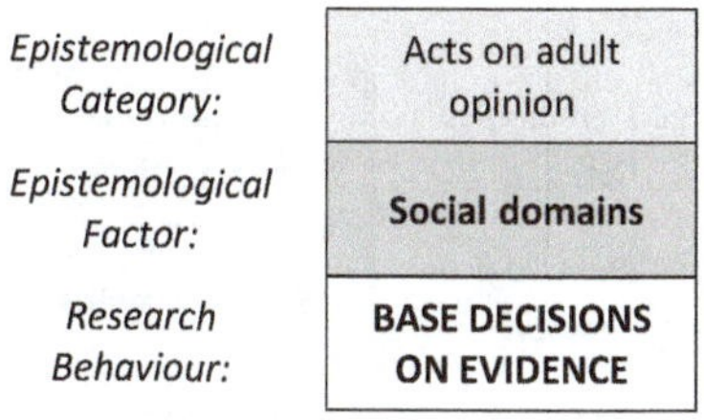

Epistemological Category:	Acts on adult opinion
Epistemological Factor:	**Social domains**
Research Behaviour:	**BASE DECISIONS ON EVIDENCE**

FIGURE 6.5 Building blocks – Acts on adult opinion

Doing up laces

One day at home, Harry (aged 5) and his brother (aged 4) were on the bottom stair and, under his father's instruction, Harry was practising doing up his laces. His father was videoing for the YCAR project, while speaking in French, his first language: 'Voilà avec tes mains, petit boucle, tournes a tours. Voila! Tu l'as trappé – voici' (*'There you go, with your hands, little loop, turn it around. There you go: you've caught it – here'*). As his father spoke, Harry made a loop, held it with his left hand and wrapped the lace around it.

This dyad was an adult:child interaction which included features of 'scaffolding' (Wood *et al.*, 1976) and 'guided participation' or 'apprenticeship' (Rogoff, 1995). It was not an equal discourse. While he engaged in 'goal-directed behaviour in the presence of options' (Hansson, 1994: 6), Harry's options were (i) to follow his father's instructions or (ii) not to follow his father's instructions to achieve his goal: doing up his shoelaces. Harry based his decisions about what to do on the evidence provided by his father.

FORMS OF KNOWLEDGE

- ✓ A posteriori reasoning
- ✓ Explicit knowledge
- ✓ Mode 1 knowledge

THE ADULT'S ROLE

The interaction between Harry and his father limited Harry's decision-making options; we do not know on what evidence Harry based his decision to comply with his father's instructions but there is evidence that he decided to do so. The dyad exemplifies the observation that 'children are often the most silenced participants in the educative process' (Fleet and Britt, 2011: 143).

> **REFLECTION POINTS**
>
> What do you think might have been the reasons that informed Harry's decision to follow all his father's instructions?

(v) Values peer perspectives

Epistemological Category:	Values peer perspectives
Epistemological Factor:	**Social domains**
Research Behaviour:	**BASE DECISIONS ON EVIDENCE**

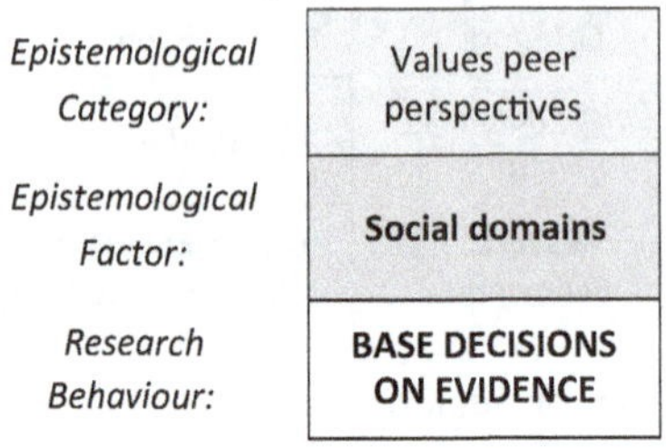

FIGURE 6.6 Building blocks – Values peer perspectives

There were numerous examples of children in the YCAR study valuing peers' perspectives; these tended to prevail in their settings, probably because there were simply more children in settings than there were in the children's own homes.

Singing assembly

One morning in Beech Setting school hall, all the children aged 4–11 years from the whole school were sitting cross-legged in rows in the hall. It was a summer day and the weather was very hot. Taped music was playing and children were chatting quietly to one another as they waited for assembly to begin. India (aged 5) was sitting cross-legged near the front, facing the front, between two boys from her reception setting, Andrew (aged 5) and Owen (aged 5). The teacher at the front of the hall said to the children 'We'll do our songs for this week – let's start with "oil in my lamp"' Sevison and Williams, n.d.). The music began, the song started, and the children began to sing, with the teacher modelling at the front. India joined in, her arms folded as she looked ahead. The children continued singing the verse 'Give me love in my heart, keep me singing...' India stopped singing. She looked around her at the other children, then stared at Andrew to her left, then Owen to her right. The children began to sing the chorus 'Sing Hosanna...' loudly. India looked ahead again and joined in singing the chorus words confidently.

When she was confident of the song words, India behaved as her peers, looking ahead at her teacher and singing. However, when she did not know the words her attention turned from looking at the teacher to looking at her peers. Once the chorus began, she knew the words, so she behaved as her peers again, looking forward and singing. Social referencing is linked to emotional support and is 'the tendency of a person to look to a significant other in an ambiguous situation in order to obtain clarifying information' (Dickstein and Parke, 1988); India's actions suggest that she engaged in social referencing but in relation to her peers, whom she seemed to regard as more 'significant others' than the teacher who was leading the assembly. First, in a situation where she knew and understood what was happening – singing familiar words – she behaved as her peers did. Second, when she was unsure of the song words, she looked around herself, 'seeking information cues' from her peers (McLain, 2014: 425). India's reference to her peers indicates a cognitive and emotional need to engage with them (Johnson-Laird and Shafir, 1993; Damasio, 2006): to be part of their 'togetherness' (Van Oers and Hännikäinen (2001: 187).

FORMS OF KNOWLEDGE

✓ Knowing how
✓ Tacit knowledge

THE ADULT'S ROLE

The teachers had organised a whole school assembly so children could practise singing together; this was an attempt to guide them 'into being competent users of the cultural tools of their society' (Anning and Edwards, 2010: 14). India attempted to conform, but when she was uncertain of what to do, she looked to her peers, rather than adults, for information and emotional support.

REFLECTION POINTS

You observed young children engaging in social referencing with peers: looking 'to a significant other in an ambiguous situation in order to obtain clarifying information' (Dickstein and Parke, 1988)? What were the antecedents?

What happened next?

How did their relationships develop?

Autonomy as a factor for young children basing decisions on evidence

During the YCAR project, young children behaved autonomously when basing decisions on evidence in the context of enacting their personal preferences.

(vi) Enacts personal preference

Epistemological Category:	Enacts personal preference
Epistemological Factor:	**Autonomy**
Research Behaviour:	**BASE DECISIONS ON EVIDENCE**

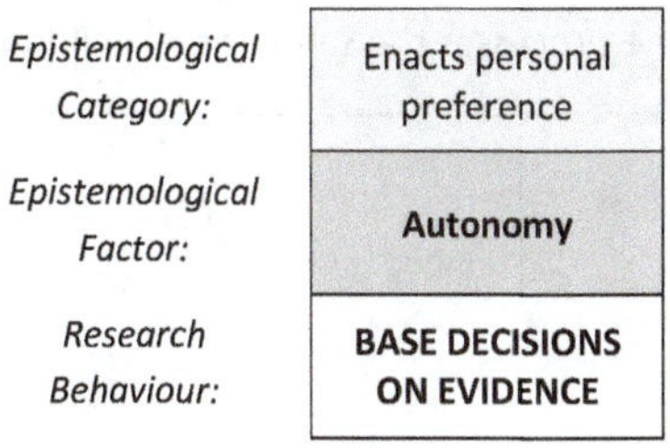

FIGURE 6.7 Building blocks – Enacts personal preference

Tyres, then tricycle

One hot afternoon in Cherry Setting, following a whole class literacy lesson, children began free-flow play activities and Martin chose to go outside. He went to the tricycles but by the time he got there, other children were riding them. Martin looked around, then went to the tyres that were lying on the ground, near the tricycles. He stepped into one tyre, then pulled a second over his head. He reached out to a third tyre and pulled that over his head so he was standing in three tyres. He looked around and saw a tricycle with nobody on it. He got out of the tyres and ran to the tricycle. He sat on the tricycle and began pedalling.

Martin wanted to play on a tricycle but realised he could not do so immediately as other children were riding them so he chose to do something else near the wheeled toys, placing himself conveniently to play on a tricycle when one became free so he could enact his personal play preference. Martin located himself 'flexibly and strategically within a particular social context' (James and Prout, 1995: 78); he engaged in 'goal-directed behaviour in the presence of options', indicative of decision theory (Hansson, 1994: 6) and his actions were autonomous, since they originated from him and were his own (Deci and Ryan, 1987: 1024).

FORMS OF KNOWLEDGE

- ✓ Knowing that
- ✓ A posteriori reasoning
- ✓ Tacit knowledge

THE ADULT'S ROLE

Martin was relatively free of adult control, since he had 'options' (Hansson, 1994: 6). However, those options had been limited and controlled by the practitioners who decided before the play session which resources – and how many – would be available to the children.

REFLECTION POINTS

With ethical protocols in place, observe young children in a setting to see how they engage in making decisions: 'goal-directed behaviour in the presence of options' (Hansson, 1994: 6). Are the processes the same for all children?

Material contexts as a factor for young children basing decisions on evidence

Children's senses often provided them with evidence for action, enabling them to base their decisions on evidence in 'material contexts'.

(vii) Senses provide evidence for action

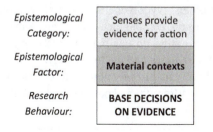

Epistemological Category:	Senses provide evidence for action
Epistemological Factor:	**Material contexts**
Research Behaviour:	**BASE DECISIONS ON EVIDENCE**

FIGURE 6.8 Building blocks – Senses provide evidence for action

White button

Martin (aged 5) was filming with the camcorder one day at home. He said to his mother: 'Pause. How do you record?' Martin panned round with the camcorder but the image on the camcorder screen was shaky. He said 'Oh yeah – you press the white button.'

Martin engaged in Hume's principle of verification (1748): 'experimental reasoning concerning matter of fact and existence'. He co-ordinated his senses of sight and touch intermodally (Marks, 1978) to work out how to operate the camcorder: he engaged in 'visual perception (which) includes attention and processing of visual information' (Woolfolk and Perry, 2012: 140) and his sense of touch, mediated by nerve endings just below the surface of his skin in response to pressure of movement on his skin's surface enabled him to find and 'press the white button' (Goddard Blythe, 2011).

Although this vignette could have been included as the epistemological category *Applies 'Humean' reason* within the cognitive domain, it was included here because the quality of Martin's intermodal sensory co-ordination was dominant.

FORMS OF KNOWLEDGE

✓ Knowing that
✓ A posteriori reasoning
✓ Explicit knowledge

> **THE ADULT'S ROLE**
>
> Martin's mother did not answer his question 'How do you record?' Martin then worked out for himself that he had to 'press the white button'. There may be a correlation between these points.

REFLECTION POINTS

In the 'Minimally Invasive Education' project (Mitra and Rana, 2001), computers with internet access were placed in walls in poor neighbourhoods in New Delhi, India where children had never previously had access to computers. There was no support from 'more knowledgeable others' (Vygotsky, 1978) but after a month, the children were skilfully accessing and using the internet. Mitra and Rana (2001) concluded that 'language and formal education do not seem to make any significant difference' to children's ability to learn to access and use technology.

What experiences have you had of young children teaching themselves skills and knowledge without support from 'more knowledgeable others' (Vygotsky, 1978). How did they do it?

Cognitive domains as a factor for young children basing decisions on evidence

When children based their decision-making on evidence in the YCAR project, the cognitive domains they engaged in included applications of Humean reasoning, strategic thinking, trial and error and metacognition.

(viii) Applies 'Humean' reason

Epistemological Category:	Applies 'Humean' reason
Epistemological Factor:	**Cognitive domains**
Research Behaviour:	**BASE DECISIONS ON EVIDENCE**

FIGURE 6.9 Building blocks – Applies 'Humean' reason

Children sometimes applied Humean reasoning: 'abstract reasoning concerning number or quantity' or 'experimental reasoning concerning matter of fact and existence' (Hume, 1748: 123).

In identifying these incidents, 'reasoning' refers to deductive approaches, as discussed in Chapter 4, because Hume favoured deductive approaches (BonJour, 1998). Additionally, Creswell's (2008: 300) characteristics of an experiment were adopted:

- Assigning random individuals or objects to a group.
- Control of variables.
- Manipulating treatment conditions.

Annie's thumb

During an interview in Ash Setting, Annie (aged 8) watched video footage of herself engaging in everyday activity in her class; I had asked Annie to talk about what she thought was happening on the video footage. Annie observed a literacy session focused on the digitext *Fergal Fly, Private Eye*, during which she sucked her thumb, took it out of her mouth and looked at it. In the interview conversation, Annie said: 'I do this…' she sucked her thumb then took it out of her mouth and looked at it.

Annie interpreted footage of herself sucking her thumb, taking it from her mouth and looking at it as 'matter of fact and existence' (Hume, 1748: 123) and she used her observation as a basis to decide to re-enact the event in the interview. As part of recounting the thumb-sucking event in the interview, Annie addressed two of Creswell's three characteristics (2008) for experimenting by controlling variables and manipulating conditions to mirror exactly what was on the screen: sucking her thumb, taking it out of her mouth and looking at it.

Annie also adopted deductive reasoning as she drew on 'formally demonstrable' evidence in the video footage (Ayer, 1940: 190–191):

- *Main premise:* Video footage provides 'formally demonstrable' evidence.
- *Minor premise:* Annie appeared on the video footage sucking her thumb.
- *Conclusion:* The video footage provided Annie with 'formally demonstrable' evidence that she had been sucking her thumb.

In this way, Annie engaged in 'experimental reasoning concerning matter of fact and existence' (Hume, 1748: 123) as a basis of evidence for deciding to recount the thumb-sucking event.

FORMS OF KNOWLEDGE

✓ Knowing that
✓ A posteriori reasoning
✓ Explicit knowledge

DISCUSSION POINT – THE ADULT'S ROLE

The adult provided provocations and the context in which Annie applied Humean reason. She had filmed the video and set up the interview with the video footage available for Annie to watch. She also asked Annie to talk about what she thought was happening on the video footage.

REFLECTION POINTS

What are some sources of 'formally demonstrable' evidence that you have known young children to use as a basis of evidence for decision-making?

(ix) Thinks strategically

Epistemological Category:	Thinks strategically
Epistemological Factor:	**Cognitive domains**
Research Behaviour:	**BASE DECISIONS ON EVIDENCE**

FIGURE 6.10 Building blocks – Thinks strategically

'Mental states are unobservable entities' (Lillard, 2001: 174), so in relation to the research behaviour that is basing decisions on evidence, children's strategic thinking may be considered counter-intuitive. However, children's thinking was expressed in multiple ways, at least some of which presented explicitly in their behaviours.

Cable reel

One day, Harry (aged 5) was sitting outside on his drive at home with a cable reel. He had just reeled in the cable and his mother asked him: 'Are you going to pick it up and put it away for me?' Harry stood, picked up the cable reel and began walking. He walked into the garage, saying to his mother: 'You come and help me', then put down the cable reel and said to her: 'I'll just put it down then you can sort it out'.

Harry's task to put away the cable reel was a goal; goal-centred behaviour is identified as characteristic of strategic thinking (Bjorklund, 1990; Flavell, 1979; Siegler and Jenkins, 1989). Bjorklund (1990) also lists intention, planning and a procedure resulting in task completion as characteristics of strategic thinking. Harry's behaviour exemplified these criteria: he demonstrated intention to put away the cable reel by walking into the garage. However, he did not put it away immediately, indicating uncertainty but he devised a plan, saying to his mother: 'You come and help me'. Finally, Harry achieved his goal by employing his mother: 'you can sort it out.'

FORMS OF KNOWLEDGE

✓ A priori knowledge
✓ Tacit knowledge

THE ADULT'S ROLE

Here, Harry and his mother seem to exemplify the 'meeting place' advocated by Dahlberg and Lenz Taguchi (1994): 'a way of relating (that) starts from the view of the child as a competent and capable child, a rich child, who participates in the creation of themselves and their knowledge' (1994: 2). At one point, Harry's mother leads in the interaction by saying 'Are you going to pick it up and put it away for me?' but later, Harry leads when he tells her: 'you can sort it out.'

REFLECTION POINTS

Using ethical protocols, observe young children in a setting to identify if and how they engage in behaviours that are characteristic of strategic thinking: goal-centred, intentional, planned and including a procedure that results in task completion (Bjorklund, 1990).

(x) Trial and error

Epistemological Category:	Trial and error
Epistemological Factor:	**Cognitive domains**
Research Behaviour:	**BASE DECISIONS ON EVIDENCE**

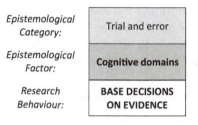

FIGURE 6.11 Building blocks – Trial and error

Popper (1972/1979) regards trial and error-elimination as highly logical; he argues that 'deliberation always works by trial and error…by tentatively proposing various possibilities and eliminating those which are not adequate…new reactions, new forms, new organs, new modes of behaviour, new hypotheses, are tentatively put forward and controlled by error-elimination' (pp. 242–243).

Ribbon in the hedge

One day in Ash Setting it was playtime and all the children were outside in the playground. Edward (aged 8) was on the football pitch. He moved to the hedge by the football pitch and touched a piece of red and white ribbon on the hedge. Edward tried to pull the red and white ribbon off the hedge but it would not move. He went around to the other side of the hedge and looked for the red and white ribbon. He put his arm through the hedge and tried to pull the ribbon again but could not loosen it from the hedge. He left the hedge and went to play football with his friends.

Edward had a 'new reaction' when he saw then touched the ribbon at first; he made a 'new hypothesis' that he could pull it from one side of the hedge but he trialled a solution and found he could not, so he had eliminated that error. He then made a second 'new hypothesis': that he could pull the ribbon from the other side of the hedge. He trialled that solution but it did not work, so he eliminated that second error. In this process, Edward enacted Swann's (2009: 260) schema representing the trial and error-elimination process, where 'P represents a problem, *TS* a trial solution applied to the problem, and *EE* stands for error-elimination:

$$P_1 > TS > EE > P_2$$

Based on the evidence that resulted from his trial and error elimination process, Edward decided to stop trying to retrieve the ribbon and he went to play football instead.

FORMS OF KNOWLEDGE

✓ Knowing that

✓ A posteriori reasoning

THE ADULT'S ROLE

Edward engaged in the process of trial and error elimination using his own initiative, without the direction of an adult. However, Swann (2009) observes that children rarely engage in trial and error at school, because teachers 'penalise the student for failing to understand, failing to give the prescribed answer' (p. 267). Does this happen in settings you know?

REFLECTION POINTS

What examples can you recall of young children engaging in trial and error elimination, according to Swann's schema:

$P_1 > TS > EE > P_2$

Did anything help the trial and error process? What?

Did anything hinder the trial and error process? What?

KEY:
P = Problem
TS = Trial Solution applied to the problem
EE = Error Elimination

(xi) Metacognition

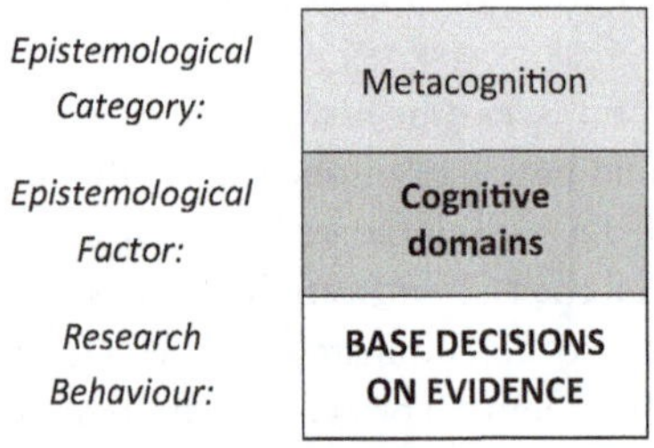

Epistemological Category:	Metacognition
Epistemological Factor:	**Cognitive domains**
Research Behaviour:	**BASE DECISIONS ON EVIDENCE**

FIGURE 6.12 Building blocks – Metacognition

Metacognition is defined as 'active monitoring and consequent regulation and orchestration of these processes in relation to the cognitive objects or data on which they bear' (Flavell,

1976: 232). In other words, it is a person's active awareness of her own behaviour that she may then channel to control her own actions.

'He didn't scare me'

One day at home, in her family focus group, Gemma (aged 5) shared a photograph. She based her decisions about what she said on the evidence of what she saw in the photograph, combined with her memory of the event photographed:

FIGURE 6.13 'He didn't scare me'

Gemma explained: 'We were playing a game and…he (her brother) was banging a thing – going like that at everybody.' I asked: 'Was he scaring everybody?' and Gemma responded: 'He didn't scare me though – because I know he was going to do it because he did it to Grandma and Grandad.'

Gemma 'surveyed' her personal behaviours and feelings in her analysis (Flavell, 1979: 909), engaging in metacognition to assert that her brother did not scare her 'because I know he was going to do it'. Annie's 'feeling' of not being scared appeared to express 'meta-cognitive experience' – active awareness of her own behaviour. Equally, Annie recounted a strategy – a goal-centred action (Flavell, 1979): she recognised that her experience of her brother attempting to scare their grandparents served as her warning. Gemma's ability to 'study (her) mind from within' (James, 1890: 225) and to articulate her thoughts regarding her own thinking seemed to help her to gain knowledge and understanding (Magnussen and

Palinscar, 2006) and given Lillard's point that 'mental states are unobservable entities' (2001: 174), acted as a vehicle to reveal Gemma's thinking.

FORMS OF KNOWLEDGE

✓ Knowing that
✓ A posteriori reasoning
✓ Explicit knowledge

THE ADULT'S ROLE

Gemma's grandparents' experience had provided her with evidence on which Gemma based her decision that she did not need to be scared of her brother. She revealed her metacognitive thinking in this regard in a discussion with another adult: the researcher.

REFLECTION POINTS

Identify some activities that might help young children to develop metacognition: a person's active awareness of her own behaviour that she may then channel to control her own actions.

Methodological issues as a factor for young children basing decisions on evidence

Three categories formed the epistemological factor 'Methodological Issues': '*Basing Decisions on Evidence* ***is*** *research*' '*Sampling Issue*' and '*Methodological issue*'. Each relates directly to the YCAR research methodology which was part of the everyday experiences of children who participated in the YCAR project while the data were being collected and analysed.

(xii) Basing decisions on evidence is *research*

Epistemological Category:	Basing decisions on evidence ***is*** research
Epistemological Factor:	**Methodological issues**
Research Behaviour:	**BASE DECISIONS ON EVIDENCE**

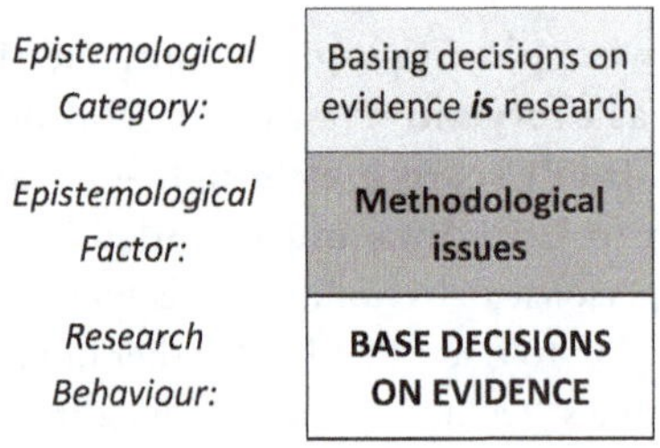

FIGURE 6.14 Building blocks – Basing decisions on evidence *is* research

Annie learns best

During an interview Ash Setting practitioner Mr Brown watched footage of Annie in a class literacy session. He observed: 'Annie learns best when she gets a teacher who is understanding of her needs. Indeed, she loved doing this project'.

Here Mr Brown suggested that Annie (aged 8) decided that she 'loved doing this project', based on the evidence she perceived that her 'needs' were accommodated and her enjoyment derived from participating in it with the researcher who was also a teacher (Invernizzi and Williams, 2008).

FORMS OF KNOWLEDGE

✓ Knowing that

✓ A priori knowledge

THE ADULT'S ROLE

Annie enjoyed participating in the project because she liked working with the adult researcher.

REFLECTION POINTS

Reflect on experiences you have had of young children basing their decisions to engage in activities on the quality of the relationships they have with you.

(xiii) Sampling issue

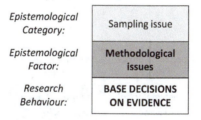

Epistemological Category:	Sampling issue
Epistemological Factor:	**Methodological issues**
Research Behaviour:	**BASE DECISIONS ON EVIDENCE**

FIGURE 6.15 Building blocks – Sampling issue

A sampling issue presented between Phases II and III, related to one participant: Nora.

Dropping out

Two children from each setting were originally going to join Phase III – six altogether – but one of these children – Nora (aged 5) – decided just before Phase III was about to begin that she would not continue. She said 'I don't want to do those things at home'.

The 'things' Nora alluded to were data collection and sharing analysis, activities that she had contributed to Phase II. Nora based her decision on experience and she justified it explicitly. As this was a methodological issue that was embedded in the YCAR research, it presented as an epistemological category.

FORMS OF KNOWLEDGE

✓ Knowing that
✓ A posteriori reasoning
✓ Explicit knowledge

THE ADULT'S ROLE

Nora's withdrawal from the study was entirely congruent with the ethical requirements for the study. Adults involved in the research were bound to respect Nora's decision and also to check that she and her parents were happy for her Phase II data to continue to be part of the project, which they were.

REFLECTION POINTS

What ethical protocols are important to you for working with children? For example...

Do you secure parents' consent for observing their children?

Do you secure children's assent to observe them?

Do you inform parents and children about how you will use observation data you collect?

If so, how? If not, why not? What other ethical protocols do you consider?

(xiv) Methodological issue

Epistemological Category:	Methodological issue
Epistemological Factor:	**Methodological issues**
Research Behaviour:	**BASE DECISIONS ON EVIDENCE**

FIGURE 6.16 Building blocks – Methodological issue

No sound

Having watched video footage of herself, her class and her practitioners during an interview in Ash Setting, Annie (aged 8) was invited to watch more. She was listening through headphones and she said: 'I can't hear it'. The sound was not working but Annie managed to find a way to turn it on.

Annie exposed a methodological issue: she could not hear the video sound, established through sensory experience. She then found a way to turn on the sound, using mental activity to identify what needed to be done and do it. Annie combined her first-hand sensory experience with mental activity to derive a conclusion, so engaged in a posteriori reasoning (Kant, 1787). Shrum, Duque and Brown (2005) acknowledge the challenges of using video technology in research; nonetheless, Shrum *et al.* (2005) argue that its 'advantages are marked' (p. 17).

FORMS OF KNOWLEDGE

✓ Knowing that
✓ A posteriori reasoning
✓ Explicit knowledge

THE ADULT'S ROLE

The adult needed help from Annie to make the sound work. This enabled Annie to demonstrate a posteriori reasoning.

REFLECTION POINTS

Should early childhood practice include information technology for young children?

If so, why?

If not, why not?

What are the disadvantages and advantages of including technology as part of the early childhood curriculum?

Conclusion

This chapter has defined and addressed basing decisions on evidence and it has considered how the YCAR project revealed 14 epistemological categories that provided 'building blocks' that enabled young children to construct knowledge by basing decisions on evidence during everyday activities at home and in their settings. These included:

- Extrapolates.
- Applies mental model.
- Applies prior experience.
- Acts on adult opinion.
- Values peer perspectives.
- Acts on adult opinion.
- Senses provide evidence for action.
- Applies 'Humean' reason.
- Thinks strategically.
- Trial and error.

- Metacognition.
- Basing decisions on evidence *is* research.
- Sampling issue.
- Methodological issue.

These epistemological categories acted as building blocks that supported young children to construct knowledge by basing decisions on evidence during their everyday activities at home and in their settings (Figure 6.1). Each of the building blocks for children basing decisions on evidence has been linked with related forms of knowledge, and the chapter has discussed ways that adults in the YCAR project supported children to construct knowledge by basing decisions on evidence (Murray, 2017). Reflection points have been provided to help practitioners to consider ways they can apply the YCAR findings about young children basing decisions on evidence to their own practice and at the end of the book, you will find a useful tool for practitioners and parents – *Observation notes for young children basing decisions on evidence* (see appendices, p. 161). Practitioners and parents can photocopy the tool and use it to record observations of young children engaging in the 14 epistemological categories for young children basing decisions on evidence: ways we can know that young children base decisions on evidence in order to construct knowledge.

7

CONCLUSIONS

Young children build knowledge, young children are researchers

This book has interwoven practice with research and theory in the field of early childhood education to suggest practical ways for setting leaders, tutors, practitioners, parents and students and others to recognise how young children construct knowledge in sophisticated ways the academy regards as research behaviour. The book builds on existing perspectives that young children's constructions of knowledge resonate with aspects of scientific theorising. However, it moves beyond earlier perspectives that have tended to regard young children's understanding as 'developing' (Gopnik, 1996: 485; Piaget, 1972b), to align with new sociological ideas that position young children as competent social actors (Corsaro, 2005: 3; OHCHR, 2005).

This final chapter has four sections. The first revisits the warrant for the YCAR project claim that young children aged 4–8 years behave as researchers and can be considered to be researchers on the academy's terms. The second section highlights what is new and different about the *Young Children As Researchers* findings. The third section focuses on how the findings may be put to good use by practitioners and others then the chapter and the book conclude with some final thoughts.

The warrant of the *Young Children As Researchers* project

The connections this book makes between research and practice are based on research evidence drawn from the *Young Children As Researchers* project. YCAR indicated ways that young children construct knowledge in their everyday activities and showed their congruence with research behaviours that were identified by professional academics who participated in the study. These connections were highlighted and linked to extant theory in the YCAR project to generate a 'plausible account' (Charmaz, 2006: 149) that conceptualised ways young children aged 4–8 years behave as researchers and can be considered researchers on the academy's terms.

Four questions framed the YCAR project:

- What might research be like in early childhood education?
- How can a study be conducted to establish young children as researchers?

- What enquiries are important to young children and how can they engage in them?
- What support structures might encourage young children to participate in research? What barriers might prevent this?

The responses that the YCAR project made to address these questions are outlined here, grouped in pairs.

What might research be like in early childhood education? How can a study be conducted to establish young children as researchers?

The YCAR project was concerned with two aspects of research in the field of early childhood education. The first aspect was the project itself: a research study conducted in the field. The second aspect was the young children's research activity, bound into their constructions of knowledge that presented in everyday activities.

As part of the first aspect, the argument was made that the lack of recognition for young children as researchers by the academy is unjust. Such exclusion denies young children respect as 'experts' in their own lives and respect as competent social actors (Langsted, 1994: 29; OHCHR, 2005). To make this argument, it was necessary to show that young children's behaviours had congruence with those of adult academics. In Phase I of the YCAR project, 39 research behaviours comprising the Research Behaviour Framework (RBF) (Chapter 2) were identified by academics in the fields of education and early childhood education; those academics also highlighted four of the research behaviours as more important than the others: exploration, finding solutions, conceptualisation and basing decisions on evidence.

Phases II and III of the YCAR project were concerned with matching these behaviours to young children's everyday behaviours. This was achieved using participatory, emancipatory and inductive approaches that were about sharing power with the children, parents and practitioners who participated in the YCAR project. Rather than imposing an immutable methodological rubric from the beginning of the project, a pluralist paradigm, jigsaw methodology and multiple methods unfolded in response to data that were co-constructed with participants. Analysis was also characterised by co-construction. This was a useful model because it worked in regard to form and function: YCAR was about addressing young children's marginalisation from recognition as researchers, particularly in matters of concern to them. It did so it by including and recognising young children as co-researchers, along with their parents and practitioners who were their advocates.

The YCAR project established that young children aged 4–8 years engaged in research behaviours. Given the study's inductive approach, paradoxically the argument for this is based on deductive logic (BonJour, 1998; Johnson-Laird and Byrne, 1991), the academy's dominant methodology (Hanna, 2006):

- *Major premise:* The research behaviour framework is populated with behaviours identified by academy members as research.
- *Minor premise:* Young children engaged in behaviours on the RBF.
- *Conclusion:* Young children engaged in research on the academy's terms.

The multiple voices and methods that contributed to the YCAR project added further verification to this claim.

What enquiries are important to young children and how can they engage in them? What support structures might encourage young children to participate in research and what barriers might prevent this?

The process of constructing knowledge begins with cognitive conflict – the experience of encountering a new idea that is at odds with your current understanding, in other words, a challenge. This may provide an incentive for enquiry that in turn may lead to the construction of new knowledge (Hutt, 1979; Robson, 2012). Children in the YCAR project engaged in many diverse enquiries, often of their own device, in varied contexts and in different ways. Together with the constructions of knowledge that followed, these enquiries emerged as part of the children's everyday activities in their settings and homes. A range is exemplified in vignettes in Chapters 3–6. Altogether YCAR captured 1,601 examples of young children engaging in the four important research behaviours when they constructed knowledge in their everyday activities. Participating children also engaged in the other research behaviours on the RBF but within the scope of the YCAR project, it was only possible to account for the most important four research behaviours in the full analysis and the final report.

Analysis and interpretation led to the identification of 68 epistemological categories (Figure 2.4) in the YCAR project. These were the building blocks that the children in the YCAR project used to construct knowledge, the provocations that enabled young children to adopt research behaviours and the support structures that encouraged young children to participate in research. 12 epistemological barriers were also identified (Figure 2.3); these were the barriers that seemed to prevent young children from participating in research. Analysis attributed all 12 barriers to the research behaviour 'Find a Solution'. The reasons for this are not entirely clear but may be due to the fact that finding a solution results in a tangible product: the solution. Conversely, exploration is a process so it may be difficult to establish clearly that it is not happening. Equally, conceptualisation and basing decisions on evidence are contingent on mental processes which may not be readily observable (Lillard, 2001: 174).

Because this book is about the ways young children build knowledge and how adults can support them in doing this, focus throughout has been on the epistemological categories, rather than the epistemological barriers that may inhibit such activity. Nevertheless, it is useful to look briefly at the epistemological barriers that emerged in the YCAR project findings, if only to consider how they can be avoided in practice. The epistemological barriers seemed to fall into three themes, each characterised by a deficit:

i. Lack of cognitive conflict
   - Reproducing knowledge s/he already had
   - Responding to an adult's semi-open questions
   - Responding to an adult's closed questions
   - Following an adult's direction
ii. Lack of appreciation by others
   - Solution not shared with or witnessed by others
   - Solution not shared with or witnessed by others: unconfirmed
   - Denied opportunity to share solution
   - Solution unconfirmed

iii. Young children's lack of motivation
   - Believes s/he has failed
   - Unmotivated
   - Has become disinterested
   - Gives up

(i) Epistemological barriers caused by lack of cognitive conflict may occur when a curriculum is blindly followed without knowing or respecting what a young child knows, can do and is interested in. These barriers may also occur when adults regard pedagogic engagement as the transmission of knowledge, rather than the co-construction of learning with children. They can be avoided if adults ask young children questions that are authentically challenging about ideas that are new to the children (Siraj-Blatchford and Manni, 2008), if centralised curriculum requirements are minimal and if adults are knowledgeable about their young children, about subject matter, about pedagogy, and are motivated to create a stimulating environment which inspires young children to make new enquiries leading to new constructions of knowledge.

(ii) Epistemological barriers caused by lack of appreciation by others can happen when young children believe that their voices are not heard, when their interests are disregarded and when social interaction is somehow limited. They can be avoided if adults make time to listen to their young children, are genuinely interested in the concerns their young children have and create environments in which social interactions flow and power relationships are equalised. Dahlberg and Moss (2005: 105) propose that such practice is characterised by an 'ethics of encounter' in which each person values others equally (Levinas, 1980) to create a pedagogy of listening and 'a laboratory or a workshop of learning and knowledge'.

(iii) Epistemological barriers caused by young children's lack of motivation have resonance with the themes above. They may happen when young children lack incentive to engage in research behaviour or construct new knowledge because they do not experience cognitive challenge. They may also present when young children perceive their own actions to be deficient which may be less likely to happen in a context where children feel valued by others (Dahlberg and Moss, 2005; Levinas, 1980).

Final analysis and interpretation of the YCAR data grouped the epistemological categories and barriers into nine epistemological factors that effect *and* affect children's capacity to engage in research behaviours that enable them to construct knowledge (Figure 2.4). The YCAR project revealed children's engagements with research behaviour through epistemological categories as an explicit expression of their 'philosophy of what counts as knowledge and truth', in other words, epistemology (Strega, 2005: 201).

Summary

Understanding how to use methodological approaches with flexibility, a highly participatory approach, and rigorous application of rational argument have emerged from the YCAR findings in response to these research questions:

- What might research be like in early childhood education?
- How can a study be conducted to establish young children as researchers?

The YCAR findings also provide a response to the research questions:

- What enquiries are important to young children and how can they engage in them?
- What support structures might encourage young children to participate in research and what barriers might prevent this?

The examples of the 68 epistemological categories that appear in Chapters 3–6 provide an indication of the enquiries that are important to young children as well as how they engage in them. The YCAR findings revealed the epistemological categories as support structures that encourage young children to participate in research behaviour. Conversely, the epistemological barriers identified in the YCAR project seem to hinder young children from participating in research behaviour.

What is different about *Young Children As Researchers*?

This book is based on the *Young Children As Researchers* project which offers some new and different ways to look at the ways young children construct knowledge.

The book and the YCAR project revisit some well-established constructivist themes. However, far from Piaget's perspective (1972a: 15) that the origins of knowledge are only in 'their most elementary forms' in young children and Gopnik's view (1996: 485) that young children's cognitive understanding is 'developing', the YCAR project corroborates Isaacs' assessment (1944: 322) that the 'factor of epistemic interest and inquiry…is in every respect the same in the child as in the adult'. It makes important links between young children's constructions of knowledge in their everyday activities and engagement in research behaviour; the YCAR findings reconceptualise and reveal young children's authentic, naturalistic behaviours as research on the academy's terms.

A new taxonomy of research behaviours proposed by academics in the field of education and early childhood education emerged as an important aspect of the YCAR findings (Table 2.1). In the fields of education and early childhood, the Research Behaviour Framework has value for research and also for practice where there is a need to identify actions that contribute to the production and construction of knowledge.

Mirroring the realities of practice in early childhood education (Gammage, 2002; Waller and Davis, 2014), the YCAR project draws on a wide range of disciplines in its uses of literature to construct meanings from its data. Theoretical perspectives are built into the examples of the epistemological categories highlighted in the book (Chapters 3–6). The book makes links between the things young children do and relevant research and theory, providing a ready resource to help practitioners, parents and others who work with young children to interpret their young children's actions.

There is relatively little empirical research concerning children's experiences in their own homes (Pellegrini *et al.*, 2004). In the YCAR project data were not only gathered in early childhood settings but young children and their families also gathered data at home and co-constructed analysis from them. This resulted in valuable new findings about young children's lives at home as well as the ways they constructed knowledge and engaged in research behaviour at home during the project. Information about young children's experiences at home may be valuable for practitioners wishing to provide a stimulating learning environment which takes account of young children's interests. Whalley and the

Pen Green Centre Team (2007) recognise the value of such practice and the Pen Green Loop is a useful model for gathering data at home and in a child's setting and sharing them across these important spaces in young children's lives. The YCAR Research Behaviour Framework and epistemological categories provide alternative new ways for parents and practitioners to interpret young children's actions at home.

The YCAR epistemological categories are specific means that children naturally adopt research behaviours as modes of knowledge construction. They indicate how young children's everyday actions can be interpreted to inform us about children's cognitive processes. They are a resource for practitioners, early childhood leaders, parents, researchers, tutors and early childhood students wishing to gain deep understanding of children's activity in order to optimise their constructions of knowledge, understanding and skills.

Young Children As Researchers in practice

This book has set out how the YCAR findings link research, theory and practice: three key elements that are inextricably intertwined in the field of early childhood education. The YCAR findings emerged from the everyday lives of young children, their parents and their practitioners who were co-researchers and researchers in the YCAR project. High calibre practitioners and strong leaders in early childhood education understand the importance of the connections between research, theory and practice for helping us to recognise what young children already know and using it as a starting point for optimising provision for what young children may come to know.

How you choose to use the findings from the *Young Children As Researchers* project that are shared in this book will depend on your role, your experience, your setting and the colleagues, children and families you work with. Suggested '*Ways you can choose to use the book*' are outlined in Chapter 1 to help you make decisions in this regard. You might use those suggestions to inform your practice or as a basis for new research with young children or by young children. Ultimately, however, you are in the best position to decide how this book will be most useful for you and those you work with and why that may be.

Final thoughts

This book's connections between practice, theory and research highlight ways young children construct knowledge by behaving as researchers on the academy's terms in their everyday activities. The book is based on empirical research conducted in partnership with children aged 4–8 years, their practitioners and parents. Based on empirical evidence, the YCAR study concluded that young children engage in research on the academy's terms; in other words, young children *are* researchers.

There is now well established recognition of young children's capacity as competent social actors and 'experts' in their own lives from birth (Alderson, Hawthorne and Killen, 2006; Langsted, 1994: 29; OHCHR, 2005). It can therefore be argued that the main conclusion of the *Young Children As Researchers* project that young children engage in research on the academy's terms may be applied from birth. The key to recognising this possibility is in adults finding ways to understand young children's research behaviours, since the ways adults tend to interpret young children's thoughts and behaviours often make children's meanings 'incomprehensible' to adults (Hardman, 1973: 95). The epistemological categories and Research Behaviour Framework that are products of the YCAR project provide ways to help adults understand the meanings that are inherent in young children's thoughts and behaviours (Murray, 2017).

The *Young Children As Researchers* findings that inform this book support the argument that young children's exclusion from the academy can no longer be justified on the grounds of their incapacity (Redmond, 2008). Young children behave naturally as researchers in matters that concern them and it is appropriate that this is recognised. This book also provides a toolkit for practitioners and other adults who work with young children to use for reflecting on – and in – their practice (Schön, 1983), in order to optimise young children's constructions of knowledge at home, in their early childhood settings and beyond.

APPENDICES

A.1 Practitioner's tool: Observation notes for young children's explorations

Young children are exploring when they are...		YCAR Young Children Are Researchers – Young Children Explore –		
		Record your own snapshot observations of young children exploring...		
Engaging in patterned behaviour p. 31		*Name:*............................ engaged in patterned behaviour when s/he		*Name:*............................ engaged in patterned behaviour when s/he
Experimenting p. 34		*Name:*................................ experimented when s/he		*Name:*................................ experimented when s/he
Engaging in social encounters p. 35		*Name:*......................... engaged in a social encounter when s/he		*Name:*............................ engaged in a social encounter when s/he
Developing their own agenda p. 37		*Name:*......................... developed his/her own agenda when s/he		*Name:*......................... developed his/her own agenda when s/he
Interested in their context p. 39		*Name:* .... showed interest in his/her context when s/he		*Name:* .... showed interest in his/her context when s/he

Young children are exploring when they are...	YCAR Young Children Are Researchers – Young Children Explore – **Record your own snapshot observations of young children exploring...**	
Showing interest in different materials p. 40	*Name:*.............................. showed interest in materials when s/he	*Name:*.............................. showed interest in materials when s/he
Identifying cause and effect p. 42	*Name:*.......................... identified cause and effect when s/he	*Name:*.......................... identified cause and effect when s/he
Focused on a task p. 44	*Name:*............................ focused on a task when s/he	*Name:*............................ focused on a task when s/he
Curious p. 45	*Name:*............................ showed curiosity when s/he	*Name:*............................ showed curiosity when s/he
Seeking p. 46	*Name:*................................ was seeking when s/he	*Name:*................................ was seeking when s/he

A.2 Practitioner's tool: Observation notes for young children finding solutions

Young children are finding solutions when they are …	YCAR Young Children Are Researchers – Young Children Find Solutions – **Record your own snapshot observations of young children finding solutions …**	
Applying a rule to create a solution p. 51	*Name:* .... applied a rule to create a solution when s/he	*Name:* .... applied a rule to create a solution when s/he
Finding a practical use for a solution p. 53	*Name:*......................... found a practical use for a solution when s/he	*Name:*......................... found a practical use for a solution when s/he
Wanting to preserve what s/he is doing p. 54	*Name:*............................ wanted to preserve what s/he was doing when s/he	*Name:*............................ wanted to preserve what s/he was doing when s/he
Using their ability to read to find a solution p. 56	*Name:*.............................. used ability as a reader to find a solution when s/he	*Name:*.............................. used ability as a reader to find a solution when s/he

Young children are finding solutions when they are...	YCAR Young Children Are Researchers – Young Children Find Solutions – **Record your own snapshot observations of young children finding solutions...**	
Finding their *own* solution p. 58	*Name:*............................ found his/her own solution when s/he	*Name:*............................ found his/her own solution when s/he
Creating a problem to solve p. 59	*Name:*................................ created a problem to solve when s/he	*Name:*................................ created a problem to solve when s/he
Devising a practical method to create a solution p. 62	*Name:*......................... devised a practical method to create a solution when s/he	*Name:*......................... devised a practical method to create a solution when s/he
Resolving another person's problem p. 63	*Name:*.......................... resolved another person's problem when s/he	*Name:*.......................... resolved another person's problem when s/he
Sharing a solution p. 65	*Name:*................................ shared a solution when s/he	*Name:*................................ shared a solution when s/he
Employing others to help with finding a solution p. 66	*Name:*............................ employed others to help find a solution when s/he	*Name:*............................ employed others to help find a solution when s/he

Young children are finding solutions when they are...	YCAR Young Children Are Researchers – Young Children Find Solutions – **Record your own snapshot observations of young children finding solutions...**	
Demonstrating Theory of Mind p. 67	*Name:*............................ showed Theory of Mind when s/he	*Name:*............................ showed Theory of Mind when s/he
Self-regulating p. 69	*Name:*................................ self-regulated when s/he	*Name:*................................ self-regulated when s/he
Focusing on something of personal interest p. 70	*Name:*......................... focused on something of personal interest when s/he	*Name:*......................... focused on something of personal interest when s/he
Experiencing time and freedom to explore, investigate, experiment with something of personal interest p. 71	*Name:*.......................... explored, investigated and experimented with something of personal interest when s/he	*Name:*.......................... explored, investigated and experimented with something of personal interest when s/he
Exploring properties of materials p. 73	*Name:*................................ explored properties of materials when s/he	*Name:*................................ explored properties of materials when s/he
Engaged in deductive reasoning p. 74	*Name:*............................ reasoned deductively when s/he	*Name:*............................ reasoned deductively when s/he

<table>
<tr><td>Young children are finding solutions when they are...</td><td></td><td colspan="3">YCAR
Young Children Are Researchers
– Young Children Find Solutions –</td></tr>
<tr><td></td><td></td><td colspan="3">Record your own snapshot observations of young children finding solutions...</td></tr>
<tr><td>Engaged in inductive reasoning
p. 76</td><td></td><td>Name:...........................
reasoned inductively when s/he</td><td></td><td>Name:...........................
reasoned inductively when s/he</td></tr>
<tr><td>Persevering to resolve a problem
p. 77</td><td></td><td>Name:.................................
persevered to resolve a problem when s/he</td><td></td><td>Name:.................................
persevered to resolve a problem when s/he</td></tr>
<tr><td>Motivated by finding a solution
p. 78</td><td></td><td>Name:.................................
was motivated by finding a solution when s/he</td><td></td><td>Name:.................................
was motivated by finding a solution when s/he</td></tr>
<tr><td>Excited by finding a solution
p. 80</td><td></td><td>Name:.................................
was excited by finding a solution when s/he</td><td></td><td>Name:.................................
was excited by finding a solution when s/he</td></tr>
<tr><td colspan="5">Notes</td></tr>
</table>

A.3 Practitioner's tool: Observation notes for young children's conceptualisations

Young children are conceptualising when they are...	YCAR Young Children Are Researchers – Young Children Conceptualise – **Record your own snapshot observations of young children conceptualising...**	
Thinking through a problem by applying concepts p. 86	*Name:* .... thought through a problem by applying concepts when s/he	*Name:* .... thought through a problem by applying concepts when s/he
Thinking tangentially p. 87	*Name:*......................... thought tangentially when s/he	*Name:*......................... thought tangentially when s/he
Synthesising concepts p. 88	*Name:*................................ synthesised concepts when s/he	*Name:*................................ synthesised concepts when s/he
Linking prior knowledge to a new application p. 89	*Name:*.............................. linked prior knowledge to a new application when s/he	*Name:*.............................. linked prior knowledge to a new application when s/he
Recalling instructions p. 91	*Name:*................................ recalled instructions when s/he	*Name:*................................ recalled instructions when s/he
Inventing a process or method p. 92	*Name:*............................. invented a process or method when s/he	*Name:*............................. invented a process or method when s/he

Young children are conceptualising when they are...	YCAR Young Children Are Researchers – Young Children Conceptualise – **Record your own snapshot observations of young children conceptualised...**	
Developing own idea/s from external stimulus p. 93	*Name:*........................ developed his/her own ideas from an external stimulus when s/he	*Name:*............................... ... developed his/her own ideas from an external stimulus when s/he
Creating an imagined space or persona p. 94	*Name:*.......................... created an imagined space or persona when s/he	*Name:*............................... ... created an imagined space or persona when s/he
Identifying an anomaly p. 95	*Name:*......................... identified an anomaly when s/he	*Name:*........................... identified an anomaly when s/he
Working with others to conceptualise p. 96	*Name:*.......................... worked with others to conceptualise when s/he	*Name:*.......................... worked with others to conceptualise when s/he
Following an adult's direction to conceptualise p. 98	*Name:*.......................... followed an adult's direction to conceptualise when s/he	*Name:*............................... ... followed an adult's direction to conceptualise when s/he
Conceptualising after an adult stopped conceptualisation p. 99	*Name:*.......................... conceptualised after an adult stopped conceptualisation when s/he	*Name:*............................... ... conceptualised after an adult stopped conceptualisation when s/he

Young children are conceptualising when they are...	YCAR Young Children Are Researchers – Young Children Conceptualise – **Record your own snapshot observations of young children conceptualised...**	
Creating a problem p. 100	*Name:*............................ created a problem when s/he	*Name:*............................ created a problem when s/he
Autonomously deciding what needs to be done and doing it p. 101	*Name:*............................. autonomously decided what needs to be done and did it when s/he	*Name:*............................ autonomously decided what needs to be done and did it when s/he
Making decision/s based on own criteria p. 103	*Name:*.......................... made decision/s based on his/her own criteria when s/he	*Name:*.......................... made decision/s based on his/her own criteria when s/he
Creating a new use for object/s p. 104	*Name:*.......................... created a new use for an object when s/he	*Name:*.......................... created a new use for an object when s/he
Predicting p. 106	*Name:*............................ predicted when s/he	*Name:*............................ predicted when s/he
Involved in pursuing a train of thought p. 108	*Name:*............................ was involved in pursuing a train of thought when s/he	*Name:*............................ was involved in pursuing a train of thought when s/he

Young children are conceptualising when they are...	YCAR Young Children Are Researchers – Young Children Conceptualise – **Record your own snapshot observations of young children conceptualising...**	
Using imagination p. 109	*Name:*............................ used his/her imagination when s/he	*Name:*............................ used his/her imagination when s/he
Using language to support their thinking p. 110	*Name:*................................ used language to support thinking when s/he	*Name:*................................ used language to support thinking when s/he
Engaging in symbolic representation p. 112	*Name:*......................... engaged in symbolic representation when s/he	*Name:*......................... engaged in symbolic representation when s/he
Planning p. 113	*Name:*.......................... planned when s/he	*Name:*.......................... planned when s/he
Making links – analogy p. 114	*Name:*................................ made links – used analogy – when s/he	*Name:*................................ made links – used analogy – when s/he
Applying anthropomorphism p. 116	*Name:*............................ applied anthropomorphism when s/he	*Name:*............................ applied anthropomorphism when s/he

A.4 Practitioner's tool: Observation notes for young children basing decisions on evidence

Young children are basing decisions on evidence when they are ...	YCAR Young Children Are Researchers – Young Children Base Decisions on Evidence – **Record your own snapshot observations of young children basing decisions on evidence...**	
Extrapolating p. 122	*Name:* .... extrapolated when s/he	*Name:* .... extrapolated when s/he
Applying a mental model p. 123	*Name:*......................... applied a mental model when s/he	*Name:*......................... applied a mental model when s/he
Applying prior experience p. 125	*Name:*................................. applied prior experience when s/he	*Name:*................................. applied prior experience when s/he
Acting on adult opinion p. 127	*Name:*............................. acted on adult opinion when s/he	*Name:*............................. acted on adult opinion when s/he
Valuing peer perspectives p. 128	*Name:*................................ valued peer perspectives when s/he	*Name:*................................ valued peer perspectives when s/he

Young children are solving problems when they are...	YCAR Young Children Are Researchers – Young Children Base Decisions on Evidence –	
	Record your own snapshot observations of young children basing decisions on evidence...	
Enacting personal preference p. 129	*Name:* .... enacted personal preference when s/he	*Name:*.............................. enacted personal preference when s/he
Using senses to provide evidence for action p. 131	*Name:*................................ used senses to provide evidence for action when s/he	*Name:*................................ used senses to provide evidence for action when s/he
Applying 'Humean' reason p. 132	*Name:*.......................... applied 'Humean' reason when s/he	*Name:*.......................... applied 'Humean' reason when s/he
Thinking strategically p. 134	*Name:*......................... thought strategically when s/he	*Name:*......................... thought strategically when s/he
Engaging in trial and error p. 135	*Name:*................................ engaged in trial and error when s/he	*Name:*................................ engaged in trial and error when s/he

Young children are solving problems when they are...	YCAR Young Children Are Researchers – Young Children Base Decisions on Evidence –	
	Record your own snapshot observations of young children basing decisions on evidence...	
Engaging in metacognition p. 136	*Name:*............................ engaged in metacognition when s/he	*Name:*............................ engaged in metacognition when s/he
Identifying evidence they use to make a decision (*Basing Decisions on Evidence is research*) p. 138	*Name:*................................ identified evidence s/he used to make a decision when s/he	*Name:*................................ identified evidence s/he used to make a decision when s/he
Reasoning why they should work with specific peer/s (*sampling issue*) p. 139	*Name:*......................... reasoned why s/he should work with specific peer/s when s/he	*Name:*......................... reasoned why s/he should work with specific peer/s when s/he
Redesigning an activity that did not go according to plan (*methodological issue*) p. 140	*Name:*.......................... redesigned an activity that did not go according to plan when s/he	*Name:*.......................... redesigned an activity that did not go according to plan when s/he

Notes

REFERENCES

Abbott, L. and Langston, A. (2005) *Birth to Three Matters*. Maidenhead: Open University Press.

Ackermann, E. K. (2001) Piaget's Constructivism, Papert's Constructionism: What's the difference? Available online at http://citeseerx.ist.pse.edu/viewdoc/download?doi=10.1.1.132.4253&rep=rep1&type=pdf

Ackermann, L., Feeny, T., Hart, J. and Newman, J. (2003) *Understanding and Evaluating Children's Participation*. London: Plan International.

Aguerrondo, I. (2009) *Complex Knowledge and Education Competences. IBE Working Papers on Curriculum Issues No. 8*. Geneva: UNESCO International Bureau of Education.

Alderson, P., Hawthorne, J. and Killen, M. (2006) The Participation Rights of Premature Babies. In H. Van Beers, A. Invernizzi and B. Milne (Eds) (2006) *Beyond Article 12: Essential Readings on Children's Participation*. Bangkok: Black and White Publications, pp. 57–65.

Alderson, P. and Morrow, V. (2004) *Ethics, social research and consulting with children and young people*. Ilford: Barnardo's.

Alexander, R. J. (2008) *Towards Dialogic Teaching: Rethinking classroom talk*. 4e. York: Dialogos.

Alexander, R. J. (Ed.) (2009) *The Cambridge Primary Review Research Surveys*. London: Routledge.

Alkire, S. and Deneulin, S. (2009) The Human Development and Capability Approach. In S. Deneulin and L. Shahani (Eds) (2009) *An Introduction to the Human Development and Capability Approach*. London: Earthscan, pp. 22–48.

Anand, P. (1993) The Philosophy of Intransitive Preference. *The Economic Journal*. **103** (417): 337–46.

Anderson, L. W. and Krathwohl, D. R. (Eds) (2001) *A Taxonomy for Learning, Teaching, and Assessing: A Revision of Bloom's Taxonomy of Educational Objectives*. New York: Longman.

Anning, A. and Edwards, A. (2010) Young children as learners. In L. Miller, C. Cable and G. Goodliff (Eds) (2010) *Supporting Children's Learning in the Early Years*. 2e. London: Routledge, pp. 77–101.

Aristotle (350 BCE) Metaphysics, Book 1 (trans. W. D. Ross). Available online at http://classics.mit.edu/Aristotle/metaphysics.html (accessed 30 June 2016).

Arnold, C. (2009) Understanding 'Together and Apart': A case study of Edward's explorations at nursery, *Early Years*. **29** (2): 119–130.

Ashcraft, M. H. (2006) *Cognition*. 3e. Upper Saddle River, NJ: Prentice-Hall.

Ashley, J. and Tomasello, M. (1998) Cooperative Problem-Solving and Teaching in Preschoolers. *Social Development*. **7** (2): 143–163.

Astington, J. W., Harris, P. L. and Olson, D. R. (1988) (Eds) *Developing Theories of Mind*. Cambridge: Cambridge University Press.

Athey, C. (2007) *Extending Thought in Young Children*. London: PCP.

Atkinson, J. (2000) *The Developing Visual Brain*. Oxford: Oxford University Press.

Audi, R. (1998) *Epistemology*. London: Routledge.

Axline, V. (1964) *Dibs: In search of self*. London: Pelican.

Ayer, A. J. (1940) *The Foundations of Empirical Knowledge*. London: Macmillan and Co., Ltd.

Ayer, A. J. (Ed.) (1959) *Logical Positivism*. New York: The Free Press.

Baddeley, A. D. (1992) Working Memory. *Science*. **255** (5044): 556–559.

Bae, B. (2009) Children's Right to Participate: Challenges in everyday interactions. *European Early Childhood Education Research Journal*. **17** (3): 391–406.

Bae, B. (2010) Realising Children's Right to Participation in Early Childhood Settings: Some critical issues in a Norwegian context. *Early Years*. **30** (3): 205–21.

Bailey, A. and Barnes, S. (2009) Where Do I Fit in? Children's spaces and places. In R. Eke, H. Butcher and M. Lee (2009) *Whose Childhood Is It?* London: Continuum, pp. 175–197.

Baillargeon, R. (2004) The Acquisition of Physical Knowledge in Infancy. In U. Goswami (Ed.) (2004) *Blackwell Handbook of Childhood Cognitive Development*. Oxford: Blackwell, pp. 47–83.

Bassey, M. (1990) On the Nature of Research in Education, Part One. *Research Intelligence*. BERA Newsletter No. 36. Summer: 35–38.

Bassey, M. (1999) *Case Study Research in Educational Settings*. Buckingham: Open University Press.

Belsky, J. (1990) Parental and Non-parental Childcare and Children's Socio-emotional Development: A decade in review. *Journal of Marriage and the Family*. **52** (4): 885–903.

Berlyne, D. E. (1954) A Theory of Human Curiosity. *British Journal of Psychology*. **54** (3): 180–191.

Biesta, G. (2007) Why 'What Works' Won't Work: Evidence-based practice and the democratic deficit in educational research. *Educational Theory*. **57** (1): 1–22.

Bjorklund, D. F. (Ed.) (1990) *Children's Strategies: Contemporary views of cognitive development*. Hillsdale, NJ: Lawrence Erlbaum Associates.

Bloom, B. S. (Ed.) (1956) *Taxonomy of Educational Objectives, the classification of educational goals – Handbook I: Cognitive Domain*. New York: McKay.

Blumer, H. (1969) *Social Interactionism: Perspective and method*. Englewood Cliffs, NJ: Prentice-Hall, Inc.

BonJour, L. (1985) *The Structure of Empirical Knowledge*. Cambridge, MA: Harvard University Press.

BonJour, L. (1998) *In Defense of Pure Reason*. Cambridge: Cambridge University Press.

Born, M. (1949) *Natural Philosophy of Cause and Chance*. Oxford: The Clarendon Press.

Bowlby, J. (1988) *A Secure Base*. London: Routledge.

Boyzatis, C. J. and Watson, M. W. (1993) Preschool Children's Symbolic Representation of Objects through Gestures. *Child Development*. **64** (3): 729–735.

Bridges, D. (1998) Research for Sale: Moral market or moral maze? *British Educational Research Journal*. **24** (5): 593–607.

Bridges, D. (2003) *Fiction Written Under Oath*? Dordrecht: Kluwer Academic Publishers.

Bridges, D. (2006) The Disciplines and Discipline of Educational Research. *Journal of Philosophy of Education*. **40** (2): 259–272.

Bridges, D., Smeyers, P. and Smith, R. (Eds) (2009) *Evidence-based Education Policy*. Chichester: Wiley Blackwell.

British Educational Research Association (BERA) (2011) *Ethical Guidelines for Educational Research*. London: British Educational Research Association.

Broadhead, P. (2001) Investigating Sociability and Cooperation in Four and Five Year Olds in Reception Class Settings. *International Journal of Early Years Education*. **9** (1): 23–35.

Bronson, M. B. (2000) *Self-Regulation in Early Childhood: Nature and nurture*. New York: Guilford.

Brookhart, S. M. (2010) *How to Assess Higher-Order Thinking Skills in Your Classroom*. Alexandria, VA: ASCD.

Brown, A. L. and Campione, J. C. (2002) Communities of learning and thinking or a context by any other name. In P. Woods (Ed.) (2002) *Contemporary Issues in Teaching and Learning*. London: Routledge, pp. 120–126.

Brown, A. L. and Kane, M. J. (1988) Preschool Children can Learn to Transfer: Learning to learn and learning from example. *Cognitive Psychology*. **20** (4): 493–523.

Brown, L. and Strega, S. (Eds) (2005) *Research as Resistance*. Toronto: Canadian Scholars' Press.
Bruner, J. S. (1961) The Act of Discovery. *Harvard Educational Review*. **31** (1): 21–32.
Bruner, J. S. (1966) *Toward a Theory of Instruction*. Cambridge, MA: Harvard University Press.
Bruner, J. S. and Olson, D. R. (1978) Symbols and Texts as Tools of Intellect. *Interchange*. **8** (4): 1–15.
Bruner, J., Olver, R. and Greenfield, P. (1967) *Studies in Cognitive Growth*. New York: John Wiley.
Bulotsky-Shearer, R. J., Bell, E. R., Romero, S. L. and Carter T. M. (2012) Preschool Interactive Peer Play Mediates Problem Behavior and Learning for Low-income Children. *Journal of Applied Developmental Psychology*. **33** (1): 53–65.
Burke, K. (1966) *Language and Symbolic Action*. Berkeley: University of California Press.
Byrnes, J. P. and Wasik, B. A. (1991). Role of Conceptual Knowledge in Mathematical Procedural Learning. *Developmental Psychology*. **27** (5): 777–786. DOI: 10.1037//0012-1649.27.5.777
Cannella, G. S. (2002) *Deconstructing Early Childhood Education*. New York: Peter Lang.
Carr, M. (2001) *Assessment in Early Childhood Settings*. London: Paul Chapman Publishing.
Carr, M. (2011) Young Children Reflecting on their Learning: Teachers' conversation strategies. *Early Years*. **31** (3): 257–270. DOI: 10.1080/09575146.2011.613805
Carr, W. and Kemmis, S. (1986) *Becoming Critical. Education, knowledge and action research*. Lewes: Falmer Press.
Carspecken, P. (1996) *Critical Ethnography in Educational Research*. London: Routledge.
Cartoon Network (2016) *Ben 10*. Available online at www.cartoonnetwork.co.uk/show/ben-10 (accessed 30 June 2016).
Chak, A. (2007) Teachers' and Parents' Conceptions of Children's Curiosity and Exploration. *International Journal of Early Years Education*. **15** (2): 141–159.
Charmaz, K. (2006) *Constructing Grounded Theory*. London: Sage.
Clark, A. (2010) *Transforming Children's Spaces*. London: Routledge.
Clark, A. and Moss, P. (2001) *Listening to Young Children*. London: National Children's Bureau.
Clore, G. C. and Palmer, J. (2009) Affective Guidance of Intelligent Agents: How emotion controls cognition. *Cognitive Systems Research*. **10** (1): 21–30.
Cobb-Moore, C., Danby, S. and Farrell, A. (2010) Locking the Unlockable: Children's invocation of pretence to define and manage place. *Childhood*. **17** (3): 376–395.
Conway, M. A. (2010) Memory. In J. M. Brown and E. A. Campbell (Eds) (2010). *The Cambridge Handbook of Forensic Psychology*. New York: Cambridge University Press, pp. 230–235.
Coon, D. and Mitterer, J. O. (2009) *Introduction to Psychology: Gateways to Mind and Behavior*. 12e. Belmont, CA: Wadsworth.
Cordova, D. and Lepper, M. (1996) Intrinsic Motivation and the Process of Learning: Beneficial effects of contextualization, personalization, and choice. *Journal of Educational Psychology*. **88** (4): 715–730.
Corsaro W. (2003) *We're Friends, Right? Inside kids' culture*. Washington, DC: Joseph Henry Press.
Corsaro, W. (2005) A *Sociology of Childhood*. 2e. Thousand Oaks, CA: Sage.
Cowan, N. (1988) Evolving Conceptions of Memory Storage, Selective Attention, and their Mutual Constraints within the Human Information Processing System. *Psychological Bulletin*. **104** (2): 163–191.
Cox, R. and Smitsman, A. (2006) Action Planning in Young Children's Tool Use. *Developmental Science*. **9** (6): 628–641.
Cox, S. and Robinson-Pant, A. (2010) Children as Researchers: A question of risk? In S. Cox, A. Robinson-Pant, C. Dyer and M. Schweisfurth (Eds) (2010) *Children as Decision Makers in Education*. London: Continuum, pp. 143–151.
Cox, S., Robinson-Pant, A., Dyer, C. and Schweisfurth, M. (Eds) (2010) *Children as Decision Makers in Education*. London: Continuum.
Craik, K. (1943) *The Nature of Explanation*. Cambridge: Cambridge University Press.
Creswell, J. (2008) *Educational Research*. 4e. Upper Saddle River, NJ: Pearson.
Creswell. J. (2013) *Qualitative Inquiry and Research Design*. 3e. Thousand Oaks, CA: Sage.
Csíkszentmihályi, M. (1990) *Flow: The psychology of optimal experience*. New York: Harper and Row.

Dahlberg, G. and Lenz Taguchi, H. (1994) *Förskola och skola och om visionen om en mötesplats*, [Preschool and school and the vision of a meeting-place]. Stockholm: HLS Förlag.

Dahlberg, G. and Moss, P. (2005) *Ethics and Politics in Early Childhood Education*. London: Routledge.

Dahlberg, G. and Moss, P. (2006) Introduction: Our Reggio Emilia. In C. Rinaldi (2006) *In Dialogue with Reggio Emilia: Listening, researching and learning*. London: Routledge, pp. 1–22.

Dahlberg, G., Moss, P. and Pence, A. (1999) *Beyond Quality in Early Childhood Education and Care*. London: Routledge.

Damasio, A. (2006) *Descartes' Error: Emotion, reason and the human brain*. London: Vintage.

Davies, M. and Stone, T. (1995) *Folk Psychology*. Oxford: Blackwell.

Deci, E. L. and Ryan, R. M. (1987) The Support of Autonomy and the Control of Behavior. *Journal of Personality and Social Psychology*. **53** (6): 1024–1037.

Delbecq, A. L. and Van de Ven, A. H. (1971) A Group Process Model for Problem Identification and Program Planning. *Journal of Applied Behavioral Science*. **VII** (July/August, 1971): 466–491.

DeLoache, J. S. (1989) The Development of Representation in Young Children. *Advances in Child Development and Behavior*. **22**: 1–40.

DeLoache, J. S., Miller, K. F. and Pierroutsakos, S. L. (1998) Reasoning and problem solving. In D. Kuhn and R. Siegler (Eds), *Handbook of Child Psychology. Vol. 2: Cognition, perception and language*. 5e. New York: Wiley, pp. 801–850.

Denham, S. A., Blair, K. A., Demulder, E., Levitas, J., Sawyer, K. and Auerbach-Major, S. (2003) Preschool Emotional Competence: Pathway to social competence? *Child Development*. **74** (1): 238–256.

Department for Business, Innovation and Skills (DBIS) (2011) *Innovation and Research Strategy for Growth*. London: Department for Business, Innovation and Skills.

Department for Business, Innovation and Skills (2012) *Innovation*. Available online at www.bis.gov.uk/innovation (accessed 30 June 2016).

Department for Children, Schools and Families (DCSF) (2008) *The Early Years Foundation Stage*. Annesley: Department for Children, Schools and Families.

Department for Education (DfE) (2010) *The Importance of Teaching*. London: Department for Education. Available online at www.gov.uk/government/uploads/system/uploads/attachment_data/file/175429/CM-7980.pdf (accessed 30 June 2016).

Department for Education (DfE) (2012) *Statutory Framework for the Early Years Foundation Stage*. London: Department for Education. Available online at http://webarchive.nationalarchives.gov.uk/20130401151715/https://www.education.gov.uk/publications/standard/allpublications/page1/dfe-00023-2012 (accessed 30 June 2016).

Department for Education and Employment (DfEE) and Qualifications and Curriculum Authority (QCA) (1999) *The National Curriculum*. London: Department for Education and Employment and Qualifications and Curriculum Authority.

Descartes, R. (1637) [2008] *Discourse on the Method*. Available online at www.gutenberg.org/files/59/59-h/59-h.htm (accessed 30 June 2016).

Dew, J. K. and Foreman, M. W. (2014) *How Do We Know? An introduction to epistemology*. Downers Grove, IL: InterVarsity Press.

Dewey, J. (1916) [1966] *Democracy and Education. An introduction to the philosophy of education*. New York: Free Press.

Dickstein, S. and Parke, R. (1988) Social Referencing in Infancy: A glance at fathers and marriage. *Child Development*. **59** (2): 506–511.

Donaldson, M. (1978) *Children's Minds*. New York: W.W. Norton & Co.

Drew, C. J. (1980) *Introduction to Designing and Conducting Research*. St. Louis, MI: Mosby.

Dudek, M. (Ed.) (2005) *Children's Spaces*. Oxford: Architectural Press.

Durkheim, E. (1915) *The Elementary Forms of the Religious Life* (trans. J. W. Swain). London: George Allen and Unwin Ltd.

Dweck, C. S. and Leggett, E. L. (1988) A Social-cognitive Approach to Motivation and Personality. *Psychological Review*. **95** (2): 256–273.

Dyson, A. H. (1997) *Writing Superheroes: Contemporary childhood, popular culture, and classroom literacy*. New York: Teachers' College Press.

Edmiston, B. (2008) *Forming Ethical Identities in Early Childhood Play*. London: Routledge.

Edwards, A. (2010) Qualitative Designs and Analysis. In G. MacNaughton, S. A. Rolfe and I. Siraj-Blatchford (Eds) (2010) *Doing Early Childhood Research*. 2e. Maidenhead: Open University Press/ McGraw-Hill, pp. 155–176.

Edwards, A., Sebba, J. and Rickinson, M. (2007) User Engagement in Research: Implications for research design. *British Educational Research Journal*. **33** (5): 647–661

Edwards, C. (1998) Partner, Nurturer, and Guide: The role of the teacher. In C. Edwards, L. Gandini and G. Forman (Eds) (1998) *The Hundred Languages of Children*. Westport, CT: Ablex, pp. 179–198.

Edwards, C., Gandini, L. and Forman, G. (Eds) (1998) *The Hundred Languages of Children*. Westport, CT: Ablex Publishing.

Einarsdóttir, J. (2011) Reconstructing Playschool Experiences. *European Early Childhood Education Research Journal*. **19** (3): 387–402. DOI: 10.1080/1350293X.2011.597970

Eisele, P. (2003) Groups, Group Members and Individual Decision Processes: The effects of decision strategy, social interaction style and reception of decision-threatening information on post-decision processes. *Scandinavian Journal of Psychology*. **44** (5): 467–477.

Eisenberg, N., Fabes, R. A., Guthrie, I. K. and Reiser, M. (2000). Dispositional Emotionality and Regulation: Their role in predicting quality of social functioning. *Journal of Personality and Social Psychology*. **78** (1): 136–157.

Else, P. (2009) *The Value of Play*. London: Continuum.

Ennew, J. (2008) Children as 'Citizens' of the United Nations. In A. Invernizzi and J. Williams (Eds) (2008) *Children and Citizenship*. London: Sage, pp. 66–78.

Epley, N., Waytz, A., Akalis, S. and Cacioppo, J. T. (2008) When we Need a Human: Motivational determinants of anthropomorphism. *Social Cognition*. **26** (2): 143–155.

Fantz, R. L. (1961) The Origin of Form Perception. *Scientific American*. **204** (5): 66–72.

Fantz, R. L. (1965) Visual Perception from Birth as Shown by Pattern Selectivity. In H. E. Whipple (Ed.) New Issues in Infant Development. *Annals of New York Academy of Science*. **118**: 793–814.

Fernyhough, C. (2010) *The Baby in the Mirror: A Child's World from Birth to Three*. London: Granta Publications.

Feuer, M. J., Towne, L. and Shavelson, R. J. (2002) Scientific Culture and Educational Research. *Educational Researcher*. **31** (8): 4–14.

Feyerabend, P. (1993) *Against Method*. London: Verso.

Field, T. (2007) *The Amazing Infant*. Malden, MA: Blackwell.

Fielding, M. (2001) Students as Radical Agents of Change. *Journal of Educational Change*. **2** (2): 123–141.

Fielding, M. and Moss, P. (2011) *Radical Education and the Common School: A democratic alternative*. London: Routledge

Fisher, K. R., Hirsh-Pasek, K., Golinkoff, R. M. and Gryfe, S. G. (2008) Conceptual Split? Parents' and experts' perceptions of play in the 21st century. *Journal of Applied Developmental Psychology*. **29** (4): 305–316. DOI: 10.1016/j.appdev.2008.04.006.

Flavell, J. H. (1976) Metacognitive Aspects of Problem Solving. In L. B. Resnick (Ed.) *The nature of intelligence*. Hillsdale, NJ: Lawrence Erlbaum, pp. 231–236.

Flavell, J. H. (1979) Metacognition and Cognitive Monitoring: A new area of cognitive-developmental inquiry. *American Psychologist*. **34** (10): 906–911.

Flavell, J. H., Green, F., Flavell, E. and Grossman, J. (1997) The Development of Children's Knowledge of Inner Speech. *Child Development*. **68** (1): 39–47.

Fleet, A. and Britt, C. (2011) Seeing Spaces, Inhabiting Places. In D. Harcourt, B. Perry and T. Waller (Eds) *Researching Young Children's Perspectives*. London: Routledge, pp. 142–162.

Fontanesci, G., Gandini, L. and Soncini, M. (1998) The Voice of Parents. In C. Edwards, L. Gandini and G. Forman (Eds) (1998) *The Hundred Languages of Children*. Westport, CT: Ablex, pp. 149–160.

Foreman-Peck, L. and Murray, J. (2008) Action Research and Policy. *Journal of Philosophy of Education.* **42** (S1): 87–119.

Forman, G. (1982) *Action and Thought: From sensorimotor schemes to symbolic operations.* New York: Academic Press.

Forman, G. (2006) Constructive Play. In D. P. Fromberg and D. Bergen (Eds) (2006) *Play from Birth to Twelve.* London: Routledge, pp. 103–110.

Formosinho, J. and Oliveira Formosinho, J. (2012) Towards a Social Science of the Social: The contribution of praxeological research. *European Early Childhood Education Research Journal.* **20** (4): 591–606. DOI: 10.1080/1350293X.2012.737237

Forrester, J. (1975) Counter-intuitive Behavior of Social Systems. In J. W. Forrester (1975) *Collected Papers of J. W. Forrester.* Cambridge, MA: Wright-Allen Press Inc., pp. 211–244.

Freire, P. (1972) *Pedagogy of the Oppressed.* Harmondsworth: Penguin.

Froebel, F. (1826) *On the Education of Man.* Keilhau/Leipzig: Wienbrach.

Fumerton, E. (2010) *Foundationalist Theories of Epistemic Justification.* Available online at http://plato.stanford.edu/entries/justep-foundational/ (accessed 30 June 2016).

Fumoto, H., Robson, R., Greenfield, S. and Hargreaves, D. (2012) *Young Children's Creative Thinking.* London: Sage.

Galinsky, E. (2010) *Mind in the Making.* New York: Harper Collins.

Gallas, K. (1994) *The Languages of Learning: How children talk, write, dance, draw, and sing their understanding of the world.* New York: Teachers' College Press.

Gallo, A. (2003). The Fifth Vital Sign: Implementation of the neonatal infant pain scale. *Journal of Obstetric, Gynecologic, and Neonatal Nursing,* **32** (2): 199–206.

Gammage, P. (1999) The Once and Future Child. *European Early Childhood Education Research Journal.* **7** (2): 103–117.

Gammage, P. (2002) Early Childhood Education and Care Vade Mecum for 2002. *Early Years.* **22** (2): 185–188. DOI: 10.1080/09575140220000012048

Gammage, P. (2006) Early Childhood Education and Care: Politics, policies and possibilities. *Early Years.* **26** (3): 235–248.

Garner, B. P. and Bergen. D. (2006) Play Development from Birth to Age Four. In D. P. Fromberg and D. Bergen (Eds) (2006) *Play from Birth to Twelve.* London: Routledge, pp. 3–11.

Garvey, C. (1991) *Play.* London: Fontana Press.

Gaut, B. and Gaut, M. (2012) *Philosophy for Young Children.* London: Routledge.

Gerhardt, S. (2015) *Why Love Matters: How affection shapes a baby's brain.* London: Brunner-Routledge.

Gettier, P. (1963) Is Justified True Belief Knowledge? *Analysis.* **23** (6): 121–123.

Gibbons, M., Limoges, C., Nowotny, H., Schwartzman, S., Scott, P. and Trow, M. (1994) *The New Production of Knowledge.* London: Sage.

Giddens, A. (1984) *The Constitution of Society.* Berkeley: University of California Press.

Glaser, B. and Strauss, A. L. (1967) *The Discovery of Grounded Theory: Strategies for qualitative research.* New York: Aldine.

Goddard Blythe, S. (2011) *The Genius of Natural Childhood.* Stroud: Hawthorn Press.

Goldacre, B. (2013) *Building Evidence into Education.* Available online at http://media.education.gov.uk/assets/files/pdf/b/ben%20goldacre%20paper.pdf (accessed 30 June 2016).

Goldschmied, E. and Jackson, S. (2004) *People Under Three.* London: Routledge.

Göncü, A. (1993) Development of Intersubjectivity in Social Pretend Play. *Human Development.* **36** (4): 185–198.

Goouch, K. and Lambirth, A. (2011) *Teaching Early Reading and Phonics.* London: Sage.

Gopnik, A. (1996) The Scientist as Child. *Philosophy of Science.* **63** (4): 485–514.

Gopnik, A. (2009) *The Philosophical Baby.* New York: Farrar, Straus and Giroux.

Gopnik, A., Mektzoff, A. N. and Kuhl, P. (1999) *How Babies Think.* London: Weidenfeld and Nicolson.

Goswami, U. (1991). Analogical Reasoning: What develops? A review of research and theory. *Child Development.* **62**: 1–22.

Goswami, U. (1992) *Analogical Reasoning in Children.* Hove: Psychology Press.

Goswami, U. (2007) Analogical Reasoning in Children. In J. C. Campione, K. Metz and S. Palinscar (Eds) *Children's Learning in Laboratory and Classroom.* London: Routledge, pp. 55–70.

Gray, D., Goldstein, H. and Thomas, S. (2004) Of Trends and Trajectories: Searching for patterns in school improvement. *British Educational Research Journal.* **29** (1): 83–88.

Gray, H. M., Gray, K. and Wegner, D. M. (2007) Dimensions of Mind Perception. *Science.* **315** (5812): 619.

Griffiths, M. (1998) *Educational Research for Social Justice.* Buckingham: Open University Press.

Griffiths, M. and MacLeod, G. (2008) Personal Narratives and Policy. *Journal of Philosophy of Education.* **42** (S1): 121–143.

Guba, E.G. and Lincoln, Y. (1989) *Fourth Generation Evaluation.* Newbury Park, CA: Sage.

Gura, P. (1992) Developmental Aspects of Blockplay. In P. Gura (Ed.) *Exploring Learning.* London: Paul Chapman.

Gussin Paley, V. (2004) *A Child's Work: The importance of fantasy play.* Chicago: Chicago University Press.

Habermas, J. (1984) *The Theory of Communicative Action.* Cambridge: Polity Press.

Habermas, J. (1987) *Knowledge and Human Interests.* Cambridge: Polity Press/Oxford: Blackwell.

Hansson, S. O. (1994) *Decision Theory: A brief introduction.* Stockholm: Royal Institute of Technology. Available online at http://home.abe.kth.se/~soh/decisiontheory.pdf (accessed 30 June 2016).

Harcourt, D., Perry, B. and Waller, T. (Eds) (2011) *Researching Young Children's Perspectives: Debating the ethics and dilemmas of educational research with children.* London: Routledge.

Hardman, C. (1973) Can there Be an Anthropology of Children? *Journal of the Anthropology Society of Oxford.* **4** (1): 85–99.

Hargraves, V. (2014) Children's Theorising about their World: Exploring the practitioner's role. *Australasian Journal of Early Childhood.* **39** (1): 30–37.

Hargreaves, D. (1996) *Teaching as a Research-Based Profession: Possibilities and prospects. Teacher Training Agency Annual Lecture.* London: Teacher Training Agency.

Harlen, W. (1994) Developing Public Understanding of Education: A role for educational researchers. *British Educational Research Journal.* **20** (1): 3–16.

Hatch, J. A. (1995) Studying Childhood as a Cultural Invention. In J. A. Hatch (Ed.) *Qualitative Research in Early Childhood Settings.* Westport, CT: Praeger, pp. 117–133.

Hatch, J. A. (2007) Back to Modernity? Early childhood qualitative research in the 21st century. In J. A. Hatch (Ed.) (2007) *Early Childhood Qualitative Research.* London: Routledge, pp. 7–24.

Hedges, H. (2014) Young Children's 'Working Theories': Building and connecting understandings. *Journal of Early Childhood Research.* **12** (1): 35–49.

Heidegger, M. (1962) *Being and Time.* New York: HarperCollins.

Hekman, S. (1990) *Gender and Knowledge: Elements of a postmodern feminism.* Cambridge: Polity Press.

Helm, J. H. and Katz, L. (2001) *Young Investigators.* New York: Teachers' College Press.

Hetherington, S. (2009) The Gettier Problem. In S. Bernecker and D. Pritchard (Eds) *The Routledge Companion to Epistemology.* New York: Routledge, pp. 119–130.

Hillage, J., Pearson, R., Anderson, A. and Tamkin, P. (1998) *Excellence in Research on Schools.* London: Department for Education and Employment.

Holyoak, K. J. and Thagard, P. (1995) *Mental Leaps.* Cambridge, MA: MIT Press.

Hoyuelos, A. (2004) A Pedagogy of Transgression. *Children in Europe.* **6**: 6–7.

Hughes, B. (2002) *A Playworker's Taxonomy of Play Types.* UK: PLAYLINK.

Hughes, M. M. (1979) Exploration and Play Revisited: A hierarchical analysis. *International Journal of Behavioural Development.* **2** (3): 215–24.

Hughes, P. (2010) Paradigms, Methods and Knowledge. In G. MacNaughton, S. A. Rolfe and I. Siraj-Blatchford (Eds) (2010) *Doing Early Childhood Research.* 2e. Maidenhead: Open University Press/McGraw-Hill, pp. 35–62.

Hume, D. (1739/1896) *A Treatise of Human Nature* (ed. L. A. Selby-Bigge). Oxford: Clarendon Press.

Hume, D. (1748) An Enquiry Concerning Human Understanding. In T. Beauchamp (Ed.) (2000) *David Hume: An enquiry concerning human understanding.* Oxford: Oxford University Press, pp. 5–123.

Hutt, C. (1979) Play in the Under 5s: Form, development and function. In J. G. Howells (Ed.) *Modern Perspectives in the Psychiatry of Infancy*. New York: Brunner/Mazel Publishers.

Hutt, C., Tyler, S., Hutt, C. and Christopherson, H. (1989) *Play, Exploration and Learning*. London: Routledge.

Invernizzi, A. and Williams, J. (2008) Constructions of Childhood and Children's Experiences. In A. Invernizzi and J. Williams (Eds) (2008) *Children and Citizenship*. London: Sage, pp. 79–83.

Isaacs, N. (1944) Children's 'Why' Questions. In S. Isaacs and N. Isaacs (1944) *Intellectual Growth in Young Children*. London: Routledge, pp. 291–354.

Isaacs, S. (1929) *The Nursery Years*. London: Routledge.

Isaacs, S. and Isaacs, N. (1944) *Intellectual Growth in Young Children and Children's 'Why' Questions*. London: Routledge.

James, A. and James, A. (2008) *Key Concepts in Childhood Studies*. London: Sage.

James, A., Jenks, C. and Prout, A. (1998) *Theorising Childhood*. Cambridge: Polity Press.

James, A. and Prout, A. (Eds) (1997) *Constructing and Reconstructing Childhood*. 2e. London: Falmer Books.

James, W. (1890) *The Principles of Psychology*. New York: Dover.

Jenks, C. (2005) *Childhood*. London: Routledge.

Johansson, E. (2009) 'Doing the Right Thing': A moral concern from the perspectives of young preschool children. In D. Berthelson, J. Brownlee and E. Johansson (Eds) (2009) *Participatory Learning in the Early Years*. London: Routledge, pp. 44–60.

Johnson, J. (2006) Play Development from Ages Four to Eight. In D. P. Fromberg and D. Bergen (Eds) (2006) *Play from Birth to Twelve*. London: Routledge, pp. 13–20.

Johnson-Laird, P. N. (1983) *Mental Models: Towards a cognitive science of language, inference and consciousness*. Cambridge: Cambridge University Press.

Johnson-Laird, P. N. and Byrne, R. M. J. (1991) *Deduction*. Hillsdale, NJ: Lawrence Erlbaum Associates.

Johnson-Laird, P. and Shafir, E. (1993) The Interaction between Reasoning and Decision-making: An introduction. *Cognition*. **49** (1/2): 1–9.

Jones, P. and Welch, S. (2010) *Rethinking Children's Rights*. London: Continuum.

Kahneman, D. and Tversky, A. (1979) Prospect Theory: An analysis of decisions under risk. *Econometrica*. **47** (2): 263–291.

Kahneman, D., Slovic, P. and Tversky, A. (1982) *Judgment Under Uncertainty: Heuristics and biases*. New York: Cambridge University Press.

Kant, I. (1787) *The Critique of Pure Reason*. Prepared in e-text by C. Aldarondo (2003) Project Gutenberg. Available online at www.gutenberg.org/dirs/etext03/cprrn10.txt (accessed 30 June 2016).

Katz, L. (1994) *The Project Approach*. ERIC Digest. Champaign, IL: ERIC Clearinghouse on Elementary and Early Childhood Education. ED 368 509. Available online at www.ericdigests.org/1994/project.htm (accessed 30 June 2016).

Karpov, Y. V. (2005) *The Neo-Vygotskian Approach to Child Development*. Cambridge: Cambridge University Press.

Kaufman, P. (1998) Poppies and the Dance of World Making. In C. Edwards, L. Gandini and G. Forman (Eds) (1998) *The Hundred Languages of Children*. Westport, CT: Ablex, pp. 285–289.

Keen, R. (2011) The Development of Problem Solving in Young Children: A critical cognitive skill. *Annual Review of Psychology*. **62**: 1–21.

Kelley, D. (1991) Evidence and Justification. *Reason Papers*. **16**: 165–179.

Kemmis, S. and McTaggart, R. (2005) Participatory Action Research: Communicative action and the public sphere In N. Denzin and Y. Lincoln (Eds) (2005) *Handbook of Qualitative Research*. 3e. Beverly Hills, CA: Sage, pp. 559–603.

Kerlinger, F. N. (1973) *Foundations of Behavioural Research*. New York: Holt, Rinehart and Winston.

King, D. L. (1966) A review and interpretation of some aspects of the infant–mother relationship in mammals and birds. *Psychological Bulletin*. **65** (3): 143–155.

Klein, H. and D'Esposito, M. (2007) Neurocognitive Inefficacy of the Strategy Process. *Annals of the New York Academy of Sciences*. **1118**: 163–185.

Klentschy, M. P. (2008) *Using Science Notebooks in Elementary Classrooms*. Arlington, VA: National Science Teachers' Association.

Knauff, M. (2007) How our Brains Reason Logically. *Topoi*. **26**: 19–36.

Kohlberg, L. (1984) *The Psychology of Moral Development*. San Francisco: Harper and Row.

Kuhn, T. (1970) *The Structure of Scientific Revolutions*. Chicago: Chicago University Press.

Kyrönlampi-Kylmänen, T. and Määttä, K. (2011) What is it Like to Be at Home: The experiences of five- to seven-year-old Finnish children. *Early Child Development and Care*. **182** (1): 71–86. DOI: 10.1080/03004430.2010.540013.

Laevers, F. (Ed.) (1994) *Defining and Assessing Quality in Early Childhood Education*. Studia Paedagogica. Leuven: Leuven University Press.

Laevers, F. (2000) Forward to Basics! Deep-level-learning and the experiential approach. *Early Years. An International Journal of Research and Development*. **20** (2): 20–29.

Laevers, F. (2005) *Deep-level-learning and the Experiential Approach in Early Childhood and Primary Education*. Leuven: Research Centre for Early Childhood and Primary Education.

Lane, J. D., Wellman, H. M. and Evans, E. M. (2010) Children's Understanding of Ordinary and Extraordinary Minds. *Child Development*. **81** (5): 1475–148.

Langsted, O. (1994) Looking at Quality from the Child's Perspective. In P. Moss and A. Pence (Eds) (1994) *Valuing Quality in Early Childhood Services: New approaches to defining quality*. London: Paul Chapman.

Lansdown, G. (2005) *The Evolving Capacities of Children: Implications for the exercise of rights*. Florence: UNICEF Innocenti Research Centre.

Lansdown, G. (2010) The Realisation of Children's Participation Rights. In B. Percy-Smith and N. Thomas (Eds) (2010) *A Handbook of Children and Young People's Participation*. London: Routledge, pp. 11–23.

Lash, M. (2008) Classroom Community and Peer Culture in Kindergarten. *Early Childhood Education Journal*. **36** (1): 33–38.

Lee, L. (2009) Young American Immigrant Children's Interpretations of Popular Culture: A case study of Korean girls' perspectives on royalty in Disney films. *Journal of Early Childhood Research*. **7** (2): 200–215.

Lees, L. (1999) Critical Geography and the Opening up of the Academy: Lessons from 'real life' attempts. *Area*. **31** (4): 377–383.

Lehmann, E. L. (1950) Some Principles of the Theory of Testing Hypotheses. *The Annals of Mathematical Statistics*. **21** (1): 1–26.

Lehmann, E. L. (1957) A Theory of Some Multiple Decision Problems. *The Annals of Mathematical Statistics*. **28** (1): 1–25.

Leslie, A. (1987) Pretense and Representation: The origins of 'theory of mind'. *Psychological Review*. **94** (4): 412–426.

Levin, I. P. and Hart, S. (2003) Risk Preferences in Young Children: Early evidence of individual differences in reaction to potential gains and losses. *Journal of Behavioral Decision Making*. **16** (5): 397–341.

Levinas, E. (1980) *Totality and Infinity: An essay on exteriority*. Dordrecht: Kluwer Academic Publishers.

Lewars, J. (2010) *Nil Desperandum* as long as you *Carpe Diem*. In B. Percy-Smith and N. Thomas (Eds) (2010) *A Handbook of Children and Young People's Participation*. London: Routledge, pp. 270–276.

Lillard, A. (2001) Explaining the Connection: Pretend play and theory of mind. In S. Reifel (Ed.) (2001) *Theory in Context and Out*. Westport, CA: Ablex Publishing, pp. 173–177.

Löfdahl, A. and Hägglund, S. (2006) Spaces of Participation in Pre-School: Arenas for establishing power orders? *Children and Society*. **21**: 328–338.

Lovatt, D. and Hedges, H. (2015) Children's Working Theories: Invoking disequilibrium. *Early Child Development and Care*. **185** (6): 909–925, DOI: 10.1080/03004430.2014.967688

Lowrie, T. (2002) Designing a Framework for Problem Posing: Young children generating open-ended tasks. *Contemporary Issues in Early Childhood*. **3** (3): 354–364.

Luper, S. (2004) *Essential Knowledge: Readings in epistemology*. New York and Oxford: Pearson Longman.

Lyotard, J-F. (1992) *Phenomenology*. Paris: Presses Universitaires de France.

Macintyre, C. (2001) *Enhancing Learning through Play*. London: David Fulton.

McClelland, M. M., Acock, A. C., Piccinin, A., Rhea, S. A. and Stallings, M. C. (2013) Relations between Preschool Attention Span-persistence and Age 25 Educational Outcomes. *Early Childhood Research Quarterly*. **28** (2): 314–324.

McGinley, B. and Grieve, A. (2010) Maintaining the Status Quo? In B. Percy-Smith and N. Thomas (Eds) (2010) *A Handbook of Children and Young People's Participation*. London: Routledge, pp. 254–261.

McLain, D. L. (2014) Sensitivity to Social Information, Social Referencing, and Safety Attitudes in a Hazardous Occupation. *Journal of Occupational Health Psychology*. **19** (4): 425–436. Available online at http://dx.doi.org/10.1037/a0037126 (accessed 20 November 2016).

McNiff, J. (2010) *Action Research for Professional Development*. Dorset: September Books. Available online at www.septemberbooks.com/actionresearchforprofessionaldevelopment.asp (accessed 30 June 2016).

Magnussen, S. and Palinscar, A. (2006) The Application of Theory to the Design of Innovative Texts Supporting Science Instruction. In M. Constas and R. Sternberg (Eds) (2006) *Translating Theory and Research into Educational Practice*. Mahwah, NJ: Lawrence Erlbaum Associates, pp. 31–52.

Malaguzzi, L. (1993) For an Education Based on Relationships. *Young Children*. **49** (1): 9–12.

Malaguzzi, L. (1996) The Right to Environment. In T. Filippini and V. Vecchi (Eds) (1996) *The Hundred Languages of Children: The exhibit*. Reggio Emilia: Reggio Children.

Malaguzzi, L. (1998a) History, Ideas and Basic Philosophy. In C. Edwards, L. Gandini and G. Forman (1998) *The Hundred Languages of Children: The Reggio Emilia Approach Advanced Reflections*. Westport, CT: Ablex Publishing, pp. 49–98.

Malaguzzi, L. (1998b) The Hundred Languages of Children. In C. Edwards, L. Gandini and G. Forman (Eds) (1998) *The Hundred Languages of Children*. Westport, CT: Ablex Publishing, pp. 2–3.

Manning-Morton, J. and Thorp, J. (2003) *Key Times for Play*. Maidenhead: Open University Press and McGraw-Hill Education.

Market Research Society (MRS) (2012) *Occupation Groupings*. London: Market Research Society Available online at www.mrs.org.uk/publications/publications.htm (accessed 30 June 2016).

Marks, L. F. (1978) *The Unity of the Senses: Interrelations among the modalities*. New York: Academic Press.

Markström, A. and Halldèn, G. (2009) Children's Strategies for Agency in Preschool. *Children in Society*. **23** (2): 112–122.

Marsh, J. (2000) 'But I Want to Fly Too!': Girls and superhero play in the infant classroom. *Gender and Education*. **12** (2): 209–220.

Mayall, B. (2006) Values and Assumptions Underpinning Policy for Children and Young People in England. *Children's Geographies*. **4** (1): 9–17.

Meade, A. and Cubey, P. (2008) *Thinking Children: Learning about schemas*. Maidenhead: McGraw-Hill and Open University Press.

Meadows, S. (2006) *The Child as Thinker*. London: Routledge.

Meins, E., Fernyhough, C., Johnson, F. and Lidstone, J. (2006) Mind-mindedness in Children: Individual differences in internal state-talk in middle childhood. *British Journal of Developmental Psychology*. **24** (1): 189–196.

Melion, W. S., Rothstein, B. and Weemans, M. (2014) *The Anthropomorphic Lens*. Leiden: Brill Academic Publishers.

Meltzoff, A. N. (1995) Understanding the Intentions of Others: Re-enactment of intended acts by 18-month-old children. *Developmental Psychology*. **31** (5): 838–850.

Meltzoff, A. N. (2011) Social Cognition and the Origins of Imitation, Empathy and Theory of Mind. In U. Goswami (Ed.) (2011) *The Wiley-Blackwell Handbook of Childhood Cognitive Development*. 2e. Malden, MA: Wiley-Blackwell, pp. 49–75.

Meltzoff, A. N. and Prinz, W. (Eds) (2002) *The Imitative Mind: Development, evolution, and brain bases*. Cambridge: Cambridge University Press.

Mensch, J. (2011) Intuition and Nature in Kant and Goethe. *European Journal of Philosophy*. **19** (3): 431–453.

Merleau-Ponty, M. (2002) *Phenomenology of Perception*. London: Routledge.

Metcalfe, M. (2007) Problem Conceptualisation Using Idea Networks. *Systematic Practice and Action Research*. **20** (2): 141–150.

Michail, S. and Kellett M. (2013) Child-led Research in the Context of Australian Social Welfare Practice. *Child and Family Social Work*. **20** (4): 377–508.

Mitra, S. and Rana, V. (2001) Children and the Internet: Experiments with minimally invasive education in India. *The British Journal of Educational Technology*. **32** (2): 221–232.

Montessori, M. (1916) *The Montessori Method*. New York: Schocken Books.

Moore, K. and Meltzoff, A. N. (2008) Factors Affecting Infants' Manual Search for Occluded Objects and the Genesis of Object Permanence. *Infant Behavior and Development*. **31** (2): 168–180.

Morgenthaler, S. K. (2006) The Meanings in Play with Objects. In D. Fromberg and D. Bergen (Eds) (2006) *Play from Birth to Twelve*. London: Routledge, pp. 65–73.

Morrow, V. (2008) Dilemmas in Children's Participation in England. In A. Invernizzi and J. Williams (Eds) (2008) *Children and Citizenship*. London: Sage, pp. 120–130.

Moss, P. and Petrie, P. (2002) *From Children's Services to Children's Spaces*. London: Routledge.

Moyles, J., Adams, S. and Musgrove, A. (2002) *Study of Pedagogical Effectiveness in Early Learning* (SPEEL). London: Department for Education and Skills.

Murray, J. (2012) Young Children's Explorations: Young children's research? *Early Child Development and Care*. **182** (9): 1209–1225. DOI: 10.1080/03004430.2011.604728

Murray, J. M. (2013) Young Children's Research Behaviour? Children aged four to eight years finding solutions at home and at school. *Early Child Development and Care*. **183** (7/8): 1147–1165.

Murray, J. (2014) Researching Young Children's Worlds. In T. Waller and G. Davis (Eds) (2014) *An Introduction to Early Childhood*. 3e. London: Sage, pp. 325–345.

Murray, J. (2015a) Can Young Children be Researchers? In H. McLaughlin (Ed.) (2015) *Children and Young People's Participation in Policy, Practice and Research*. London: National Children's Bureau, pp. 48–63.

Murray, J. (2015b) Young Children As Researchers in Play. In J. Moyles (Ed.) (2015) *The Excellence of Play*. 4e. Maidenhead: McGraw-Hill Education, pp. 106–124.

Murray, J. (2016) Young Children are Researchers: Children aged 4–8 years engage in important research behaviour when they base decisions on evidence. *European Early Childhood Education Research Journal*. **24** (5): 705–720. Available online at http://dx.doi.org/10.1080/1350293X.2016.1213565 (accessed 22 November 2016).

Murray, J. (2017, in production) Welcome In! How the academy can warrant recognition of young children as researchers. *European Early Childhood Education Research Journal*. **25** (2).

Napier, N. and Sharkey, A. (2004) Play. In D. Wyse (2004) *Childhood Studies*. Oxford: Blackwell, pp. 149–152.

National Playing Fields Association, Children's Play Council and Playlink (2000) *Best Play. What play provision should do for children*. London: National Playing Fields Association.

Nelissen, J. M. C. and Tomic, W. (1996) *Representation and Cognition*. Heerlen: Open University.

Nelson, R. (2012) *Self-Improvement Guide: The art of solving problems*. Raleigh, NC: Lulu Publications.

Newson, J. and Newson, E. (1979) *Toys and Playthings*. New York: Pantheon Books.

Norris, C. (2000) McDowell on Kant: Redrawing the bounds of sense. *Metaphilosophy*. **31** (4): 382–411.

Norwegian Ministry of Education and Research (2006) *Kindergarten Act. 2006*. Oslo: Norwegian Ministry of Education and Research.

Nutbrown, C. (1999) *Threads of Thinking: Young children learning and the role of early education*. London: PCP.

Oancea, A. and Pring, R. (2008) The Importance of Being Thorough: On systematic accumulations of 'what works' in educational research. *Journal of Philosophy of Education*. **42** (S1): 15–40.

Oancea, A. and Pring, R. (2009) The Importance of Being Thorough: On systematic accumulations of 'what works' in educational research. In D. Bridges, P. Smeyers and R. Smith (Eds) (2009) *Evidence-based Education Policy*. Chichester: Wiley Blackwell, pp. 11–35.

Office of the High Commissioner for Human Rights (OHCHR) (1989) *The United Nations Convention on the Rights of the Child*. Available online at www.ohchr.org/Documents/ProfessionalInterest/crc.pdf (accessed 30 June 2016).

Office of the High Commissioner on Human Rights (OHCHR) (2005) *Convention on the Rights of the Child: General Comment No. 7. Implementing child rights in early childhood*. Geneva: United Nations. Available online at www2.ohchr.org/english/bodies/crc/docs/AdvanceVersions/GeneralComment7Rev1.pdf (accessed 30 June 2016).

Oliver, R. and Oliver, H. (1997) Using Context to Promote Learning from Information-Seeking Tasks. *Journal of the American Society for Information Science*. **48** (6): 519–526.

Papert, S. (1993) *The Children's Machine*. New York: Basic Books.

Pascal, C. and Bertram, T. (2012) Praxis, Ethics and Power: Developing praxeology as a participatory paradigm for early childhood research. *European Early Childhood Education Research Journal*. **20** (4): 477–492. DOI: 10.1080/1350293X.2012.737236

Pascal, C., Bertram, A. D., Ramsden, F., Georgeson, J., Saunders, M. and Mould, C. (1996) *Evaluating and Developing Quality in Early Childhood Settings: A professional development programme*. Worcester: Amber Publications.

Payton, O. D. (1979). *Research: The validation of clinical practice*. Philadelphia: F. A. Davis.

Pellegrini, A. D., Symons, F. J. and Hoch, J. (2004) *Observing Children in their Natural Worlds*. Mahwah, NJ: Lawrence Erlbaum Associates.

Pells, K. (2010) 'No-one Ever Listens to Us'. In B. Percy-Smith and N. Thomas (Eds) (2010) *A Handbook of Children and Young People's Participation*. London: Routledge, pp. 196–203.

Penn State LeHigh Valley (2016) *Biology 110 Laboratory Independent Research Project*. Available online at www2.lv.psu.edu/jxm57/irp/sci_inv1.html (accessed 30 June 2016).

Perry, B. (2001) Curiosity: The fuel of development. *Early Childhood Today*. **15** (6): 22.

Pestalozzi, J. (1801) *How Gertrude Teaches her Children*. Bern and Zurich: Heinrich Gessner.

Peters, M., Seeds, K., Goldstein, A. and Coleman, N. (2008) *Parental Involvement in Children's Education 2007*. London: Department for Education and Skills.

Piaget, J. (1929) *The Child's Conception of the World*. London: Routledge and Kegan Paul.

Piaget, J. (1945) *Play, Dreams, and Imitation in Childhood*. New York: W.W. Norton & Co.

Piaget, J. (1952) *The Origins of Intelligence in Children*. New York: W.W. Norton & Co.

Piaget, J. (1969) *The Mechanisms of Perception*. New York: Basic Books.

Piaget, J. (1972a) *The Principles of Genetic Epistemology*. London: Routledge and Kegan Paul.

Piaget, J. (1972b) *Psychology and Epistemology: Towards a theory of knowledge* (trans. P. A. Wells). London: Allen Lane.

Piaget, J. and Inhelder, B. (1956) *The Child's Conception of Space*. London: Routledge and Kegan Paul.

Pintrich, P. R. and Zusho, A. (2002) Student Motivation and Self-regulated Learning in the College Classroom. In J. C. Smart and W. G. Tierney (Eds) (2002) *Higher Education: Handbook of Theory and Research, Volume XVII*. New York: Agathon Press.

Plato (369 BC) *Theaetetus* (ed. John M. Cooper). (1997) Indianapolis: Hackett, pp. 157–234.

Polanyi, M. (1958) *Personal Knowledge. Towards a Post Critical Philosophy*. Chicago: University of Chicago Press.

Polanyi, M. (1967) *The Tacit Dimension*. New York: Anchor Books.

Popper, K. (1965) *Conjectures and Refutations: The growth of scientific knowledge*. New York: Basic Books.

Popper, K. R. (1979) [1972]. *Objective Knowledge: An evolutionary approach*. Oxford: Oxford University Press.

Postman, N. (1994) *The Disappearance of Childhood*. New York: Vintage.

Prawat, R. S. and Floden, R. E. (1994) Philosophical Perspectives on Constructivist Views of Learning. *Educational Psychologist*. **29** (1): 37–48.

Punch, S. (2002) Research with Children: The same or different from research with adults? *Childhood.* **9** (3): 321–341.

Qvortrup, J. (1994) Childhood Matters: An introduction. In J. Qvortrup, M. Bardy, G. Sgritta and H. Wintersberger (Eds) (1994) *Childhood Matters: Social theory, practice and politics.* Aldershot: Avebury.

Ramdass, D. and Zimmerman, B. J. (2011) Developing Self-Regulation Skills: The important role of homework. *Journal of Advanced Academics.* **22** (2): 194–218.

Redmond, G. (2008) *Children's Perspectives on Economic Adversity: A review of the literature. SPRC Discussion Paper No. 149.* Sydney: The Social Policy Research Centre.

REF 2014 (2011) *Assessment Framework and Guidance on Submissions.* Available online at www.ref.ac.uk/media/ref/content/pub/assessmentframeworkandguidanceonsubmissions/GOS%20including%20addendum.pdf (accessed 30 June 2016).

Ritchie, J., Lewis, J., McNaughton Nicholls, C. and Ormston, R. (2003) *Qualitative Research Practice: A guide for social science students and researchers.* London: Sage.

Roach, J. A. (2003) Stimulation: Preventing over-stimulation is key for optimal growth and well-being. *Nursing for Women's Health.* **7** (6): 530–535.

Roberts-Holmes, G. (2014) *Doing Your Early Years Project.* London: Sage Publications.

Robinson, M. (2008) *Child Development Birth to Eight.* Maidenhead: McGraw-Hill and Open University Press.

Robson, C. (1993) *Real World Research.* Oxford: Blackwell.

Robson, S. (2012) *Developing Thinking and Understanding in Young Children.* London: Routledge.

Rogoff, B. (1990) *Apprenticeship in Thinking: Cognitive development in social context.* New York: Oxford University Press.

Rogoff, B. (1995) Observing Sociocultural Activity on Three Planes: Participatory appropriation, guided participation, and apprenticeship. In J. V. Wertsch, P. del Rio and A. Alvarez (Eds) (1995) *Sociocultural Studies of Mind.* New York: Cambridge University Press, pp. 139–164.

Rose, J. (2006) *Independent Review of the Teaching of Early Reading. Final Report (The Rose Review).* London: Department for Education and Skills.

Rosen, M. (1993) *We're Going on a Bear Hunt.* London: Walker Books.

Rousseau, J-J. (1762) [1911] *Émile.* London: Dent.

Rudduck, J. and McIntyre, D. (2007) *Improving Learning through Consulting Pupils.* London: Routledge.

Rutter, M. (2002) Nature, Nurture and Development: From evangelism through science toward policy and practice. *Child Development.* **73** (1): 1–21.

Ryle, G. (1949) *The Concept of Mind.* London: Penguin.

Ryle, G. (1968) The Thinking of Thoughts: What is 'Le Penseur' doing? *'University Lectures', No. 18. Saskatchewan: The University of Saskatchewan.* Available online at http://lucy.ukc.ac.uk/csacsia/vol11/papers/ryle_1.html (accessed 30 June 2016).

Samelson, P. (2008) *Three Types of Justification.* Available online at www.samelsonmagic.com/linkedItems/Justification.pdf (accessed 30 June 2016).

Sanchez, R. (2005) *'Tacit Knowledge' versus 'Explicit Knowledge' Approaches to Knowledge Management Practice.* Available online at www.knowledgeboard.com/download/3512/Tacit-vs-Explicit.pdf (accessed 30 June 2016).

Schaffer, H. (1992) Joint Involvement Episodes as Context for Development. In H. McGurk (Ed.) (1992) *Childhood Social Development: Contemporary perspectives.* Hove: Lawrence Erlbaum Associates, pp. 99–130.

Schechter, J. (2013) Deductive Reasoning. In H. Pashler (Ed.) (2013) *Encyclopedia of the Mind.* London: Sage, pp. 226–230.

Schleicher, A. (2007) Can Competencies Assessed by PISA be Considered the Fundamental School Knowledge 15-year-olds Should Possess? *Journal of Educational Change.* **8** (4): 349–357.

Schön, D. (1983) *The Reflective Practitioner. How professionals think in action*, London: Temple Smith.

Schostak, J. F. (2002) *Understanding, Designing and Conducting Qualitative Research in Education.* Buckingham: Open University Press.

Schweinhart, L., Barnes, H., and Weikart, P. (1993) *Significant Benefits: The High/Scope Perry Pre-school Study through age 27*. Ypsilanti, MI: HighScope Press.

Scruton, R. (2001) *Kant*. Oxford: Oxford University Press.

Sen, A. K. (1985) *Commodities and Capabilities*. Amsterdam: North-Holland.

Senju, A., Southgate, V., Snape, C., Leonard, M. and Csibra, G. (2011) Do 18-Month-Olds Really Attribute Mental States to Others? A critical test. *Psychological Science*. **22** (7): 878–880.

Sevison, A. and Williams, J. P. (n.d.) *Give Me Oil in My Lamp*. S.l. S.n.

Sherman, A. and MacDonald, A. L. (2006) Children's Perspectives on Building Science Models. *Education 3–13*. **34** (1): 89–98.

Shevlin, M. and Rose, R. (2003) *Encouraging Voices: Respecting the insights of young people who have been marginalised*. Dublin: National Disability Authority.

Shevlin, M. and Rose, R. (2008) Pupils as Partners in Education Decision-making: Responding to the legislation in England and Ireland. *European Journal of Special Needs Education*. **23** (4): 423–430.

Shrum, W., Duque, R., and Brown, T. (2005) Digital Video as Research Practice: Methodology for the millennium. *Journal of Research Practice*. **1** (1): Article M4, pp. 1–19.

Siegler, R. S., and Jenkins, E. (1989) *How Children Discover New Strategies*. Hillsdale, NJ: Lawrence Erlbaum Associates.

Silverman, D. (2006) *Interpreting Qualitative Data*. London: Sage.

Singer-Freeman, K. E. and Bauer, P. J. (2008) The ABCs of Analogical Abilities: Evidence for formal analogical reasoning abilities in 24-month-olds. *British Journal of Developmental Psychology*. **26** (3): 317–335.

Singer-Freeman, K. E. and Goswami, U. (2001) Does Half a Pizza Equal Half a Box of Chocolates?: Proportional matching in an analogy task. *Cognitive Development*. **16** (3): 811–829.

Siraj-Blatchford, I. and Manni, L. (2008): 'Would you Like to Tidy up now?' An analysis of adult questioning in the English Foundation Stage. *Early Years*. **28** (1): 5–22.

Siraj-Blatchford, I., Sylva, K., Muttock, S., Gilden, R. and Bell, D. (2002) *Researching Effective Pedagogy in the Early Years*. London: Department for Education and Skills.

Smeyers, P. (2008) On the Epistemological Basis of Large-Scale Population Studies and their Educational Use. *Journal of Philosophy of Education*. **42** (S1): 63–86.

Smilansky, S. and Shefatya, L. (1990) *Facilitating Play*. Gaithersburg, MD: Psychosocial and Educational Publications.

Sosa, E. (2003) Chisholm's Epistemic Principles. *Metaphilosophy*. **34** (5): 553–562.

Spencer, C. (2004) Place Attachment, Place Identity and the Development of the Child's Self-identity. In S. Catling and F. Martin (Eds) (2004) *Researching Primary Geography*. Special Publication No. 1. August. London Register of Research.

Stavy, R. and Tirosh, D. (2000) *How Students (Mis)Understand Science and Mathematics*. New York: Teachers' College Press.

Stebbins, R. A. (2001) *Exploratory Research in the Social Sciences*. Thousand Oaks, CA: Sage.

Stenhouse, L. (1975). *An Introduction to Curriculum Research and Development*. London: Heinemann Educational Books.

Stern, D. (1985) *The Interpersonal World of the Infant*. New York: Basic Books.

Strega, S. (2005) The View from the Poststructural Margins. In L. Brown and S. Strega (Eds) (2005) *Research as Resistance*. Toronto: Canadian Scholars' Press, pp. 199–236.

Suggate, S. (2011) Viewing the Long-term Effects of Early Reading with an Open Eye. In R. House (Ed.) (2011) *Too Much, Too Soon?* Stroud: Hawthorn Press, pp. 236–246.

Swann, J. (2009) Learning: An evolutionary analysis. *Educational Philosophy and Theory*. **41** (3): 256–269.

Sylva, K., Melhuish, E., Sammons, P., Siraj-Blatchford, I. and Taggart, B. (Eds) (2010) *Early Childhood Matters: Evidence from the Effective Pre-school and Primary Education Project*. London: Routledge.

Tarini, E. and White, L. (1998) Looking in the Mirror: A reflection of Reggio practice in Winnetka. In C. Edwards, L. Gandini and G. Forman (Eds) (1998) *The Hundred Languages of Children*. 2e. Westport, CT: Ablex Publishing Ltd, pp. 135–404.

Thomas, G. (2007) *Education and Theory: Strangers in paradigms*. Maidenhead: Open University Press/McGraw-Hill.

Tizard, B. and Hughes, M. (1984) *Young Children Learning*. London: Fontana Paperbacks.

Topping, K. J., Miller, D., Murray, P., Henderson, S., Fortuna, C. and Conlin, N. (2011) Outcomes in a Randomised Controlled Trial of Mathematics Tutoring. *Educational Research*. **53** (1): 51–63.

Tsai, J. L., Louie, J. Y., Chen, E. and Uchida, Y. (2007) Learning What Feelings to Desire: Socialization of ideal affect through children's storybooks. *Personality and Social Psychology Bulletin*. **33** (1): 17–30.

Tunteler, E. and Resing, W. (2007) Effects of Prior Assistance in Using Analogies on Young Children's Unprompted Analogical Problem-solving over Time: A microgenetic study. *British Journal of Educational Psychology*. **77** (1): 43–68.

Turri, J. (2012) In Gettier's Wake. In S. Hetherington (Ed.) (2012) *Epistemology: The key thinkers*. London: Continuum, pp. 214–229.

Van Beers, H., Invernizzi, A. and Milne, B. (2008) *Beyond Article 12: Essential readings on children's participation*. Bangkok: Black and White Publications.

Van Deth, J., Abendschön, S. and Vollmar, M. (2011) Children and Politics: An empirical reassessment of early political socialization. *Political Psychology*. **32** (1): 147–174.

Van Oers, B. and Hännikäinen, M. (2001) Some Thoughts About Togetherness: An introduction. *International Journal of Early Years Education*. **9** (2): 101–108.

Vig, S. (2007) Young Children's Object Play: A window on development. *Journal of Developmental and Physical Disabilities*. **19** (3): 201–215.

Von Hofsten, C., Feng, Q. and Spelke, E. S. (2000) Object Representation and Predictive Action in Infancy. *Developmental Science*. **3**: 193–205.

Vygotsky, L. S. (1962) *Thought and Language*. Cambridge: MIT Press.

Vygotsky, L. S. (1976) Play and its Role in the Mental Development of the Child. *Soviet Psychology*. **5** (3): 6–18.

Vygotsky, L. S. (1978) *Mind in Society: The development of higher psychological processes*. Cambridge, MA: Harvard University Press.

Warren, L. and Boxall, K. (2009) Service Users In and Out of the Academy: Collusion in exclusion? *Social Work Education: The International Journal*. **28** (3): 281–297.

West, A. (2010) High Stakes Testing, Accountability, Incentives and Consequences in English Schools. *Policy and Politics*. **38** (1): 23–39.

Waller, T. and Davis, G. (Eds) (2014) *An Introduction to Early Childhood*. 3e. London: Sage.

Whalley, M. and the Pen Green Centre Team (2007) *Involving Parents in Their Children's Learning*. 2e. London: Paul Chapman Publishing.

Whitebread, D. (2010) Play, Meta-cognition and Self-regulation. In P. Broadhead, J. Howard and E. Wood (Eds) (2010) *Play and Learning in the Early Years*. London: Sage, pp. 161–176.

Whitebread, D. (2012) *Developmental Psychology and Early Childhood Education*. London: Sage.

Whitebread, D., Coltman, P., Pino Paternak, D., Sangster, C., Grau, V., Bingham, S., Almeqdad, Q. and Demetriou, D. (Eds) (2009) The Development of Two Observational Tools for Assessing Metacognition and Self-regulated Learning in Young Children. *Metacognition and Learning*. **4** (1): 63–85.

Whyte, W. F. (1949) The Social Structure of the Restaurant. *American Journal of Sociology*. **54**: 302–310.

Williams, B. (2002) *Truth and Truthfulness: An essay in genealogy*. Princeton, NJ: Princeton University Press.

Wimmer, H. and Perner, J. (1983) Beliefs about Beliefs: Representation and constraining function of wrong beliefs in young children's understanding of deception. *Cognition*. **13** (1): 103–128.

Wood, A. (2008) The Duty to Believe According to the Evidence. *International Journal of Philosophy and Religion*. **63** (7): 7–24.

Wood, D. (1988) *How Children Think and Learn*. Oxford: Blackwell.

Wood, D., Bruner, J. and Ross, G. (1976) The Role of Tutoring in Problem Solving. *Journal of Child Psychology and Psychiatry*. **17** (2): 89–100.

Woolfolk, A. and Perry, N. (2012) *Child and Adolescent Development*. Upper Saddle River, NJ: Pearson.

Worthington, M. (2010) 'This is a Different Calculator – with Computer Games on': Reflecting on children's symbolic play in the digital age. In J. Moyles (Ed.) *Thinking about Play*. Maidenhead: Open University Press and McGraw-Hill Education, pp. 179–196.

Yin, R. K. (2012) *Applications of Case Study Research*. London: Sage.

INDEX